Microsociology

Microsociology

Discourse,
Emotion, and
Social Structure

Thomas J. Scheff

The University of Chicago Press   Chicago and London

The University of Chicago Press, Chicago 60637
The University of Chicago Press, Ltd., London
© 1990 by The University of Chicago
All rights reserved. Published 1990
Paperback edition 1994
Printed in the United States of America

99 98 97 96 95 94   5 4 3 2

Library of Congress Cataloging in Publication Data

Scheff, Thomas J.
    Microsociology : discourse, emotion, and social structure / Thomas
  J. Scheff.

        p.   cm.
    Includes bibliographical references.
    ISBN 0-226-73666-0 (cloth)
    ISBN 0-226-73667-9 (paper)
    1. Social interaction.   2. Emotions.   3. Motivation (Psychology)
  I. Title.
    HM291.S288   1990   89-20540
    302—dc20   CIP

⊛ The paper used in this publication meets the minimum requirements of
the American National Standard for Information Sciences—Permanence
of Paper for Printed Library Materials, ANSI Z39.48-1984.

The Godhead is broken like bread. We are the pieces.
—W. H. Auden, "Herman Melville"

Contents

Foreword

This book is by any token a major contribution to some central debates in social theory at the present time. On the face of things, the argument seems to concern the development of a "microsociology," concerned with the details of social interaction. It is a much more profound study than such a characterization suggests. What Thomas Scheff seeks to develop is essentially a quite novel account of the nature of social life, its relation to language and human reflexivity, in which he insists upon the importance of a theory of emotion.

The core of Scheff's analysis concerns his discussion of the connection between emotion and motivation, in which he places a special stress upon the significance of pride and shame as more or less continuous aspects of human experience. Scheff then relates this motivational analysis to what is to my mind a quite brilliant account of the massive complexity of the everyday understanding of meaning between speakers and agents. He demonstrates this complexity both by direct empirical analysis and by taking literary texts as exemplifications. In the interpretation of meaning, he suggests, human actors routinely employ what the philosopher Peirce called "abduction," which in this instance refers to rapid "searches" that continuously have to be employed to create an intelligible social world. Not content to leave things there, he then moves on to attempt to work out a theory of individuality and genius. I found these sections particularly arresting and important.

This is not a book which fits easily into conventional categories. It is not written in a strictly narrative form, but combines insights drawn from a variety of sources in an eclectic fashion. The style is quite often idiosyncratic. Yet it is a work of true originality and jolting impact.

To appreciate how important this new book is, one must understand something about the current state of development of sociology. With some exceptions, most sociological work, particularly on a theoretical level, has been dominated by cognitive interpretations of action and institutions. The major debates in social theory have concerned issues such as how far methodological individualism or holism is appropriate as a model for social analysis, or how far human activity can be understood in terms of models of rational choice.

Scheff's work breaks away from these more traditional concerns. In particular, he focuses upon the significance of *emotion* in human social relations, showing that no approach to sociology can be complete which fails to analyze

this. He also develops a highly innovative account of emotional life, giving a
central place to pride and shame in the sustaining of self-identity. He relates
this account of pride and shame to the social bond, the structuring foundation
of day-to-day life and of larger social systems.

As a result of these new perspectives, he is able to make major contributions to rethinking preexisting conceptions of self and society. Scheff ranges
over an extraordinary diversity of sources, which stretch well beyond those
ordinarily associated with sociological investigation. The reader should be
forewarned: this is not a simple book to follow, nor does it fit snugly into the
usual categories of sociological thought, but these very characteristics help
give the work its originality and intellectual power.

In presenting some of the aforementioned themes of the book, let me, in
true hermeneutic fashion, begin in the middle, work back to the beginning,
and from there move to the end of the volume. In chapter 7, the fulcrum of his
study, Scheff offers a discussion of an incident from Goethe's *Werther*. Why
do we find an analysis of a literary text in an academic work of sociology?
Goethe's intellectual career captures some of the features of both art and science which Scheff wants to address in his own work. Goethe was one of the
greatest scientists of his time as well as a leading literary figure. Goethe's
work in both spheres illustrates a fundamental principle with which Scheff is
concerned: the relation between concrete phenomena, in all their idiosyncratic
richness, and more abstract characteristics or generalizations.

Goethe's fiction provides many detailed accounts of episodes of interaction,
describing inner thoughts and feelings as well as outer behavior. *Werther,*
Scheff thinks, was probably an "as if" autobiography. Goethe was a man of
middle-class background, seeking to make a place for himself in a society
dominated by a traditional aristocracy. He did in fact forge an acceptable
status for himself in that society; his literary genius and scientific accomplishments brought him considerable fame, and he also held high governmental
positions. *Werther* might be regarded as a literary thought experiment: What
would Goethe's own life have been like if he were a more ordinary man from a
middle-class background, not a person of exceptional talent and energy?

Werther is ordinarily seen purely as a story of unrequited love. Werther
falls into a state of despair, having conceived a passion for a woman who is
promised to another, and eventually kills himself. Scheff points out that
Werther's failures in love are actually part of a wider series of setbacks or
humiliations he experiences. Werther's life is haunted by shame, never fully
acknowledged either by himself or by others. His tribulations are caused less
by the rebuffs he has to endure than by his denial of his emotional reactions to
them. He is caught in a "feeling trap," in which emotions of shame and anger
intensify internally without finding full external expression. Feeling traps,
Scheff argues, are characteristic of most systems of social deference or un-
equal status. Goethe's story therefore allows us to move from the particular

incidents of the narrative to a generalized account of patterns of deference and inequality.

The notion of the feeling trap (which Scheff derives from the psychologist Helen B. Lewis) is used in other parts of Scheff's book to explore the origins of self-esteem and the nature of the social bond. The theme of genius is pursued by Scheff in relation to a discussion of language acquisition. "Genius" is normally taken to refer to the talents and accomplishments of a few, very rare individuals, like Goethe himself. Modern linguistics, however, has demonstrated that in a certain sense all human beings possess qualities of genius, demonstrated in their capability to master a natural language. Learning such a language is an enormously complicated endeavor, so complicated that even the most advanced computers cannot manage to come to terms with it. Yet virtually all children, by the age of four or five, have somehow gained access to the rules, procedures, tactics, social knowledge, and other items involved in everyday language use. Why are there so few geniuses in fields of invention, discovery, or artistic attainment when genius in this sense is a general characteristic of the human species?

According to Scheff, exposure to language, coupled with instruction from supremely competent teachers—in other words, adult language users—saturates the child's early life. No other forms of symbolic learning or instruction—music or mathematics, for example—are so intense, save for a few people brought up in constant contact with them. Most of the great musical composers, Scheff points out, had one or more relatives who were gifted musicians and were exposed to musical instruction from the very early years of their lives onward. This is one condition of exceptional accomplishment in music or other creative spheres. Taken on its own, it is not sufficient: to produce genius, it has to be coupled to a firmly entrenched base of self-esteem. The person who has such inner confidence from early years retains access to the intuitions and perceptions that in most people become constrained or repressed.

We find here some key dynamics of pride, shame, and self-identity. For a person to be possessed of genius, in the individualistic sense, she or he must have escaped the shame-rage dynamics which afflict the less gifted. Scheff does not suggest that this interpretation provides a complete explanation of individual genius, a phenomenon which in any case admits of no very precise definition. It is particularly relevant, he suggests, to the "easy" creator—the person who produces exceptional work quickly and with little revision. Creativity of this sort is released when there is a relative absence of self-censure, and where the individual can draw directly upon the original fund of ideation which all human beings possess, but only the few can harness in boldly innovative fashion. Goethe was just such an easy creator.

Perception of the self by others, in relation to the bonds of day-to-day life, is the main focus of feelings of pride and shame. Goffman's celebrated analy-

sis of embarrassment, in Scheff's view, opens up some of the main connections here. The risk of embarrassment, Goffman points out, is contained in
every social encounter. Embarrassment is loss of face, which occurs when an
individual is "caught out" in a process of interaction, inadvertently revealing
to another something which should stay hidden, or witnessing another person
thus being caught out. For all its virtues, however, Goffman's account of embarrassment does not relate loss of face to inner emotions—the crucial emphasis of Scheff. The conception of the feeling trap allows for a more profound
understanding of what Scheff calls the "deference-emotion system" in social
interaction than is possible using Goffman's account alone. Embarrassment,
Goffman tends to presume, may be agonizing but is usually transitory. If we
understand that embarrassment is integral to shame, and linked to anger, we
see that it often has enduring consequences. Moreover, interaction rituals between large collectivities, even nations, may incorporate spirals of shame and
anger, linked to conceptions of honor, insult, and retribution, which can have
far-reaching implications for social life.

The achievement of joint attention and feeling in interaction Scheff describes as *attunement*. It follows from his analysis that social bonds presume
not just a cognitive but an emotional connectedness between participants.
Scheff shows how this is so in even the simplest contexts of day-to-day talk.
Little of what gets said in everyday conversation, as sociolinguists have demonstrated, is in the words themselves; grasping what another person means by
an utterance demands an intricate knowledge of the cultural settings of interaction. Such taken-for-granted forms of knowledge include factors directly
bound up with the deference-emotion system. Speakers demand mutual esteem from one another in any situation of talk. For instance, someone who
breaks in when another person is speaking shows disregard for the other's au-
tonomy and integrity; a person who allows too lengthy a pause between conversational exchanges risks being seen as disrespectful. Codes of deference
are therefore built into the minutiae of everyday talk. Emotional attunement is
necessary to the interpretative understanding upon which interpersonal communication depends. Understanding what another person says thus presumes
not only generalized social knowledge but the constant gauging of the other's
(and one's own) inner feelings. A subtle process of tacking backward and forward between observation and imaginative inference is incorporated within
everyday talk—a process very similar to that which Charles Peirce described
as abduction when analyzing the creative character of scientific activity. Abduction in day-to-day talk, as in science, is heavily counterfactual: individuals
are, as it were, continually imagining what might happen if certain utterances
or actions were not produced. Scientific thought here rejoins art, as Scheff
initially points out in his discussion of Goethe.

Writing a foreword to another person's book is a difficult affair, however
much one might admire both the individual and the work. I am not sure how
far I am properly attuned to Scheff's discourse, or how far my own powers of

abduction have proved up to the task of whetting the reader's appetite for what is to follow. Inevitably I have some disagreements with, or worries about, aspects of Scheff's presentation. For instance, he does not consider at any length the question of what emotions actually are, a problem of very considerable difficulty. But then any and every book is open to critical reservations. This is a work of exceptional interest, which bears witness to the very creativity which it puts at the center of human social conduct.

ANTHONY GIDDENS

Preface

This book proposes a new theory and method for the human sciences. The *theory* asserts that social bonds generate the primary motives in human conduct; pride and shame, signals of the state of the bond, are also fundamental motives. The *method* is based on Peirce's idea of abduction, the rapid shuttling back and forth between imagination and observation, between deduction and induction. As I hope to show, my approach unifies seeming opposites: individual-group, qualitative-quantitative, micro-macro, theory-research, art-science.

The writing of this book involved five years of hard labor, struggle, and excitement. It would have been impossible to complete without the help of what might be deemed either a large committee or a small army. To begin on a formal note: my thanks to the *American Sociological Review, Sociological Theory,* and *Theory, Culture, and Society,* for permission to publish chapters 5, 6, and 7, which appeared in earlier versions in those journals. My thanks also to the editors and anonymous referees, whose comments helped to shape the chapters in their present form. Further acknowledgments are made in footnotes in these and the other chapters for comments that have been particularly decisive.

Clerical assistance and goodwill was provided by Chris Allen, Kristin Freese, and Art Morin; research assistance by Dawn New, Heide Schmittel, and Lori Terry; advice and counsel on word processing and printing by Bill Hyder and Joan Murdoch, and word processing by Francesca Guerra-Pearson, Val Jenness, and Jan Sallinger McBride.

The following persons helped by commenting on one or more chapters, or by publishing work which I found stimulating and relevant to my own: Donald E. Brown, T. D. Kemper, Melvin Lansky, Aaron Lazare, Donald N. Levine, the late Helen B. Lewis, Jonathan Turner, and Frederic Turner. I am also indebted to Donald N. Levine for ending my search for a publisher; on the basis of an early draft of one of the chapters, he recommended my book to the University of Chicago Press.

My debt to the late Donald Cressey is not easy to describe in a few words. For much of my career, he functioned as my adviser, advocate, and court of last appeal. Although he did not particularly approve of the direction he saw me taking in the early stages of this book, he gave me the benefit of the doubt. Somehow that cleared the space for me that I needed. I miss him sorely.

Only a few persons read and commented on the entire manuscript, starting with three persons who functioned almost as a team. Anthony Giddens made valuable suggestions about form and content. His views were particularly important in encouraging me to enlarge the overall scope of my claims. Two sets of extremely detailed and expert advice were provided by reviewers appointed by the University of Chicago Press: Mel Pollner and an anonymous reviewer. Pollner's advice was especially helpful. Giddens, Pollner, and the other reviewer particularly pointed to ways of linking the chapters into a single theme.

My largest indebtedness is to my partner, Suzanne M. Retzinger. First, she introduced me to the meaning and significance of authors and fields little known to me: Nietzsche, Scheler, McDougall, Bowlby and Bowen, and the sizable literatures on family systems, on communication, on infant-caretaker interaction, and on conflict.

Second, together we explored the details and ramifications of the literature on anger and shame, particularly the work of Helen Lewis. As is the case with other emotions, access to the shame literature is not easy. Although there are many brilliant contributions, the field lacks coherence; it is scattered over many disciplines, with the contributors speaking virtually different languages. Suzanne's insight was so vital in this process that she is a hidden collaborator in everything I have to say on this topic.

A third contribution was made by her own work. Since I serve as a sounding board for it, as she does for mine, I am familiar with the details of her research. Her discovery of patterns of meaning and emotion in sequences of videotaped social interaction has been a source of stimulation and inspiration.

A fourth contribution has been her role as reviewer and listener. Of all the members of my supporting committee-army, she is the only one who has suffered through *all* drafts and revisions. My last thanks is for her continuing emotional support. It is difficult to convey the extent and depth of my indebtedness. A stanza by Edna St. Vincent Millay comes to mind:

> The man who ventures forth alone
>   When other men are snug within,
> Walks on his marrow, not his bone,
>   And lacks his outer skin.

This passage is from the poem "How Naked, How Without a Wall." My relationship with Suzanne has clothed and sheltered me during the writing of this book.

Addendum to second printing: *The History of Manners* by Norbert Elias (New York: Pantheon, 1978) suggests, in a general way, many of the same ideas about both theory and method that are featured in this book. See page 95, below, for further comment.

Part 1

Introduction

1

Human Nature and the Social Bond

This book should be seen as a first pass, a preview, perhaps, of a new kind of sociology. It is based on an underlying conception of human nature quite different from those current in the social sciences. Although the very concept of human nature is unfashionable at the moment, it serves as the unnoticed backdrop of every investigation into human conduct. I am referring here not to the models that the various schools of thought use in their published work but to an underlying orientation so primitive that it is seldom discussed even between the closest colleagues. My purpose is to stimulate discussion of this issue by proposing a theory radically different from the prevailing ones. In this chapter I provide a brief sketch of the basic ideas and will return to them, and to some of them repeatedly, in subsequent chapters.

Even though motivational systems are usually not discussed, every analysis of human behavior implies them. Most approaches emphasize a single motive, such as money, power, or prestige. Some are more complex, assuming a system of motives involving several vectors. Orthodox psychoanalytic theory, for example, points to the seeking of pleasure, such as sexual or oral fulfillment, as a positive motive, and the avoidance of anxiety and guilt as negative ones, a system for maximizing pleasure and minimizing pain. The motives in this system are specific. Learning theory also assumes pleasure and pain as basic motives but is extremely broad and vague about their sources—any kind of repetitive reinforcement in the environment.

The prevailing approaches initially appear quite different from each other, but a closer examination shows important similarities among them. First of all, the theories can be divided into two broad groups: those that are narrow, like psychoanalysis, emphasizing only a few specific motives, and those that are extremely broad, like learning theory, so abstract that they explain everything and therefore nothing.

Common to all the various approaches is the simplicity of the system that they assume. For the most part they treat human beings as if they were no more complex than an input-output device, like a transistor. As will be discussed below, human understanding is much more complex than the most complex computer, which contains thousands of transistors and other devices. I will return to this issue.

A final similarity is that most approaches to motives focus on isolated individuals. At least in Western thinking, motives, almost by definition, occur within individuals. Current approaches to motives are based on theoretical and methodological individualism. The way in which laboratory experiments and sample surveys are usually conducted provides a striking example of this point. These designs employ isolated individual subjects without reference to their webs of social relationships, as if they were irrelevant.

Social Bonds

Although not denying the usefulness of the prevailing approaches, or the reality of the underlying motives they assume, this book proposes *maintenance of bonds* as the most crucial human motive. This motive is seldom discussed, yet it may underlie or at least color virtually all human behavior. The concept of the bond to be sketched here is quite complex, ramifying into many seemingly disparate aspects of conduct. It does not assume isolated individuals but connects individual behavior with social structure and process.

Secure social bonds are the force that holds a society together. In my definition, this force involves a balance between closeness and distance, what Bowen (1978; Bowen and Kerr 1988) has called "differentiation." (Bowen, a psychiatrist, is one of the originators of family system theory.) Optimal differentiation defines an intact social bond, a bond which balances the needs of the individual and the needs of the group. It involves being able to maintain ties with others who are different from self.

The family that defines loyalty in terms of conformity, of being like other members of the family rather than different from them, exemplifies underdifferentiation. In such a family, the other members feel betrayed by a member who develops his or her own direction rather than conforms to the direction taken by the family. In this family, the individual members are *engulfed*. At the other pole are families in which the bonds are too loose, the individual is everything, the group is nothing; the individual members are *isolated*.

Optimal differentiation involves closeness since it requires knowledge of the other's point of view. But it also involves distance, the acceptance of the other's independence from self. An intact social bond does not imply agreement but knowledge and acceptance of both agreement and disagreement.

The usefulness of the concept of level of differentiation is not limited to family systems but can be extended to all social relationships. The idea of optimal differentiation is implied by Durkheim's typology of suicide: egoistic suicide implies relationships in which there is too much distance; altruistic-fatalistic, too little. His analysis suggests that suicide is caused by pathological social bonds. Significantly, however, Durkheim did not discuss the structure of a normal bond; it goes without saying in his analysis.

The degree and type of differentiation in a social system may be crucial for its survival since it determines its adaptive capacity. As Bowen (1978) indicates for the family, level of differentiation seems to generate the degree of rigidity or adaptiveness of the unit as a whole. Too little distance produces overconformity, just as too much produces underconformity. Some balance seems to be necessary to allow for the system to maintain coherence, a mixture of tradition and change.

Although at first sight the level of differentiation seems similar to the distinction Durkheim made between mechanical and organic solidarity, the overlap is slight. Durkheim's distinction is strictly behavioral; it does not encompass the main elements in Bowen's idea, which concern internal as well as external states. Organic solidarity concerns cooperative *behavior*. Optimal differentiation in Bowen's sense concerns intellectual and emotional *attunement*, mutual understanding as well as behavioral interdependence.

At present there is no usable model of a normal social bond in the literature of the social sciences. Sociologists are at least aware of the bond, which sets them apart from most in the other human sciences.[1] Modern sociology, following Durkheim, postulates that social order depends upon exterior and constraining bonds.

In Etzioni's (1989) critique of the liberal-communitarian debate in political theory, he reminds both sides of the "human arch": an arch is composed of bricks, but bricks without the arch are a pile of rubble. Absent from Etzioni's discussion of the arch is any description of the forces that bind the bricks together. As Etzioni indicates, the liberal-communitarian argument suffers from a lack of specificity; neither side makes explicit what it means by the principal terms in the debate. In this book, I propose a step toward specifying the terms by outlining a model of the relationship between individual and group. Without specificity, it may be possible for such arguments to continue in perpetuity.

The social bond and its collective counterpart, social solidarity, remains a "black box" in sociological analysis, an idea of unspecified content that is accepted without discussion or criticism. Boudon (1986) makes a distinction between black and white boxes quite relevant to the current situation in social theory. The idea of black boxes originated in electrical engineering, where it has no negative connotation. In wiring diagrams of complex electronic systems, the elements of subsystems, the parts and their interconnections, are omitted. A subsystem like a transducer is represented by a box empty except for its name, since the actual wiring diagram can easily be provided on demand. In Boudon's terminology, such empty boxes would be termed white boxes, since their contents are demonstrable and discussable.

As Boudon points out, the situation in social theory is quite different. The content of the major concepts is not made explicit, even though the actual wiring diagrams, the parts and their linkages, have not been specified. As will be

---

1. The theorists of "object relations" in psychoanalysis are a partial exception. The crucial role of social bonds is implied, particularly in the early bonds in the family of origin and their relation to development over the life span. For a summary, see Guntrip (1971).

suggested below, the wiring diagrams of some of the major subsystems in social theory, concepts like solidarity, intelligence, and understanding, are complex beyond one's wildest imaginings.

My purpose is to propose a detailed model of the social bond, one that will specify at least some of the parts and connections in the subsystems. The design of the model begins by applying a theory of the social bond at the micro level, episodes of actual and fictional discourse. By relating the moment-by-moment elements of discourse to the larger context, I suggest how a micro-model might become the basis for a theory of social solidarity.

Beginning at the microscopic level is not without peril. Given the extraordinary complexity and richness of detail at this level, it is difficult to reach even to the next level, the total relationship of the particular husband and wife in the interaction, let alone to the macro level, all relationships between husbands and wives. Much of the very fine work that is done in discourse and conversation analysis (to be discussed in subsequent chapters) is limited to the level of discourse alone, the very lowest level, with almost no connection with macrotheory.

Attempts to proceed down the scale from the top, it seems to me, are even more difficult. Giddens (1984) has led the way with his analysis of slips of the tongue in discourse, using concepts and examples both from Freud and from Goffman. For most settings, however, it may be impossible to link discourse and social structure directly. The relevant parts are too small and various, the relevant wholes too large and abstract: more intermediate steps are needed. With a sufficient number of intervening steps one can play both ends against the middle: working up from the micro level to the level of society and down again, and up and down in a way that the parts illuminate the whole, and the whole the parts, *part/whole analysis*.

Goffman's analysis of the microworld can be used to provide some of the intermediate steps. His very detailed description of the ritual conditions for face-to-face interaction, of being in what he called "a state of talk," intimates a model of the social bond. Since this issue will be discussed at length in chapter 5, I will describe only the main contours here.

Communication and Emotion

Goffman's description of the conditions necessary for a state of talk points to what I will consider to be two different systems of activity, the first a *communication* system, the second a *deference-emotion* system. The first system enables the speakers to make known to each other their thoughts; the second, their evaluation of each other's status. The first system depends mostly on linguistic symbols; the second, on nonverbal gestures, of the most part.

I propose that a normal social bond involves what Goffman calls "reciprocal ratification" of each of the parties by the other as "legitimate participants" in the relationship. Although Goffman was thinking only of face-to-face interaction, his description is useful as a starting point for describing a social bond, whether the participants are co-present or not.

The key idea in Goffman's analysis is "legitimacy": reciprocal ratification of each other's participation involves both feelings and actions of legitimation. Legitimacy serves to bridge the communication and deference-emotion systems: ritually correct forms of communication develop mutual understanding and also serve to award deference.

As Goffman's discussion makes clear, ratification of the other's legitimacy must be not only felt but also expressed. Otherwise one or both of the parties might feel rejected or excluded to the point that the bond would be threatened. Threats to the social bond generate intense feelings; this proposition lies at the core of my argument.

Unlike most who discuss the social encounter, Goffman did not limit his analysis to thought and behavior but included *emotion* as an important component. The discussion of states of talk occurs as a part of his analysis of "face," which he relates to feelings and actions that are connected with the social worth of the interactants, and hence to intense feelings.

Unlike his predecessor Durkheim, Goffman was quite specific in naming the concrete emotion he saw at the core of interaction ritual: he proposed that *embarrassment* or the anticipation of embarrassment is the key to understanding face-work, as well as what he had earlier called "impression management." Although he seldom used the terms pride and shame, as Cooley did, his analysis of embarrassment is very much in the spirit of the looking-glass self and provides an extension of it. I will return to the role of emotion in social bonding below. First, however, it will be helpful to describe the process/structure of successful face work, the state of attunement.

As Goffman and others have argued, effective social encounters may result in a "single focus of thought and visual attention," which I will call attunement. By attunement I mean a mutual understanding that is not only mental but also emotional. I do not mean agreement but rather empathic intersubjectivity: mind reading. Such attunement can occur as easily in conflict as in cooperation.

I will argue, however, that conflicts in which the parties are to some degree attuned have a different *quality* than when they are not, and usually have different outcomes. By and large, conflict will be constructive to the degree that the parties are attuned, and destructive when they are not. When the social bond is intact, conflict serves the purposes of change and mutual adjustment; even in the heat of anger, one identifies the opponent as a person like oneself. Even in the act of aggression, maintenance of the bond is an issue. Prestige as a motive implies intact bonds: the person or group is concerned about its image in the eyes of others.

There are obviously conflicts in which the bond is not a consideration; it has been severed or is so threatened that one is willing to risk that it will be cut completely. The opponent is an enemy to be destroyed. In such conflicts, external objects such as money or sex or power may be the sole motives. But an analysis which assumes that such motives are general and preemptive affirms a state of bondlessness, the war of each against all.

In a society in which most bonds are intact, money, power, sex, and other such externals may appear to be motives in themselves, but they also symbolize a hidden motive, the maintenance or enhancement of one's standing in the eyes of others. An economics which objectifies money completely ignores a source of money's power as a motive, perhaps the most fundamental one. A political science which focuses on power and procedure rather than prestige and legitimacy makes a similar error. And a behavioral science which focuses on the process of external reinforcement ignores the social motives proposed here. Emerson put it very well: "Things are in the saddle; they ride Mankind."

Ambiguity and Meaning

The relationship between attunement and the social bond is by no means obvious but needs to be explained. A secure social bond in the animal world does not require intellectual and emotional attunement because bonds are determined by genetically inherited mechanisms. But in the human world, genetic guarantees of bonding have been shattered. (Recent studies of infant-caretaker interaction suggest that genetic mechanisms still function in the early years of infancy; these studies will be discussed in later chapters.) Bonding for adults has an improvised quality: the bond must be constantly tested and renewed if it is to remain intact.

For adults, each new situation becomes an arena for an exploration of the nature and degree of the bond. In interaction, the bond is being built or protected or repaired, or it is being damaged. Discourse which focuses entirely on communication, on the exchange of thoughts, which ignores deference and emotion, is apt to damage the bond. As will be suggested, most "serious" discourse in modern societies usually focuses on the words, on *what* is said, ignoring the manner, on *how* it is said. Since the bond-relevant signals are carried for the most part by manner, this practice usually results in further damage to bonds that are often already in poor repair.

Although every culture develops institutional patterns for signaling bondedness, culture itself has an improvised, and therefore massively complex, character. Bonding in the animal world is based on unambiguous physical and chemical signals. In the human world, it depends on language, a vast system of signs and signals, mostly arbitrary in nature, and therefore ambiguous in meaning (Levine 1985).

The ambiguity and complexity of human expressions is explored at some length in later chapters. At this point I will give two brief examples as background. An adult asks a five-year-old boy to explain the point of soccer. The boy says, "Everyone hates the ball." The adult asks what the boy means. The child relies, "They all kick it." He has created a motive to explain the game, because he is unaware of the sizable body of rules and understandings the players share about goals, moving the ball with head, hands, feet, and so forth. Although the child's explanation is creative, it is also ignorant and therefore laughable to adults.

Computer programs for dealing with ordinary language have similar difficulties. For example, a program furnished four paraphrases of the sentence "Time flies like an arrow" (Raphael 1976). The least erroneous, "Time moves in the same manner that an arrow moves," is not an actual paraphrase. It simply identifies the form of the sentence but gives no hint of its concrete meaning. In a sense, it takes only the first step in deciphering the meaning, recognizing the type of sentence: a simile rather than a command or statement of fact.

The three other paraphrases mistook the meaning. One of the paraphrases can be used to exemplify the others: "Measure the speed of flies in the same way that you measure the speed of an arrow." The program has run afoul of the ambiguities of the words "time" and "flies," mistaking the noun for a verb and the verb for a noun. The mistake is not an absolute error but rather misses the meaning within the English-speaking culture, if we assume that virtually every adult speaker of English would recognize the sentence as a simile rather than a command.

This example typifies the results of computer treatments of natural language. Even the most sophisticated programs cannot decipher the culturally correct meaning of a sentence in ordinary language. Like the small child confronted with the game of soccer, computer programs lack the background understandings that are necessary to solve the puzzle. The file is too large, the associative pathways too complex, and the words too ambiguous. The complexity of ordinary language was recognized by Wittgenstein long before the advent of computers. He realized that understanding and following a seemingly simple rule (stop for red lights) actually involves understanding a whole culture.

Parts and Wholes

To put it another way, a living culture is an "open system," a vast collection of small parts, each having meaning only in relationship to the other and to the whole. In this respect, cultural systems such as natural languages are like functioning organisms: they can be used and understood only by understanding the parts in relation to the whole, and the whole in relation to the parts, a vast and complex project. The parts of an open system are holograms: each stands for the whole, just as the whole is made up by the parts and their interrelationship.

A part/whole paradigm is implied in Goethe's work, especially his science.

In his far-ranging research in botany on the structure and function of plants, he sensed the importance of relating parts and wholes (1785; quoted in Fairley 1963, 195):

> In every living thing what we call the parts is so inseparable from the whole that the parts can only be understood in the whole, and we can neither make the parts the measure of the whole nor the whole the measure of the parts; and this why living creatures, even the most restricted, have something about them that we cannot quite grasp and have to describe as infinite or partaking of infinity.

The words in a living language, like the parts of a plant, are holograms: they represent and reflect the whole system, as well as serving as miniscule components in it.

If ordinary language is so complex that even the most sophisticated computer program cannot understand a single sentence, how do we ever understand each other in everyday discourse? How do we deal with our vast cultural file of ambiguous signs and symbols? This question will be the focus of several chapters. Suffice it here to refer to "intuition." Using and understanding ordinary language requires lightning-quick intuitive understanding of the meaning of expressions *in context*. By the time we are adults, we have so much experience with this process, and we are so adept at it, that it becomes invisible. Needless to say, intuition often fails, giving rise to misunderstanding, an issue that will be discussed below.

By using intuitive understanding, we learn the skill of empathy, of intersubjective awareness, of "mind reading." We learn, as Cooley (1922, 208) put it, to live in the minds of others:

> Many people of balanced mind and congenial activity scarcely know that they care what others think of them, and will deny, perhaps with indignation, that such care is an important factor in what they are and do. But this is illusion. If failure or disgrace arrives, if one suddenly finds that the faces of men show coldness or contempt instead of the kindliness and deference that he is used to, he will perceive from the shock, the fear, the sense of being outcast and helpless, that he was living in the minds of others without knowing it, just as we daily walk the solid ground without thinking how it bears us up.

What Cooley does not note, however, is that our reading of the minds of others is a varying mixture of understanding and misunderstanding. At times there is actual attunement, mutual understanding. At other times, however, we are living in the minds of others, but only in our imaginations; we have misunderstood. This possibility introduces a note of complexity into a seemingly simple idea in social science, the concept of consensus.

Consensus is ordinarily used a facile way, as if it were a matter of simple agreement. But agreement can occur between isolated individuals. Limiting consensus to simple agreement involves theoretical and methodological individualism. It ignores the vast structure and process I have been alluding to: the complex process of observation and inference that leads to varying degrees and types of mutual understanding and misunderstanding. The typical study of "conflict and consensus," since it uses surveys of isolated individuals, does not tap social relationships but only verbal indications of agreement and disagreement.

A second shortcoming of the prevailing concept of consensus is that it refers only to cognitive understanding, ignoring a component that is probably more important, overall, for social solidarity—emotional consensus. Although cognitive and emotional consensus are correlated to some degree, there are important tensions between the two levels in modern societies. Bonding between individuals and solidarity between groups both depend upon mutual trust, which in turn is usually connected to emotional as well as intellectual ties.

Treating social solidarity as if it were entirely a cognitive matter is implied by Durkheim's treatment of mechanical solidarity. He equates it with "likemindedness," implying that solidarity involves agreement at the cognitive level. Elsewhere, however, Durkheim intimates the importance of emotions for social solidarity; he devoted considerable space to what he called "the social emotion," which he saw as of central importance in welding individuals together into a society. However, his treatment is vague; he refers to emotion only in general, never to concrete emotions. He treats emotion as a residual category: that aspect of human conduct which is not behavior or cognition. For that reason, his argument about emotion is inconsequential.

Durkheim's theory is not the only one which treats emotion as a residual category. With the already noted exceptions of Cooley and Goffman, all the major social theorists follow this practice. It may be flagrant, as in the case of Skinner, who explicitly states that emotions are effects, not causes. In Parsons's theory of action, emotion in principle is given equal standing with the other components of action. However, since he treats affect only abstractly and residually, it plays little role in his theory.

At first glance, emotions seem to play a prominent role in psychoanalytic theory since, as already indicated, specific emotions, anxiety and guilt, form a central part of the psychoanalytic theory of motivation. Anxiety is particularly important in psychoanalytic formulations; it figures in virtually all major propositions. However, a close reading suggests that the concept of anxiety has been extended to the point where it has come to stand for many unnamed emotions and therefore to function as an undifferentiated and residual category. In Freud's early work, anxiety meant a specific emotion, a type of fear. Its meaning has currently expanded to include all types of diffuse or disguised emotions except for anger and guilt.

Guilt is an important ingredient of social bonding but is used in most theories in a way that disguises its social character, another instance of theoretical

individualism. Before explaining my approach to this issue, I must step back
from the particulars of my argument to the whole package, a theory that ad-
dresses some of the major contradictions in modern societies.

Basic Premise

Sociology as a discipline arose out of the realization that modernization—
the rise of urban, industrial societies—was destructive of community. With
social and geographic mobility and the free flow of information, modern societies have a potential for change that would be unthinkable in a traditional
society. Although limitless change has many advantages, it also gives rise to
a substantial disadvantage: all social bonds are at risk. Not just one bond or
another is threatened, but all bonds: one's connections to others are never
quite safe.

Suppose, as a basic premise, that all human beings require a sense of belonging, a web of secure social bonds, and that for most of us, this minimum
is never quite achieved. If that were the case, the human condition in modern
societies would be one of permanent insecurity. The sustaining web has been
lost. If one allowed oneself to be aware of the loss, every moment of daily
existence would be exquisitely painful. How might a society defend its members against this kind of pain?

One defense would be to deny the very existence of the social bond. Individualism provides a defensive myth for organizing experience in an anomic
society. Under these conditions, the need for social bonds would become an
unmentionable secret, even an unthinkable one.

I propose that modern societies have institutionalized two defenses against
the loss of secure bonds. The first myth is individualism, and the denial and
repression of the emotions that are associated with social bonds—pride and
shame. The second myth follows from the denial of complexity in human affairs: human nature and social order are simple matters, easily understood.
The last part of this chapter will outline how the concept of the bond, its massive complexity, and the feelings that accompany it are denied and disguised.

Children who have undergone the loss of parental care at an early age usually defend themselves against the pain of further separation. The case of Reggie (Burlingham and Freud 1942; quoted in Bowlby 1973, 247) illustrates the
point. Separated from his parents at five months, he formed a passionate attachment to his nurse in the orphanage. This attachment was suddenly broken when he was two years, eight months; his nurse, Mary-Ann, left to be
married.

> He was completely lost and desperate after her departure, and re-
> fused to look at her when she visited him a fortnight later. He
> turned his head to the other side when she spoke to him, but stared
> at the door, which had closed behind her, after she had left the
> room. In the evening in bed he sat up and said: "My very own
> Mary-Ann! But I don't like her."

Reggie has defended himself against the pain of his second separation; he has rejected the rejector.

Burlingham and Freud, Bowlby (1969, 1973, 1980), and others who have studied the effects of broken or threatened bonds repeatedly report the same syndrome. After a lengthy period of futile calling for the missing loved one, the child learns its lesson. In effect the child says, like Reggie; "Very well, if you are not coming, then I don't need you anyway. I am sufficient unto myself. I don't need anyone. *Ever.*" This defense is what Bowen (1978) calls "cut-off." In effect, it is a self-inflicted wound in response to a wounding social environment. Since one has suffered from separation in the past, one protects oneself by giving up hope, producing a self-perpetuating system.

One limitation of the reports in developmental psychology needs to be mentioned. Bowlby and other researchers seem to assume that severed bonds create more disruption than bonds that are threatened. In effect, they seem to be saying that being a member of a physically intact household, no matter what its emotional dynamics, is less damaging than being an orphan. However, as Bowen's (1978) analysis of family systems suggests, this may not be the case. The threat to bonds in an egoistic-anomic or altruistic family system is hidden and therefore confusing. The disruption caused by such a family may be more enduring than the disruption suffered from severed bonds.

The ideation of severed bonds can be found in the culture of peoples who have been enslaved. A spiritual of the southern black slaves provides an example:

> Sometimes I feel like a motherless child.
> Sometimes I feel like a motherless child.
> Sometimes I feel like a motherless child.
> A long, long way from home.
> A long, long way from home.

The slaves were wrenched not only from their families but also from their cultures; all bonds were severed. Since the destruction of bonds is absolutely clear, however, it may be possible to form new ones.

In the white middle-class family which is physically intact, anomie-egoism or altruism can arise which is hidden behind a facade of polite words. Conflict is so disguised that its roots are virtually invisible to family members. These are the conditions which give rise to underground conflict in the form of "interminable quarrels" or "silent impasses" (Scheff 1987). Retzinger's (1988) analysis of marital quarrels reports such relationships; they are marked by politeness but accompanied by emotional distance, lack of trust, and withdrawal of affection.

In an earlier paper (Scheff 1989a) on discourse in a family with an anorexic member, I have shown how a daughter and mother were locked in a hidden system of mutual threat: the daughter threatened self-starvation; the mother, abandonment of the daughter. The threats, recriminations, and insults exchanged were so subtle they seemed outside the awareness of the family members. In relationships marked by hidden conflict, the bond is continually threatened but in a way which makes understanding and repair of the bond extremely difficult. Since their prototypic bonds are inadequate, the typical individual in such a family might find it just as difficult to form new bonds as to repair old ones.

It is possible for the relationships in a whole society to be physically intact but based on threatened or inadequate bonds. In such a society, we would expect to find individuals willing to accept social relationships which do not meet their basic needs but are tolerated because they are felt to be better than isolation and loneliness. In these circumstances, nationalism and other kinds of sectarian grouping may arise, providing what may be thought of as "pseudobonds." Rather than attunement, which balances the needs of the individual and the needs of the society, pseudobonds in nations, sects, cults, and other exclusive groups furnish only the semblance of community. In such sects, the members give up significant parts of themselves, their individual points of view; they are engulfed. Engulfment damages both the individual and the group because competing points of view are needed for adaptation and survival.

The prevalence of highly specialized groups in a society might constitute a subtle threat to that society's existence, in a way not foreseen by Toqueville. Just as optimal differentiation in a family system balances individual and group needs, so optimal differentiation in a social system would balance group and societal needs, the tension between the parts and the whole.

An analogy to living organisms may help make the point (suggested to me by Frederic Turner). A normal cell is self-reproducing, but it is sufficiently complex that it also functions to maintain the larger organism of which it is a part. A cancer cell is simpler; it is only self-reproducing. Rather than providing service to the host, it destroys it. Hyperspecialized groups in a society, and nations in the world system, may become analogs to cancer cells. They become only self-reproducing, entirely dedicated to their own survival; they cease to serve the larger system of which they are part.

This process lies at the heart of the triumph of "incumbency" in the modern world, the ability of officeholders, no matter what their coloration, to defeat all contenders. The leaders and followers are *ideological* (Mannheim, 1936), mesmerized by the status quo. They are such devotees of the status quo that the system ceases to be adaptive to changing conditions. The Reagan-Bush ascendancy is one example; Gorbachev's difficulties suggest the USSR provides another.

The ideology of individualism, and its corollaries, such as the myth of the "self-made man" and the denial of complexity, obscures the part/whole nature of social systems. Such an ideology may be an adult parallel to a child's defenses against the intense pain that follows severed or threatened bonds. Those approaches which insist on viewing human issues in terms of isolated individuals driven by simple inner motives may be defenses against the anomic conditions in our society.

It will be useful to view these defenses in terms of the psychoanalytic idea of repression. If the ideology of the isolated, self-sufficient individual is a defense against the pain of severed and threatened bonds, what is being repressed is the *idea* of the importance of the social bond, of individuals being incomplete without a web of secure bonds. Freud, however, argued that repression concerns not only ideas but also the *feelings* that accompany them. He thought that repression could be lifted only if both idea and emotions were expressed. If modern societies repress the *idea* of the social bond, what are the associated *feelings* that are also being repressed?

I follow the lead of Cooley and Goffman, whose work implies that pride and shame are the primary social emotions. These two emotions have a signal function with respect to the social bond. In this framework, pride and shame serve as intense and automatic bodily signs of the state of a system that would be otherwise difficult to observe, the state of one's bonds to others. Pride is the sign of an intact bond; shame, a severed or threatened bond. The clearest outer marker of pride is holding up one's head in public and looking others in the eye, but indicating respect by taking turns looking and looking away. In *overt* shame, one shrinks, averting or lowering one's gaze, casting only furtive glances at the other. In *bypassed* shame, one stares, attempting to outface the other.

Pride and shame serve as instinctive signals, both to self and other, to communicate the state of the bond. We react automatically to affirmations of, and threats to, our bonds. However, if a culture is sufficiently insistent, it can teach us to disguise and deny these signals. If the idea of the social bond is repressed in modern societies, then we would expect that these two emotions would also be systematically repressed.

In the nineteenth century, pride and shame could be treated openly and directly by Darwin, McDougall, and Cooley. In current discussions, these two emotions have all but disappeared. As indicated, orthodox psychoanalysis glosses over them, and they fare little better in systematic research. Neither emotion is reported, for example, in the research on emotional universals by Ekman and Freisen (1972).

The work of Cooley, Goffman, and Lewis provides basic ingredients for developing pride and shame constructs. Cooley's and Goffman's analyses have already been mentioned. Cooley's stress on the social nature of pride and shame, particularly his insistence on the way in which we are unaware of normal pride, points in this direction, as does Goffman's analysis of the crucial role of embarrassment in interaction ritual.

The work of the late Helen Lewis, a research psychoanalyst, provides preliminary support for the conjecture about the repression of shame in modern societies. In her empirical work on affects in psychotherapy, she discovered that although other emotions (such as anger) often go unacknowledged, by far the most frequent and least often acknowledged were embarrassment, shame, and humiliation. Since her work will be discussed in later chapters, I will not attempt to outline it here.

However, one aspect of Lewis's work is particularly relevant to the conjecture under discussion. Lewis found that in contexts high in potential for shame (e.g., when the patient appears to suspect that the therapist is critical or judgmental), nonverbal indications of shame were plentiful, for example, long or filled pauses ("well," "you know," "uh-uh-uh," etc.), repetition or self-interruption, and particularly, a lowering of the voice, often to the point of inaudibility.

In these same contexts, however, shame was virtually never acknowledged by name. Instead, a wide variety of words were used, which Lewis interpreted to be a code language, a way of mentioning feelings otherwise unmentionable. Feeling words such as "insecure," "awkward," and "uncomfortable" are a few of the hundred or so similar words often found in these situations. (These same words are found in the Gottschalk-Gleser scale used for interpreting shame in verbal texts [Gottschalk, Winget, and Gleser 1969].) When feelings of shame are verbalized, a language is used which seems to deny or at least disguise the feeling itself. This language is analogous to the code language used for designating other unmentionables such as sexual or "toilet" terms. Like baby talk about body functions with children, the denial of shame is institutionalized in the adult language of modern societies.

It is of great interest that laypersons and researchers alike are apt to insist on the differences among the behaviors referenced by shame variant words (embarrassment, insecurity, etc.) rather than acknowledge the underlying similarities. The resulting Balkanization may be seen as one aspect of the process of denial and repression. Lewis's findings, like the approaches of Cooley and Goffman, suggests that shame is repressed in modern societies.

Although Goffman's and Lewis's treatments of shame are an advance over Cooley's in one way, in another they are retrograde. Their treatments are much more specialized and detailed than Cooley's, whose discussions of the "self-regarding sentiments" are quite casual and brief, conveyed in ordinary language. But Cooley had a vision of the whole system, which is lacking in the more recent discussions. His treatment is explicitly based on the polar opposition between pride and shame in everyday encounter. It therefore lays the basis for my construct of the social bond, with pride and shame as continuous signals of the state of the bond, an instant readout of the "temperature" of the relationship. The emotion of pride is completely absent from Goffman's and Lewis's formulations.

The omission of pride by Goffman is particularly disastrous. Since Lewis is dealing with psychotherapy discourse, we are free to imagine that in normal conversation there would be much more pride than shame. But Goffman's formulations concerning impression management, face, and embarrassment presume to be about normal discourse, leaving the reader with the impression that all human activity is awash in a sea of shame. He nowhere envisioned a secure social bond, much less a well-ordered society built upon secure bonds.

Goffman's omission of pride and secure bonds is a disaster because it implies that impression management is the only game in town. In this way, it indirectly sanctions what I call the "*bella figura*" syndrome. The Italians say, "*fare una bella figura*"; that is, by all means cut a good figure, no matter what the cost. To translate the *bella figura* syndrome into English, one might call it the Bush-Reagan syndrome. At the level of individuals, this syndrome is merely destructive; to the level of nations, it threatens human survival. With respect to Goffman's and Lewis's treatments of shame, it would appear that social theory has both evolved and devolved to the same time.

We are now in a position to interpret the view of guilt and anxiety as elemental emotions in psychoanalysis, and similar treatments in other disciplines also, such as anthropology and classics (Dodds 1951). I will argue, as Lewis does, that guilt is one of the many types of affect belonging to the shame family. If that were the case, then the emphasis on guilt and anxiety, individual emotions, in psychoanalytic and similar formulations can be seen as an aspect of the repression of the idea of the social bond in modern societies. That is to say that anxiety and guilt are used in most theories in a way that denies their social component, shame.

The use of catch-all emotion words functions to disguise the social components of emotion. The disguise involved is often a matter of labeling, of linguistic convention. For example, the phrases "social anxiety" and "social fear" virtually never reference the feeling of anticipated danger to life or limb. Instead they almost always involve the anticipation of embarrassment. In this usage, the suppression of the correct name of the affect is superficial, since it involves only one layer, mislabeling.

In many usages, however, the denial of shame or embarrassment is not merely a linguistic habit but also involves defenses that are at least partially automatic and unconsidered. The sentence "It was an awkward moment for me" almost always refers to embarrassment. In this usage, however, embarrassment is disguised by two defensive movements, denial and projection. "It was not *me* that was embarrassed, but the *moment* that was awkward." The disguise in this case can be envisioned as involving two layers, rather than just one layer, a misleading label, as in the case of social fear. The example of the awkward moment provides an example of the way in which our very language conspires to deny the existence of shame. The repression of shame, and thereby of the social bond, is institutionalized.

The depth of repression of pride and shame is indicated by the absence of these two emotions from the frameworks proposed by Bowlby and by Bowen, two of the principal architects of sociological thinking in psychiatry. Although Bowen has pioneered the social system approach in family therapy, and Bowlby the concept of the social bond in human development, neither of them utilizes the concepts of pride and shame. Instead, they both categorize all diffuse or ambiguous emotion as anxiety, the catch-all term.

After Lewis, Gaylin has shown the most sensitivity to pride and shame, in his typology of feelings (1979) and his treatment of the sources of rage (1989).

Although he does not provide explicit constructs of pride and shame, these two emotions play a prominent role in many of his interpretations. However, his framework is oriented toward individuals; it lacks the emphasis on social relations found in Bowen and Bowlby. Until a framework is fashioned which includes both elements, the social bond and its associated emotions of pride and shame, the human sciences will stayed entrapped in the ideology of simplicity and individualism.

Feeling Traps

Goffman's treatment of embarrassment and Lewis's of shame suggest that these emotions have a characteristic that makes them especially potent and preeminent in human conduct—*recursiveness*, acting back on themselves in never-ending loops. Goffman suggests that embarrassment is especially contagious between interactants; and Lewis, within them. Lewis suggests that the original stimulus for shame, say a comment that one takes to be critical of self, may be only the first step in a long shame sequence. Once ashamed, one can be ashamed of being ashamed, each shame state serving as stimulus for further shame. For this reason, she implies, it is possible for shame-prone persons to be in a more or less chronic shame state.

Goffman advances a parallel argument for the contagion of embarrassment between interactants. One becomes embarrassed that the other is embarrassed, who in turn becomes more embarrassed, and so on. He proposes this kind of contagion as one of the reasons that one may attempt to avoid embarrassing others, since the other's embarrassment may result in one's own.

As already suggested, I define the concept of shame in a way that will include many emotions that are often used as if they were unrelated. Embarrassment is one such affect. I will consider embarrassment to be a type of shame, one which is of lesser intensity and briefer duration and in which the pain of arousal is experienced in awareness. That is to say, embarrassment is a less intense, brief, and overtly experienced form of shame.

Given this definition, it is possible to combine Lewis's model of inner contagion of shame and Goffman's of outer. Shame states have the potential for being extraordinarily intense and protracted because they can be contagious within and between interactants. I refer to such social and psychological loops as triple spirals: one within each interactant and one between them. Triple spirals of shame contagion could give rise to shame states of unlimited intensity or duration.

I have already proposed that shame is deeply repressed and denied in modern societies because it is linked to anomie, the prevalence of threatened or severed social bonds. The recursiveness of shame suggests the fundamental basis for repression: loops of shame like those described above can be so violently painful that one might wish to avoid them at any cost. I propose that, just as normal pride and shame are necessary because they serve as signals for the state of social bonds, unacknowledged shame could be the root cause of chains of threatened bonds, of the transmission of threat from person to person in an ongoing society, and from generation to generation over time.

By studying the microworld of manner and implication that underlies discourse, one may retrieve the hidden causal chain—the unacknowledged shame that leads to compulsive behavior. The continuing repression of the idea of the social bond, of its accompanying emotions of pride and shame, and of human complexity could be the root cause, however, of the profound social disruption we are witnessing in the modern era. The language of laypersons and experts in modern societies systematically denies the social bond and the emotions: repression of the idea of the bond and of the emotions of pride and shame is institutionalized. My book proposes the need for a new language, based on models of bond-relevant behavior, with emphasis on the complexity of behavior and on the key role of sequences of emotion.

Conclusion

The attempt to capture human nature and social structure, to envision the parts and wholes of a massively complex social and psychological system within a single paradigm, is not a simple task. In writing the ensuing chapters, directed on different occasions to different aspects of the overall system, I have not been able to develop a completely linear argument. Since I have fished with many lines, they are frequently tangled. Using lines more original than mine, Wittgenstein (1953, ix) fished the same ocean. His apology to his readers I also offer to mine:

> [It is necessary to depict] landscapes by images and remarks because of the nature of the investigation. For this compels us to travel over a wide field of thought criss-cross in every direction. The . . . remarks in this book are, as it were, a number of sketches of landscapes which were made in the course of these long and involved journeyings. The same or almost the same points were always being approached from different directions, and new sketches made. . . . Thus this book is really only an album.

I have attempted to weld together parts of landscapes from the albums of Cooley, Goffman, Lewis, and many others into a coherent whole but, like them, I have also produced an album. The next step is to discuss a problem intimately connected with the social bond—the relationship between community and society.

2

Micro- and Macroworlds: Community and Society

If one is to proceed with a theory of the social bond, the first issue to be faced is the micro-macro link, the connection between the small world and the large. In sociology at least, there is currently considerable interest in this problem, thanks to the work of Collins, Giddens, and others. Much of the work to this point has been preparatory, pointing out that the problem is crucially important yet extraordinarily difficult, if not intractable. In this chapter, to find a foothold, I return to fundamentals, the basis of social *solidarity* in communities and societies.

The concept of solidarity lies at the core of sociological analysis yet is little discussed. The distinction between community and society, crucial to all sociological theory, assumes the more abstract concept of solidarity. The most explicit use of the concept is found in Durkheim's discussion of the division of labor. Most of his attention, however, is focused on his two forms of solidarity—the mechanical and the organic. He devotes little discussion to the concept of solidarity itself. Like other sociological theorists, he assumes social connectedness without specifying the details.

Another difficulty with his formulation is that it does not include an opposing process at the same level of abstraction. His discussion of anomie appears in his study of suicide and is closely related to his empirical findings. But, as incomplete as it is, Durkheim's formulation is still the best available.

Sociology began with a concern for one form that solidarity takes, the community, early in the Industrial Revolution. Conservative theorists like de Bonald, Condorcet, and Comte observed the migration of rural people to the cities with alarm. They believed that traditional rural communities were being destroyed without being replaced by equivalent structures in the cities. Concerned for the welfare of the migrants, they were also worried about the potential for anarchy. Preoccupation with loss of community has continued to form a thread in social theory. One of the many contemporary manifestations of this idea is that the family might provide, or at least it might be expected to provide, a "haven in a heartless world."

Communities involve relationships between *identified persons,* as in families, children's play groups, and neighborhoods, Cooley's (1909) three types of primary groups. Needless to say, the solidarity in these groups is not based exclusively on bonds between particular persons. Bonding occurs not only between persons but also between roles. In the family, for example, there are shared expectations governing relationships between conventional roles, such as those between wife and husband, parent and child. Nevertheless, the communal component in a relationship is the link between particular, unique persons and not between interchangeable roles. The pain of separation from a loved one is connected, for the most part, with that person's irreplaceable uniqueness and not just the loss of the function he or she fills.

Shibutani's treatise on social psychology (1961) was an attempt to encompass solidarity between persons and between roles. He contrasted relationships between *conventional* and *interpersonal* roles. For example, the social role of father may be played out in many different ways within a particular family, depending on the personalities and relationships of the members. In this way Shibutani sought to integrate community and society in a single theoretical framework. Such an analysis points toward an understanding of the personal elements within social structure. His conjecture (155) on the causal role of interpersonal relationships in "conversion" (massive attitude change), for example, can be extended to the study of changes in social structure, as I suggest below.

Shibutani's analysis placed emphasis on the role of emotions (or sentiments, as he called them) in causation. This emphasis will be a prominent feature of my own approach, as will be seen in the central role I assign to pride and shame. It is significant in this respect that his chapter "Self-Esteem and Social Control" (1961, chap, 13) anticipated, in part, my argument here. This book builds upon Shibutani's earlier work.

Although his framework has great potential, it has had little influence in sociology. Theory and research at the societal level are by far the dominant thread in modern sociology. Why has there been so little interest in communal bonds? For an answer to this question, further comment on the roots of modern sociology is in order.

In the second wave of sociological analysis, in the nineteenth century, the idea of loss of community continued to be an influence but only as a residue. Instead of absolute loss, as the earlier theorists had portrayed the change, a much milder version appeared: one form of social solidarity was being replaced by another. As communal bonds were disappearing, societal ones were taking their place. This dichotomy is so familiar by now that only a few of the variants need be mentioned: status-contract (Maine, 1887), community-society (Toennies 1887), mechanical-organic solidarity (Durkheim 1902), and primary-secondary groups (Cooley 1909).

Especially in Durkheim, the emphasis on societal relations was at the expense of interest in community. In this group of theorists, Cooley was the strongest exception since he forcefully urged the primary group as a form of community. In this respect, Cooley, proponent of community, and Durkheim, proponent of society, represented antithetical positions. Marx's critique of human relations under capitalism, his analysis of alienation, represents another plea for community in addition to Cooley's.

The dominant approach in modern sociology, following Durkheim rather than Cooley, places much more emphasis on role relationships than on relationships between persons—on society rather than community. No doubt there is a host of reasons for this emphasis. One involves the division of labor between sociology and psychology. In order to define sociology as an independent profession, sociologists sought a distinctive approach that would differentiate it from other disciplines, particularly from psychology. With the advantage of hindsight, this preoccupation has not been salutary. With its exclusive focus on individuals, the discipline of psychology has shown little interest in, or even awareness of the existence of, communal bonds. As indicated above, sociologists, although interested, have not been able to agree on an approach to the connection between community and society, the micro-macro link (Collins 1981; Giddens 1984; Alexander et al. 1987). The problem of the nature of communal bonds still remains.

In sociology, the paucity of systematic studies of communal solidarity may be due in large part to the all but overwhelming influence of Durkheim. His predominance seems to have two interrelated bases. First, of all the theorists and researchers, only Durkheim offered both a theory and a method for systematic research. Second, his empirical work, particularly his study of suicide (1897), established the effectiveness of his approach. In this study, he was able to demonstrate social effects on suicide: groups with different cultures (e.g., religious beliefs) had different rates of suicide. Although these effects were small, an issue to which I will return, they were remarkably consistent. He showed that social effects seemed to occur regardless of context. Durkheim's empirical work has justifiably become model of excellence in social science research.

Perhaps the influence of Durkheim's theory on modern sociology has been just as great as his method, but its effects have been more subtle and hidden. The formulations that may have had the greatest effect were not those in *Suicide,* which seem ad hoc, but those in *The Division of Labor in Society* (1902). In this later statement he advanced his analysis of social solidarity. He argued that solidarity in small, traditional groups is based on likemindedness of members. Each member makes identical contributions to the collective consciousness. For example, all members react to the crime of murder with abhorrence and the desire for vengeance, an instance of what he called "mechanical" solidarity.

In modern industrial societies, he argued, solidarity was based not on likemindedness but on the division of labor. The thoughts and actions of each complement those of the others. The response to crime in such groups was more sophisticated than in traditional communities, involving restitution rather than punishment. Durkheim clearly thought that bonds in this type of group, characterized as "organic" solidarity, were tougher and more advanced than those in mechanical solidarity, although this judgment is not made explicit.

Durkheim's description of organic solidarity concerned social relationships which were *irrespective of persons*. The division of labor involves relationships between social roles rather than between particular persons. In his analysis, collective conscience continues to function in modern society, but its significance is eclipsed by the division of labor. (My reference to collective emotions in the origins of WWI [chap. 5] concerns mechanical solidarity.)

As suggested, Durkheim was the only theorist to offer a methodology for systematic research. He developed a method of using statistical summaries to make inferences about levels of solidarity. His method detected patterns of solidarity which were irrespective of particular persons. His theory and his method, in this respect, were perfectly matched.

Durkheim's approach has the great advantage of providing an integrated package of theory and method. But it also labors under a severe disadvantage since it deals only with solidarity involving social roles and excludes communal solidarity. Perhaps his analysis strikes a dominant chord in modern societies because it seems to focus on universals, excluding concrete details.

Durkheim's theory and method are Cartesian; they deal only with universal elements, treated in what Pascal called "the spirit of system," in contrast to what he called the "spirit of finesse," that is, intuitively. The emphasis on system parallels the trend toward formal rationality and away from substantive rationality, to use Weber's (1946) distinction.

I am not criticizing the Cartesian method per se. Indeed, without it, modern science would never have developed. But it becomes a fetish when used in isolation from substantive rationality. Formal and substantive rationalities need not conflict; they complement one another. System alone, when not in tandem with finesse, becomes a trap, Weber's "iron cage." I return to this issue, the integration between system and finesse, in chapter 8.

Durkheim's Cartesian approach led him to ignore the specifics of context in his theory and method. The exclusion of specific personal bonds may be one of the reasons that the effects uncovered by Durkheim's original study, and those in modern studies inspired by his model, are very small. Although he was able to demonstrate a recurring correlation between culture and suicide rates, it was always so small as to suggest that other causes, perhaps many other causes, were also at work. If communal bonds could be included in research, as well as societal ones, perhaps a more complete explanation would be forthcoming.

More directly to the point of my argument, the exclusion of persons from the Durkheimian approach breaks the conceptual link between the microworld and the macroworld. The bond between persons, much more than between roles, is highly dependent on the specific details which characterize persons, even down to nuances of manner and appearance. An associated limitation is that his analysis focuses on external behavior, excluding inner events such as thoughts and feelings. This book will deal with these details in an attempt to restore the micro-macro link.

Durkheim's typology of mechanical and organic solidarity was an enormous step forward in the progress of sociological theory, but elaboration of the basic idea is needed if progress is to continue. Like the other theories of community and society, his analysis is extremely abstract, a simple dichotomy. His formulations remain somewhat vague about empirical markers. Furthermore, he implies that each type can exist only separately, in different societies. He does not consider the possibility, as Shibutani does, of the interweaving of the two types of solidarity in the same society. Finally, and most important, nowhere does he develop a detailed model that would specify the links between causes and effects. I return to this issue in chapter 5.

In the remainder of this chapter, I briefly review theories of communal relationships. Drawing upon this review, I take a step toward formulating a theory and method for studying relationships between persons and between roles, social bonds and social solidarity.

Communal Bonds

Further elaborated, Shibutani's approach to community and society could provide a framework for research on the micro-macro link. His hypothesis about interpersonal causation of conversions (1955) provides an example. He suggested that conversions depend on the emotional attitudes of the convert toward his or her significant others. Specifically, he hypothesized that a person converts because of negative attitudes toward the bearer(s) of the convert's original perspective and positive attitudes toward the holder(s) of the new perspective. For example, a convert to a religious sect like Hare Krishna would be expected to have had painful personal relationships with his or her family of origin and positive ones toward sect members.

To state the matter in a slightly different way, conversion is caused by severed or insecure bonds with the members of one's original reference group and more secure bonds with members of the new reference group. (The concepts of severed, insecure, and secure bonds are Bowlby's [1973], to be discussed below.) Although Shibutani limits his analysis to the interpersonal level, there is no inherent reason that it may not also be applied to the societal level.

What is the cause of the rapid and large changes of perspective that sometimes occur at the national or even international level? Extending Shibutani's hypothesis, one might look for a preponderance of severed or insecure bonds at the communal level in a whole society. Such a preponderance might occur in combination with the appearance of a charismatic political or religious figure with whom great numbers of persons could form personal bonds. This hypothesis offers an avenue for understanding the rapid changes in collective attitudes which sometimes occur in whole societies.

One problem with this hypothesis, already hinted at by my reference to Bowlby, is that it is posed in terms of a simple dichotomy between positive and negative attitudes toward significant others. Such a dichotomy might not lead to research difficulties at the personal level, particularly if converts were chosen who had extreme attitudes. In studies at the societal level, however, problems might arise. At this level, many relationships are probably ambivalent, a mixture of positive and negative attitudes. As a first step toward systematic research, bonds need to be described in terms more specific than the negative-positive distinction.

The work of Bowlby on attachment offers a first step in this direction. His research on children (1969, 1973, and 1980) describes the personal bond. His cases consistently show strong effects of early separation: when infants and young children are cut off from there parents or other caretakers, invariably there are enduring effects. He notes particularly how early separation leads to ambivalence in all later relationships. His descriptions should be helpful for systematic research since they involve observable markers, for example, anxiety, depression, grief, and angry protest. For brevity, I refer to the instance already mentioned in chapter 1, a case cited by Burlingham and Freud, which is also discussed by Bowlby.

Reggie was three years old when his former nurse, Mary-Ann, returned for a visit (Bowlby 1973, 247). He refused to speak to her during her visit, turning his head away. But after she left, he was overheard to say, "My very own Mary-Ann! But I don't like her." The first sentence suggests strong attachment, but the second, occurring in almost the same breath, aversion. Like most of Bowlby's cases, this one suggests not simple attachment or aversion but ambivalence. Since many of his cases showed similar conflicts, Bowlby conceived three kinds of bonds rather than the usual dichotomy (1973), as indicated above.

Although his research is a step toward developing a model of bonding, it may still be too narrow to apply to relationships at the society level. It deals entirely with extreme cases of loss, and only with children. The dramatic, highly visible ambivalence in his cases may be unusual in adults. The history of attachments for the average adult might be less extreme, or at least less visible, than in Bowlby's cases.

Even in adults who have suffered from threatened or severed bonds, conflicting feelings are probably more hidden than in children. This latter problem, particularly, might make for difficulties in studies of entire populations. Even the surface contours of adult relationships are extraordinarily complex, to say nothing of undercurrents. To formulate a theory of the communal bond, one may need to use Bowlby's ideas and those of others as starting points for the development of more complex models.

The "Attitude" of Theory

A brief digression will serve as an introduction to Goffman's approach, which, like Shibutani's, contributes to my argument. One of the limitations of existing social theory is a tendency toward oversimplification. In preparation for our descent from abstract theory into the microworld, it may be well to discuss this point further. Many theorists and researchers, even those, like Bowlby, who deal in detail with concrete instances, seem content, in the main, with the conventional concepts of their particular culture. It is true that they originate new concepts. But the number and scope of their innovations may be obscured by conventional usage, the common coin of their society.

In this light, most social theories are only slightly removed from folk theories, the ethnotheories of human nature and conduct that prevail in the theorist's society. Because theory is written largely in ordinary language, it often reflects and reiterates what Schutz (1962) called "the attitude of everyday life." Theory tends to portray the social world as an orderly, predictable, and relatively simple place, sharing the simplifying presuppositions held in the host society.

An unanalyzed backdrop of presuppositions gives rise to the attitude that relatively simple formulations are complete and virtually self-evident. This attitude impedes the development of theory which is both innovative and testable. The attitude of everyday life in theory was particularly prominent in the nineteenth century. Durkheim and Cooley, otherwise antagonists, offend equally in this respect.

To be sure, some theorists, both classic and modern, have shown attitudes toward the social world appreciative of its complexity. Kant wrote: "Two things fill the mind with awe: the starry sky above, and the moral law within." Properly awed by nature, Kant included the social world in his respectful gaze.

A similar tone can be found in several recent approaches. Many theorists have seen human communication as so complex as to be almost a miracle. Some of Dewey's statements reflect this attitude (1958, 202): "In communication, such conjunction and contact as is characteristic of animals become endearments capable of infinite idealization; they become symbols of the very culmination of nature." In a like vein, Steiner (1975) implies that the translation of text from one language to another may be the most complicated event that has ever happened in the universe. (The issue of inter- and intralingual translation will appear again in later chapters.) Levine's (1985) plea, following Simmel, for awareness of the ambiguity that pervades human affairs also points in the same direction.

A taste for complexity may be found among the analysts of discourse. An example is Pittenger, Hockett, and Danehy's (1960, 211) criticism of the position that only the statistical approach to behavior is legitimate:

> To us the most discouraging characteristic of the behavioral sciences today is the prevalence of an overweening drive for quick

nomothetic results of high statistical reliability, whatever the cost in relevance. The statistical tail wags the scientific dog. Instead of regarding statistical methods as means to an end, empirical data are viewed merely as ends to a mean. One fears and avoids direct encounter with human behavior, in all its incredible complexity, as one would shun a Gorgon's glance.

The idea that human communication is awesomely complex may be necessary to break through a fixed point of view, an intellectual "cake of custom." We are all so adept at communication that we take it for granted.

The Microworld

Studies of the microworld of ordinary discourse (such as those in the chapters to come) suggest rather a different story. It may be that the meaning of a word in context is at least as complex as a strand of DNA. As will be discussed in later chapters, creating and understanding expressions in context require almost instantaneous access to vast domains of history and culture. Contextual meanings involve the enfolded intricacies of both the human brain and the social world.

In order to visualize the domain of the microworld, one may helpfully invoke the idea of an implicate order. This idea, suggested by Bohm (1980), is being used in current discussions of the subatomic world in physics.[1] Its genealogy derives ultimately, I suspect, from Goethe's botanical research. Goethe viewed the mature plant as part of the *explicate*, or unfolded, order. The origins of this order, he argued, were hidden in the seed, which contained the *implicate*, or enfolded, order. The explicate order is the world of appearances; the implicate order, the world that underlies appearances. Its existence can only be inferred.

The analysis of discourse in the chapters to come suggests that it may clear the mind to consider the microworld as a part of the implicate social order. I am not suggesting that the microworld is particularly mysterious or inaccessible. On the contrary, my purpose is to demonstrate its accessibility. The idea of the implicate order is introduced only to signal that one needs to shift mental gears, to relinquish, for the time being, the attitude of everyday life, to enter the microworld.

Sociologists are familiar with the difficulties of observing recurring patterns in the macroworld. This world, so vast and so slow moving, requires special techniques to make its regularities visible—the statistics and mathematical models now taken for granted. The study of the microworld also requires special techniques, but for the opposite reason: the movements are too

---

1. In current sociology, the concept of the implicate order has been used by Bradley (1987) because it is connected with the concept of the hologram, the way in which the part represents the whole.

small and quick to be readily visible to the unaided eye. Microlinguistics is needed to explore the microworld. The required technique is a radical departure from those that have become standard in sociology, but it is necessary if we are to understand bonds between persons. Observing the microworld requires not a telescope, such as the sample survey, but a microscope—video- and audiotapes, or at least verbatim texts, which provide the data for discourse analysis.

The fate of the concept of the "double bind" (Bateson et al. 1956) can be used to illustrate the need for studies of the microworld. Bateson and his associates argued persuasively that mental illness might arise out of recurring situations of mixed messages, that is, families which communicated conflicting information at two or more levels. The examples used often involved conflicts between the verbal and nonverbal levels, between thoughts and feelings. Like most theorists, however, the authors failed to specify causal sequences and empirical markers. Although this concept proved useful in the clinical realm, it has been tried and discarded by researchers (Olson 1972; Abeles 1976). Since the theorists did not provide a detailed causal model or markers, the researchers used aggregate, decontextualized data that did not test the underlying idea. Neither theorists nor researchers explored the specific details of the microworld.

Of all the social theorists, the one who came closest to confronting the reality of the microworld was Erving Goffman. He sought to understand social structure by observing small events in ordinary social interaction. At least abstractly, he understood and usually achieved the shifting of gears necessary to escape "emeshment" with the attitude of everyday life; he was not afraid of nuance. A very brief review of both the achievements of his approach and its limitations may clarify my argument.

In his treatment of "impression management" (1959) and his work on face saving, deference, and demeanor (1967), Goffman established the central role of "face" in social encounter. He showed that participants are excruciatingly sensitive to the exact amount of *deference* they receive, that is, to gestures of respect and disrespect. Each gesture is a comment on, an affirmation or denial, of momentary social *status* in the encounter. Weber's term "status honor" is relevant here, although Goffman implies that status honor is not a fixed attribute but a fluid process, at hazard in every encounter. Social status is not permanent but continuously reviewed and contested.

Goffman's analysis implies a theory of motivation, although he would have vehemently denied any such implication. He demonstrated repeatedly how preoccupied each participant is with face. In his essay "The Social Organization of Embarrassment" (1967), he took an important first step toward understanding the social psychology of face. He argued that the emotion of embarrassment is the goad which produces the participants' preoccupation with face. His examples show participants are continuously involved in the exacting task of avoiding embarrassment and of avoiding embarrassing others. His analysis implies that fending off embarrassment is a crucial motive in all social encounters in the sense of being the most pressing of the participants' immediate concerns.

Goffman's description of the microworld does not exclude attention to the larger public order. On the contrary, he was usually attuned to the connection between the small world and the large. His treatment of the symptoms of mental illness (as in "Insanity and the Public Order" [1967]) provides an example. He deals with symptoms as "situational improprieties" in order to make visible what is usually invisible—the microstructure of norms about comportment that characterize our society. He is careful not to become merely a miniaturist for its own sake but to show the way in which microworld process supports and is supported by the macrostructure.

However, another step that Goffman took, important as it is for a theory of motivation, shows an uncharacteristic hesitation. In his essay "Where the Action Is" (1967), he developed an idea that has broad implications for understanding *disputes*. As usual with his writing, the exposition is informal, almost an aside to the reader. His idea of duels, feuds, and vendettas as "character contests" implies that saving and building face may be a primary motive in disputes of all kinds. That is to say, seeking pride and avoiding embarrassment may take on highly aggressive forms, as well as the more passive forms involved in polite conversation.

In this particular instance, however, Goffman's customary alertness to the connections between micro- and macroworlds seems to have failed him. He did not consider the possibility that quarrels between nations could also be character contests, with collective motivations similar to the individual ones that he detailed so precisely. Why limit the honor-insult-revenge cycle to primitive warfare and vendettas (such as those in the Italian city-states of the Renaissance and nineteenth-century Sicily)? Perhaps Goffman, like most other theorists, was unwilling to enter the microworld, the implicature and emotions in the revenge cycle, at the level of actual discourse (see chap. 5).

In his analysis of interaction ritual, the pervasive and all but invisible etiquette of social interaction, Goffman (1967) developed a forceful and immediately plausible description of the machinery of social life. His description has a strong if somewhat hidden resonance with the psychology of emotion, particularly the emotion of embarrassment. Characteristically, however, he disavowed any such association, proposing that he meant to deal only with "the syntactical relations among *acts* of persons mutually present to one another" (1967, 2; emphasis added). That is to say, he eschewed the psychological level of description, relying entirely on an analysis of behavior.

But the omission of the psychological level gives only a specialized, and therefore *partial*, analysis of encounters. Since Goffman's self-imposed program of interpretation forbade him the explicit consideration of motives, he could only describe the interaction machine but not explain why it runs. Human intelligence seems to function best when allowed to integrate all available points of view, using part/whole analysis (see the discussion of parts and wholes in chap. 10). I develop the implications of Goffman's partial analysis into a comprehensive theory and method for the study of discourse. In particular, I use the relationship between deference and embarrassment to develop an explicit theory of motivation (chaps. 5–7).

One central part of the whole of discourse as it is understood by participants is their own motives. They are usually unwilling merely to describe, as is the current fashion in discourse analysis. With the exceptions that I discuss below, modern discourse analysis is behavioral, attempting to understand discourse as if it concerned only outer behavior. Participants, however, are often likely to understand the *entire* meaning of utterances in terms of motives. The absence of analysis of motives in current studies usually fails to produce a lifelike representation. Since the motives that I will discuss are closely tied to emotions, it is understandable why so many current studies seem lifeless; they do not touch on discourse as the lived experience of the participants.

As indicated, Goffman's approach lacked an explicit theory of motivation. It also lacked a systematic method. His contributions to sociology and social psychology, and he made many more than I have mentioned, were as a specialist in theory. He was content to create a viewpoint that would increase one's intuitive understanding, no mean accomplishment.[2] Like the other theorists of the community, he had not yet devised a method that allowed him to test and modify his understanding.

The theorists of community formulated *theory without method*. The analysts of discourse, with special emphasis on the work of Pittenger et al. (1960), and Labov and Fanshel (1977), whose work will loom large in later chapters, devised *method without theory*. Helen Lewis (1971), a psychoanalyst and research psychologist, came closest to integrating theory and method. In the years to come, she may be seen as the Durkheim of social psychology. My overall framework for understanding social bonds depends heavily upon the formulations of Shibutani and Goffman. But my theory and method proper are an elaboration of Lewis's work. By enlarging the scope of her theory to include an explicit social dimension, and by formulating the methodology that is only implied in her empirical research, I delineate a theory and method for studying the social bond.

The *theory* combines Lewis's analysis of unacknowledged shame with Cooley's and Goffman's observations on the crucial role of pride and shame in virtually all social process. I propose *normal* pride and shame as the basic human motives, but shame has the potential to become pathological when it is *not acknowledged*.

The *method* I propose is based on C. S. Peirce's (1896–1908) concept of

---

2. Perhaps if Goffman had lived longer he might have become interested in method; one of his later books (1981), a close reading of forms of conversation, was a move toward discourse analysis.

abduction, the *rapid* shuttling back and forth between observation and imagination. His formulation cut across the more conventional ideas of induction and deduction. In effective social interaction and thought, one not only observes (induction) and imagines (deduction) but also constantly (in microseconds) checks one against the other. I propose that abduction is the process which enables participants to accomplish the incredibly complex process of understanding meanings *in context*. I also propose a way in which researchers can use abduction, as participants do, yet use it in a verifiable way: make verbatim recordings of the data available so that the reader can check the researcher's interpretations against the original text. This procedure may resolve the controversy surrounding "thick description," the quarrel between qualitative and quantitative viewpoints.

It would have been desirable if each of the chapters that follow employed theory and method equally, as prescribed by my theory. Since exact balance is an ideal, I was unable to accomplish it. The introductory chapters emphasize theory. The next section, on understanding, has better balance, but somewhat more emphasis on theory. The section after that, on discourse, shows balance between the two realms. Chapter 8, on science and common sense, emphasizes method. The last two chapters, one on genius, the other on the social bond, lack sufficient instances of concrete discourse. Overall, I have sought to show how theory and method used in close conjunction illuminate each other, connecting micro and macro, qualitative and quantitative, individual and group, art and science.

Part 2
Understanding: A *Verstehende Soziologie*

3

Meaning, Context, and Interpretation

This section deals with a basic problem in both social and natural sciences: the structure and process of interpretation. All signs in the social and natural worlds are inherently ambiguous. There seem to be two separate problems: (1) What is the function which transforms a set of signs into a coherent interpretation? (2) What is the goodness of fit of the transformation? In social science, both questions involve complex issues, especially the second. Both issues are usually glossed by the theorists of interpretation and go unexplicated by its practitioners. I argue that one reason may be ideological: both issues require analysis of the microworld which underlies all social encounter and therefore undercuts the *status quo*, the social arrangements which go without saying in our society.

As a starting point for delineating a model of interpretation, I examine a dialogue from a novel by George Eliot and draw three conclusions: (1) Understanding of the passage depends upon implicature: the characters do not articulate the basic *content* or *form* of their discourse. (2) For this reason, it would be almost impossible for the interactants to understand fully *what* they are talking about, at its various levels, or to understand the implications of the *form* their talk takes. (3) The extent of the imaginative activity of one of the interactants (during the pauses in the conversation) suggests the extraordinary rapidity and breadth of inner search.

The first and second conclusions suggest a fault in theories of intersubjectivity; they seem to imply almost continuous attunement between interactants. Although this may be true at the surface level, it seems untrue and misleading when applied to the many layers of meaning and implication below the surface of discourse: feelings, motives, and long-range intentions. Attunement at these deeper levels is difficult enough at the personal level; at the group level it may be precarious indeed. The implications of the third conclusion, the nature and role of inner search, will be examined in chapter 4.

Ideological and Utopian Theories

In referring to the status quo, the social arrangements that obtain in a particular time, we usually have in mind the macroworld of large institutions, particularly political and economic institutions. This world has been the traditional ground of sociological theory. Even though the tradition has been often criticized, it has been nevertheless maintained in practice.

Weber's (1947) complaint about the excessively macroscopic nature of most sociological thinking gives one pause:

> Interpretative sociology considers the individual [*Einzelindiv-iduum*] and his action as the basic unit, as its "atom"—if the disputable comparison for once may be permitted. In this approach, the individual is also the upper limit and the sole carrier of meaningful conduct. . . . In general, for sociology, such concepts as "state," "association," "feudalism," and the like, designate certain categories of human interaction. Hence it is the task of sociology to reduce these concepts to "understandable" action, that is, without exception, to the actions of participating individual men.

Sociological concepts "designate certain categories of *human interaction*," according to Weber. Although he states that theory must be applicable to the actions of individuals, he never actually carried out such an analysis, nor has any other theorist. Of course there is the danger of losing one's way in the details of a concrete event. But without the individual event, there is the equally grave danger of *reification*, of converting abstractions into realities. Concepts which are not applicable to specific events obscure social reality more than they help uncover it.

As already suggested, preparation for the microscopic analysis of social institutions can be found in the work of Goffman. Like Weber, he understood that *every* concrete action manifests social structure, even the most commonplace scene. In any social encounter, one is involved with what is perhaps the most fundamental social institution, the one which governs gatherings: "More than to any family or club, more than to any class or sex, more than to any nation, the individual belongs to gatherings, and he had best show he is a member in good standing" (Goffman 1963, 248). Goffman surveyed the rules of propriety and deportment, of language, thought, and feeling, that obtained in face-to-face gatherings. He saw that here too there was a status quo which as yet had received scant attention. This microworld is taken for granted and goes without saying. Each member of a society assumes its contours to be the only ones that are imaginable, possible, and decent.

As Schutz (1962) pointed out, the smooth functioning of the status quo requires in its members "the attitude of everyday life." That is, the intricate procedures which are used to construct social scenes and gatherings should go unnoticed and unremarked. Toward this institution, the scenes of daily life in a society, its members maintain what Mannheim (1936) called an "ideological" attitude; they accept it totally and without question. Those with this attitude are seen by others, and see themselves, as normal, sane, regular persons. They are thought of as "fitting in," as "our sort." They are *gleigeschalten;* not only do their actions, thoughts, and feelings mesh with the actions, thoughts, and feelings of others, but their emeshment is perfectly aligned; there is virtually no friction.

The attitude of Goffman and Schutz, however, is not ideological but *utopian,* to use Mannheim's (1936) term. That is, it shatters the calm surface of everyday life, it notices and comments upon what is to be taken for granted by the member in good standing, and it challenges the sanctity of daily life by implying that it, like any other social institution, is constructed, not eternal and absolute. Such thinking is not radical in the political or economic sphere; neither Schutz nor Goffman expressed any view about the nature of capitalism, socialism, or political economy. Nevertheless, their work is radical not in the macroworld but in the microworld. They might be considered to be proponents of cultural revolution, since their analysis undercuts the most fundamental of all institutions, the one which governs social gatherings and occasions, the unnoticed backdrop of all activity in any society.

By the same token, most theory and method in social science, to the extent that they take for granted the construction of the microworld, are profoundly conservative. This is the crux of Schutz's critique of modern sociology. It applies equally to theories that are politically radical, such as those of Marx, and to those that are politically conservative, such as those of Parsons. It also applies to most methods in social and behavioral sciences, both quantitative and qualitative. To the extent that the experiment, survey, or interview takes for granted the microworld, it reaffirms and therefore helps maintain it.

In ethnomethodology, Garfinkel (1967) sought to develop Schutz's critique of sociology into a program of research, as did Cicourel in cognitive sociology (1974), programs that would treat the microworld as the topic of research rather than as a hidden resource. That is to say, the proposed research would not tacitly assume, and therefore depend upon, the microworld but would describe it explicitly. Following Schutz, Garfinkel and Cicourel proposed radical approaches to social encounter that were focused on the "indexical" nature of expression. Unlike the expressions of all other living creatures, the meaning of human expressions is not fixed; it only indexes a relationship between the expression and the *context* in which it occurs. The meaning of all human expressions is contextual.

Contexual Meaning

Because the idea of contextual meaning is so crucial to my argument, and so abstract, a further example of its implication is necessary. Linguists now realize that the meanings of certain types of words, the pronouns, for example, are contextual. Words like "you," "it," "he," or "she" have little meaning in themselves; they are like blank checks; their references are determined by the context. To understand what person or object a pronoun references, the interactant must do a certain amount of work, the work of examining the context for the actual reference. That is, the interactant must *contextualize* the meaning of every pronoun.

Finding the meaning of a pronoun in context involves the interactant in a *search* that may be both external and internal. For example, the sentence "It is over there" may first require the listener to note the direction of the speaker's gaze, then look in the same direction, and finally search the environment located in that direction for the reference of the pronoun "it": an external search. If the object cannot be found, the listener may look again at the speaker, noting that she is only staring in that direction. This turn of events may require the listener to make an internal search, remembering earlier segments of the conversation, in attempting to locate "there."

Remembering the particular manner in which the phrase "over there" was uttered, and an earlier conversation about overseas travel, the listener may conclude that the speaker was referring to a particular geographic location that had been mentioned in the conversation preceding the present one. In order to locate the meaning of the pronoun, the listener was required to search not only the immediate physical and verbal context but also his memory of earlier conversations, the *extended context*.

In this hypothetical conversation the meaning of the pronoun had to be constructed by the listener, ad hoc, for this particular moment. Since the example deals with a pronoun, a flagrantly ambiguous word, we are apt to think that the intricate search process described above is the exception, that it is necessary only when ambiguous words are used. Recent work in linguistics and computer science, however, has strongly suggested that all human expressions are ambiguous and, by implication, require complex search in order to be understood. One sees this most clearly in seeking to translate an unfamiliar language. Using a dictionary is frustrating because all the most frequently used words, especially adverbs, prepositions, and verbs, have more than single meanings. Even the commonly used nouns may have several meanings. There is a basic ambiguity in language, even if we accept the simplifying myth that the meaning of a word is exactly defined by a dictionary.

Ambiguity of expression is generated not only by multiple linguistic meanings. This is the most restricted source of ambiguity. Another and much richer source of ambiguity is the *manner* of expression. The nonverbal components of utterance, the sounds (paralanguage) and the gestures (kinesics or body language), profoundly modify and enhance the linguistic meaning of expressions. In our hypothetical example, the speaker should have signaled that the phrase "over there" was to have a special meaning by using a special intonation, "heavy emphasis," a conventional paralinguistic device putting an expression "in quotation marks" (which can also be mimed by stroking the air twice, using two fingers of both hands).

There is one further source of the ambiguity of expression. Although we usually think that words and gestures have conventional and therefore fixed meanings, this is not quite the case. Conventional definitions of words serve only as an approximation of meaning in use. Human expression has an innovative character: conventional meanings may be modified or transformed. New words, gestures, and meanings may be invented on the spur of the moment to fulfill the expression that is needed. There is a creative element in human expression, as manifested in art and poetry, and in mundane settings such as spontaneously improvised metaphor, wit, and irony.

What has been said to this point can be summarized as follows: natural language, as it occurs in spontaneous conversation, is always ambiguous because most words and gestures each have more than one conventional meaning and because, in varying degrees, meanings are unconventional, improvised at the moment of encounter. It has been argued that human language functions to conceal meaning at least as much as to reveal it (Steiner 1975).

The Problem of Interpretation

How does the interactant find his or her way through the labyrinth, the maze of ambiguous expressions? This is the fundamental problem of interpretation, which has been expressed in many guises in intellectual history; the puzzle of hermeneutics, the correct interpretation of an ambiguous text, or the very similar issue that lies at the heart of semiotics, the relationship between the sign and that which it signifies. The construction of theories in science involves a variant of the problem of interpretation as it is construed here: the problem of demonstrating the reference of signs which are necessarily ambiguous.

Among the solutions to the problem of reference that have been proposed by social scientists, I will consider two that are closely related. The American pragmatists, particularly Mead (1934) and Peirce (1896–1908), approached the problem in social psychological terms. For Mead, meaning is created in the process of *role taking:* in an encounter, each person can solve the problem of reference by a method of successive approximation, which involves shuttling back and forth between imagination and observation. Observing the outer signs, the words and gestures, one imagines the reference. This sequence is the zeroth approximation. If one is sufficiently motivated, this initial inference can be checked by imagining what signs would be visible if one's inference is correct, then observing whether these are actually present. This cycle, which involves a movement from outer signs to inner experience, can be repeated, many times, if necessary, until one is virtually certain of the reference.

In Mead's solution, each interactant functions like a scientist—proposing a hypothesis, then testing it through careful observation. Peirce applied his model, which he called *abduction,* to science itself. As will be suggested below, the interactant in everyday life and the scientist face a similar task, the interpretation of ambiguous signs. Peirce suggests that the scientist seeking to explain events in nature (signs) is involved in interpretive activity. A theory is an interpretation which shows the correspondence between the signs (data) and that which is signified (the theory).

According to Peirce, the scientist also is involved in a movement between observation and imagination. He shows that the creative scientist, like Kepler, is involved not only in observation (induction), and not only in imagination (deduction), but also in a process which combines both, *abduction,* that is, cycling rapidly between observation and imagination, as in Mead's model. Both role taking and abduction involve swift alternation between inner and outer experiences as a solution to the problem of reference. I will return to the issue of the rapidity of these inner and outer processes below, and also in chapter 4.

Schutz's solution to the problem of reference represents the tradition of European idealism. Although starting from the point of view of individual phenomenology, rather than Mead's social behaviorism, Schutz proposed a solution that is similar in form. Like Mead and the pragmatists, Schutz describes the procedures which may result in intersubjectivity, the joint consciousness of interacting individuals. The basic procedure, the documentary method of interpretation, to use Mannheim's phrase (1952), involves the alternation between the signs or documents and the underlying pattern (reference) which the search presupposes.

The language Mannheim used was vague and abstract, as is most phenomenological theory. Schutz, however, described a somewhat more specific process, the prospective-retrospective method of understanding. By this phrase Schutz meant that the interactant does not limit search for reference to the immediate verbal-physical context. In order to understand the meaning of expressions, one must forage backward in memory, over what has happened, and forward, in imagination, to what might happen. Although not as explicit about inner and outer search as Mead, Schutz implies a similar process.

In order to understand the problem of interpretation further, one must state it in a form sufficiently abstract so that its application to both natural and social sciences will be apparent. An interpretation may be viewed in the following format. Given a collection of signs, S, one must determine the function, F, such that interpretation $I = F(S)$. That is, What is the procedure, F, that produces a one-to-one correspondence between each sign in S and the interpretation, I?

This formulation suggest that there are two basic questions involved in interpretation: the construction of the function, F, which serves to transform the set of signs, S, into an interpretation, I, and the testing of this transformation to determine its goodness of fit.

In natural science the function, F, is usually expressed as a mathematical equation. Newton was able to predict the orbit of Mars with his universal law of gravitation: $f = mM/D^2$. The force between a body with a mass of m and a body with a mass of M is the product of the two masses divided by the square of the distance between them. This interpretation can be tested by using the function (mM/D^2) to transform a set of signs (the observed distances between Mars and the sun) into a set of predictions (S') for the force on Mars at each observed distance. The goodness of fit, or accuracy, of I involves a simple comparison between S and S'. (Newton used Kepler's equation for the orbit of Mars to demonstrate the goodness of fit of his law.)

The same abstract formulation of the problem of interpretation may also be applied to social interaction. Although the nature of the function which translates signs into interpretations has not been much discussed (let alone determined), in principle at least, it might be similar to the one in natural science. The problem of goodness of fit is more complex, however. If we consider the signs to be interpreted in a conversation to be the words and gestures, an interpretation would be the *implicature* (Grice 1981), a verbal statement of the implications of the words and gestures (S) which were not expressed in words by the interactants.

An exchange from the session analyzed by Labov and Fanshel (1977) provides an example. In response to Rhoda's request that Aunt Editha dust the room, Editha replied, "It looks clean to me." Although Editha did not actually use the word "no," Rhoda clearly took Editha's response to mean no, as would any other person; no is implied by Editha but not stated.

One way of assessing goodness of fit between S and S' would be to compare the implicature, as understood by the other interactant or by the researcher, with the intentions of the speaker. Leaving aside the problem of assessing these intentions, this procedure would result in only a partial test, the degree of overt agreement between the two sets of data. The failure of agreement between an interpretation and a speaker's intentions would not necessarily disqualify an interpretation, however, since the speaker may have been unaware of some of the meaning of his or her own words and gestures. In the event of disagreement, it might be necessary for the researcher to use a panel of judges to decide the issue.

It is significant that none of the theorists of interpretation—not Mead, Schutz, Mannheim, Weber, Dilthey, or any other—shows us how the ideas and concepts he discusses may be applied to concrete examples. What is the point-for-point correspondence between sign and the interpretation of what is signified, and by what processes do the participants arrive at it? In studies of human expression, there is a strong tendency to gloss over both of these questions. Except for the current approaches to interpretation in artificial intelligence and in cognitive science (to be discussed in chap. 4), all approaches to a theory of interpretation have been merely conceptual.

It is true that semioticians and theorists of language (e.g., Quine), have been more venturesome than the social theorists. However, the texts they have discussed have been either very small units (words or sentences) detached form the verbal matrix in which they occur in the social world (Quine) or, in the case of the semiotic analysis of literary texts, such as a drama, divorced from the nonverbal components which enable an audience to understand and appreciate the text. Perhaps for this reason, theorists of language and semioticians are apt to be dubious about the possibility of explicating the process of interpretation and the possibility of accurate translation. Quine argues that translation is "indeterminate" (1960). As will be seen in my critique in chapter 4, explicit functions of transformation are modeled in artificial intelligence and in studies of problem solving in cognitive science.

The classical theorists of interpretation, like Mead and Dilthey, provide few examples. When they are offered, they are extremely brief. If an interpretation is offered, it will be an abstract gloss. Garfinkel (1967, 38–39), unlike most of the other theorists, provides many examples of texts but does not attempt a complete, point-for-point interpretation. Here is an example of one of his texts (for brevity, I include only the first of three exchanges between the husband and wife):

| HUSBAND: | Dana succeeded in putting a penny in a parking meter today without being picked up. | This afternoon as I was bringing Dana, our four-year-old son, home from the nursery school, he succeeded in reaching high enough to put a penny in a parking meter when we parked in a meter parking zone, whereas before he has always had to be picked up to reach that high. |
| WIFE: | Did you take him to the record store? | Since he put a penny in a meter that means that you stopped while he was with you. I know that you stopped at the record store either on the way to get him or on the way back. Was it on the way back, so that he was with you or did you stop there on the way to get him and somewhere else on the way back? |

The signs, what was said, are on the left side of the page; the signified, the interpretation, on the right. This text and its interpretation were produced by one of Garfinkel's students, who had been asked to write dialogues of what was said, on the one hand, and "what they and their partners understood that they were talking about," on the other.

The statements in the right-hand column may be taken to represent the implicature of expression, a verbal statement of what is implied but has not been stated. Although Garfinkel describes some of the abstract features of the relationship between the dialogue and its implicature, he makes no attempt to show point-to-point correspondence or the process which produced the interpretation—not in this text or in any of his other examples. He also ignores the problem of goodness of fit: To what extent would the wife agree? In this regard he is like the other theorists: their treatment of interpretation is abstract and conceptual. To find descriptions of the process of interpretation, of its inner and outer components, we must turn from its theorists to its practitioners.

Interpretive Procedures: A Literary Example

It is often noted that because of the high degree of specialization in modern societies, there is usually a pronounced split between theory and practice. The study of interpretation is no exception: the theorists provide analysis without application; the practitioners, application without analysis. Because extended examples may provide clues to the nature of the interpretive process, I will examine a small segment from a novel—a dialogue and the author's comments about it.

Although there are many literary treatments of inner search which occurs in a fictional character's social encounters, in the "stream of consciousness," these accounts often do not mention outer search. In George Eliot's novels, however, the author pays close attention to both components.

The chosen passage, from *Daniel Deronda* (1876, 114–16), concerns the heroine's first encounter with her husband-to-be, Grandcourt. To appreciate some of the fine points, the reader should know something of the extended context. Since Gwendolen and Grandcourt are considered the two most eligible persons in their community—she the most beautiful and intelligent, he the richest and most handsome—the idea of marriage is "in the air," although nothing has been said on either side. Since Gwendolen's family has been recently impoverished, and she has expensive tastes, she is under considerable pressure to consider him seriously as a suitor. (For convenience of reference, I have numbered Grandcourt's [Gr] and Gwendolen's [Gw] passages.)

> . . . conversation had begun, the first and constant element in it being that Grandcourt looked at Gwendolen persistently with a slightly exploring gaze, but without change of expression, while she only occasionally looked at him with a flash of observation a little softened by coquetry. Also, after her answers there was a longer or shorter pause before he spoke again.
>
> Gr1:   "I used to think archery was a great bore," Grandcourt began. He spoke with a fine accent, but with a certain broken drawl, as of a distinguished personage with a distinguished cold on his chest.
>
> Gw1:   "Are you converted to-day?" said Gwendolen.
> (Pause, during which she imagined various degrees and modes of opinion about herself that might be entertained by Grandcourt.)
>
> Gr2:   "Yes, since I saw you shooting. In things of this sort one generally sees people missing and simpering."
>
> Gw2:   "I suppose you are a first-rate shot with a rifle."
> (Pause, during which Gwendolen, having taken a rapid observa-

tion of Grandcourt, made a brief graphic description of him to an indefinite hearer.)

Gr3:   "I have left off shooting."

Gw3:   "Oh, then, you are a formidable person. People who have done things once and left them off make one feel very contemptible, as if one were using cast-off fashions. I hope you have not left off all follies, because I practice a great many."

(Pause, during which Gwendolen made several interpretations of her own speech.)

Gr4:   "What do you call follies?"

Gw4:   "Well, in general, I think whatever is agreeable is called a folly. But you have not left off hunting, I hear."

(Pause, wherein Gwendolen recalled what she had heard about Grandcourt's position, and decided that he was the most aristocratic-looking man she had ever seen.)

Gr5:   "One must do something."

Gw5:   "And do you care about the turf!—or is that among the things you have left off?"

(Pause, during which Gwendolen thought that a man of extremely calm, cold manners might be less disagreeable as a husband than other men, and not likely to interfere with his wife's preferences.)

Gr6:   "I run a horse now and then; but I don't go in for the thing as some men do. Are you fond of horses?"

Gw6:   "Yes, indeed; I never like my life so well as when I am on horseback, having a great gallop. I think of nothing. I only feel myself strong and happy."

(Pause, wherein Gwendolen wondered whether Grandcourt would like what she said, but assured herself that she was not going to disguise her tastes.)

Gr7:   "Do you like danger?"

Gw7:   "I don't know. When I am on horseback I never think of danger. It seems to me that if I broke my bones I should not feel it. I should go at any thing that came in my way."

(Pause, during which Gwendolen had run through a whole hunting season with two chosen hunters to ride at will.)

Gr8:   "You would perhaps like tiger-hunting or pig-sticking. I saw some of that for a season or two in the East. Every thing here is poor stuff after that."

Gw8:   "*You* are fond of danger, then?"

(Pause, wherein Gwendolen speculated on the probability that the men of coldest manners were the most adventurous, and felt the strength of her own insight, supposing the question had to be decided.)

Gr9:   "One must have something or other. But one gets used to it."

Gw9:   "I begin to think I am very fortunate, because every thing is new to me: it is only that I can't get enough of it. I am not used to any thing except being dull, which I should like to leave off as you have left off shooting."

        (Pause, during which it occurred to Gwendolen that a man of
cold and distinguished manners might possibly be a dull compan-
ion; but, on the other hand, she thought that most persons were
dull, that she had not observed husbands to be companions—and
that, after all, she was not going to accept Grandcourt.)

Gr10:   "Why are you dull?"

Gw10:   "This is a dreadful neighborhood. There is nothing to be done
in it. That is why I practiced my archery."

        (Pause, during which Gwendolen reflected that the life of an un-
married woman who could not go about, and had no command
of any thing, must necessarily be dull through all the degrees of
comparison as time went on.)

Gr11:   "You have made yourself queen of it. I imagine you will carry
off the first prize."

Gw11:   "I don't know that. I have great rivals. Did you not observe how
well Miss Arrowpoint shot?"

        (Pause, wherein Gwendolen was thinking that men had been
known to choose some one else than the woman they most ad-
mired, and recalled several experiences of that kind in novels.)

Gr12:   "Miss Arrowpoint? No—that is, yes."

Gw12:   "Shall we go now and hear what the scoring says? Every one
is going to the other end now—shall we join them? I think my
uncle is looking toward me. He perhaps wants me."

Eliot's introductory comment describes the body language of both Grandcourt
and Gwendolen over the course of the entire dialogue: both facial expressions
and direction of gaze of the interactants, how Gwendolen takes turns looking
toward Grandcourt and away, and how both his facial expression and gaze are
fixed. One immediate implication of this description is lack of deference on
Grandcourt's part. Gwendolen conforms to the convention of turn taking, indicating respect; Grandcourt violates it, suggesting either a sense of arrogant
superiority or a lack of finesse or involvement, or perhaps both.

    The author's first comment on the dialogue itself concerns the constant para-
linguistic features of Grandcourt's speech, his accent and drawl, which like
her description of his body language, seems to imply that Grandcourt has an
exaggerated and offensive sense of his own status. The remainder of Eliot's
extensive commentary on the dialogue is devoted to Gwendolen's inner experience of it. During the apparently lengthy pauses while she is waiting for
Grandcourt's response, this commentary suggests that Gwendolen has ample
time for imaginative activity.

    Like everything else in the author's description of Grandcourt, the long
pause after each of Gwendolen's remarks also implies his arrogance. Just as he
violates the convention of courteously taking turns looking and looking away,
the rule against staring, he also appears to take much too long in responding to
Gwendolen's lines, flagrantly violating the convention of promptly taking his
turn at speaking. (Long pauses are suggested by the extent of Gwendolen's
thoughts while she is waiting for his response, particularly after her first, sec-

ond, third, seventh, and eleventh turns; the content during the seventh pause suggests that it may be the longest, since she has time to "run through a whole hunting season with two chosen hunters to ride at will.")

There seem to be several layers of innuendo in Eliot's description of this one feature of Grandcourt's behavior, and perhaps some ambiguity, since, like his stare, his slowness of response could mark not only insolence but also self-absorption or the importance of the moment to him. Whatever the mixture, however, his slowness suggests too little involvement with his conversational partner and therefore too little deference toward her. I will return to the issue of deference later.

I now consider the descriptions of *inner* experience in this passage. As richly embodied as it is, from the point of view of my argument, Eliot omits an important aspect of this conversation. Following a practice common in imaginative writing, she does not describe Grandcourt's imaginative activity since she apparently wants the reader to have no sympathy for him (Scheff 1976). This practice forces the reader to take Gwendolen's point of view and excludes that of Grandcourt. Even so, Eliot's description of only Gwendolen's imaginative activity still suggests several important issues about interpretive procedures.

The first subject to be discussed is the content of the conversation and Gwendolen's experience of it: What are they talking about? Although many subjects are discussed—archery, shooting, horses and horse racing, danger, and so on—there is only one *topic,* and that is marriage, the possibility of marriage between Gwendolen and Grandcourt. Although this topic is never mentioned, not even by the author, the context in which the conversation took place, as already suggested, the implicature of each utterance, and each thought of Gwendolen's suggest this single topic. The most basic meaning of the transaction is never stated, only implied.

In his opening comment, Grandcourt pays what both seem to recognize as a compliment to Gwendolen, implying that he is at least positively inclined toward her, a step that would be expected if a proposal were intended. In (Gw1) however, Gwendolen pretends not to understand his implied meaning. While waiting for his response, Gwendolen imagines "various degrees and modes" of his possible opinion of her. That it, while pretending not to be sure what he meant, and thus faintly deriding the offhanded casualness of his attempted compliment, she wonders what his actual opinion might be, rather than what he implied: whether he likes her and, if so, how much and in what role, that is, as a mistress or as a wife?

In (Gr2), he affirms his compliment. Gwendolen, in the guise of returning the compliment, begins a series of questions about his interests—shooting, hunting, and "the turf" (horse racing, i.e., gambling). This is again an appropriate opening step toward ultimately accepting an offer of marriage: What manner of man are you? What are your virtues and vices?

In (Gw3), Gwendolen begins a series of comments about herself parallel, to some extent, to her questions about Grandcourt. On the path to marriage, she would be expected to let him know what manner of person she is, as she expects to know the same about him. In the pause after (Gw4), Gwendolen acknowledges to herself that she is favorably impressed by Grandcourt's appearance.

The question about Gwendolen's fondness for horses and her answer (Gr6 and Gw6) have a significant implication for the reader on the issue of marriage. The reader knows that Gwendolen wants, but cannot afford, a fine horse and that Grandcourt could easily satisfy this desire if she married him. This implication is confirmed, indirectly, in Gwendolen's thoughts in the pause after (Gr7), when she rides through an entire hunting season, possessing not one but two horses.

The situation at this moment is somewhat comical, partly because Gwendolen's thoughts make patently clear to the reader what the actual dialogue carefully disguises, that she is considering marrying Grandcourt and that her decision might depend on such grossly material considerations. It is also comical because, at this juncture, she is so completely disconnected from him: he is talking about danger, both in (Gr7) (whether she likes danger) and in (Gr8) (in which he seems to imply that he likes it). Since he continues on this topic, he seems to be thinking about it, perhaps implying that liking danger is a trait they both share. She does not seem to be attending to him or to his topic but to be off in another world with her two horses.

However, as (Gw8) indicates, her romp through a fox-hunting season does not prevent her from listening intently to Grandcourt when he finally responds, because she picks up the implication of (Gr8): she asks if it is he that is fond of danger. While she is waiting for his answer, she further considers his potential as a husband, seeking a positive interpretation of his offensive manner. After contrasting herself with Grandcourt's description of himself, she continues with her evaluation of his potential, but this time alternating: first taking a negative view of him, then a positive one. She ends this train of thought on a note that seems somewhat self-contradictory. Even though she has been carefully evaluating Grandcourt as a potential husband, in the end she indicates to herself that she will not accept him no matter what.

The seesaw battle in Gwendolen's mind continues in the pause after (Gw10): by implication, she once more reverses herself, as she now considers her disadvantaged position as an unmarried and penniless woman. A further sally in the direction of accepting Grandcourt is implied by (Gw11): she tests the strength of her chances by questioning him about her most obvious rival, Miss Arrowpoint. While awaiting his response, she hits upon a new thought, that it may be Grandcourt who rejects her rather than the other way around. This thought further implies her inclination to accept him.

Apparently Gwendolen is not reassured by his answer; she breaks off the conversation. As the reader learns later in the novel, this moment is characteristic of Gwendolen: she is self-deceiving; she usually takes up a new activity or line of thought rather than face an unpleasant one. What is most important about the topic of the conversation, however, is that it is not acknowledged by either of the principals, not by Grandcourt, not by Gwendolen—and not even by the author, who leaves the reader to infer it. It is true that the author hints at it by some of the contents of Gwendolen's imaginative activity. But even in this sphere, which is completely private, Gwendolen manages both to acknowledge and deny what she is actually doing: considering marrying Grandcourt. In this passage, at least, although there are plentiful clues, the actual topic of discourse is never directly articulated.

If the *content* of the dialogue concerns marriage, what is its form? That is, what can be said about the *manner* in which this topic is being discussed? One crucial aspect of the form this dialogue takes has already been mentioned in passing, the amount of deference being shown: Gwendolen's manner is conventionally deferential, Grandcourt's flagrantly lacking in deference. This issue takes on new importance given the topic of discourse, the possibility of marriage.

Presumably Gwendolen should be alarmed by Grandcourt's manner, since it could (and does, as we later learn) portend disaster for her should they marry. Gwendolen considers the issue during three of the pauses. In the first two (after [Gw5] and [Gw8]), she thinks that his coldness might even benefit her. In the last, after (Gw9), she momentarily considers that it might cause difficulty but immediately discounts the possibility in three different ways. But, for the purpose of my argument about interpretation, what seems most important is that neither Gwendolen nor the author makes the matter explicit; it goes without saying in a way that exactly parallels the treatment the topic received.

It probably would have been in Gwendolen's interest in this or subsequent conversations to comment on, and further investigate, the content and form of their discourse. Borrowing from usage in linguistics, I will imagine a "counterfactual" comment she could have made (as indicated by the conventional asterisk): * "I don't know you very well, or your class, for that matter. You seem to be interested in me, but your manner is flagrantly offensive. What is going on?" With luck, direct talk like this may have led to a marriage *contract,* which could have protected her from some of the grosser forms of domination to which she is later subjected in the novel. As it usually seems to happen in polite society, however, neither the basic form nor content of discourse is explicitly referred to but is ignored, glossed, or denied. As will be further discussed in later chapters, a close look at ordinary conversations suggests that *deception* and *self-deception* are often practiced, particularly with respect to meanings that are relevant to the state of the social bond.

A second component of this dialogue involves the degree of attunement or connectedness between the participants, the basic issue of the interpretation by one person of the thoughts and feelings of another. Since Eliot describes Gwendolen's inner monologue, some aspects of her interpretive process and its outcome can be discussed. In what is roughly the first half of the passage, she seems to be intensely involved in abduction, first imagining Grandcourt's inner experience, then observing his outer expressions. In the first six exchanges, there is a rhythm of alternation in her inner experience between imagination and observation: in the pauses after (Gw1, Gw3, and Gw6), she is imagining what he is experiencing; after (Gw2 and Gw6), she is reflecting on her observations of his appearance and manner. There is only one break in the rhythm, after (Gw4 and Gw5), in which she reflects on the implications of his appearance rather than imagines his inner experience.

In the pause after (Gw6), envisioning a whole season of riding to the hounds, she leaves this cycle and does not return to it. She seems to have lost interest in Grandcourt himself; she gives herself over to considerations of marriage to him and its implications. One possibility is that the difficulty of connecting with him demoralizes her; she notes his arrogance, terseness, and flat understatement. However, a possibility which seems to account for most of what happens in the last half of the passage is that during the pause after (Gw6), she makes her decision: she will marry him. Although she does not acknowledge this decision to herself, the evaluation of his suitability in the remaining pauses can be seen as rationalization of a decision already made, with a note of panic during the last pause that she might not get what she wants.

The way in which interactants avoid directness, naming the actual topic and commenting on manner or form, usually involves either deception or self-deception, or both. Deception is often encouraged by social convention. "Leveling" (Satir 1972, chap. 5), directly stating what one thinks, feels, or needs, is often associated with coarseness or selfishness; innuendo and irony may be seen as marks of good breeding. There is a comic parody of this practice in one of the early scenes in *Swann's Way*. Marcel's great-aunts are so indirect in thanking Swann for his gift that he is simply baffled by their comments.

In the present case, Grandcourt seems to be motivated in part by this practice. Gwendolen's motives for deception are more complex, perhaps driven both by fear of rejection, on the one hand, and by shame or guilt about her motives for being even faintly interested in a monster like Grandcourt, on the other. This latter motive may be the source of her self-deception; after deciding that she will marry him, she denies to herself that she has made the decision. Her self-deceiving practices, together with their joint deception of each other, form what might be called a conspiracy to deny the reality of their relationship. The components in this conspiracy are subtle; in chapter 7, the analysis of the dialogue between Werther and his employer suggests more obvious and grosser forms of deception and self-deception, as well as much more intense indications of unacknowledged shame (see also chap. 5).

Gwendolen's imaginative activity suggests an important qualification of Mead's model of role taking and Schutz's of intersubjectivity. Although never stating it explicitly, these models seem to suggest a more or less continuous state of attunement between interactants. The concrete case discussed here presents a quite different picture. At best, in the first half of the passage, when Gwendolen seems to be intent on understanding Grandcourt, there is an alternating rhythm of connecting and detaching. In the second half of the passage, although Gwendolen is still paying sufficient attention to allow civil courtesy, in her imagination she is almost entirely alienated from the encounter, obsessing about the possibility of marriage. In this case at least, such joint attention and feeling as there are, occur only momentarily, interspersed with much detachment and alienation.

Perhaps this concrete example can be used to suggest one of the reasons that models of interpretive understanding such as those proposed by Mead and Schutz are not more widely accepted. As these models have never been applied to concrete instances, but described only abstractly, they give the reader the impression of continuous attunement. These models, at least in their exposition, have been biased toward cooperative activity and reflective intelligence. The average reader, whose experience of social encounter is apt to be like Gwendolen's—a fast-moving blur of misunderstanding, error, folly, and alienation, with only rare and all too brief moments of attunement—is justifiably skeptical of descriptions which suggest continuous interpretive understanding.

To be sure, there is enough attunement in the example for Gwendolen and Grandcourt to have a surface understanding of each other's words. At one point, in (Gw8), she even picks up an implication which lies below the surface. But, as already indicated, the basic content and form of discourse are never acknowledged by either. For this reason, it would be very difficult for the interactants to get below the surface to each other's motives, intentions, and character, even though they have every interest in doing so.

In this passage, there is only sufficient attunement for the interactants to understand each other's spoken words, but not their unstated thoughts and feelings. They are worlds apart. Gwendolen ignores the implications of their separation, and we are led to infer that Grandcourt assumes that all encounters are like this one. As it turns out, Grandcourt wants Gwendolen as one of his possessions, like a dog or horse. Although there are indications of this possibility in his manner, Gwendolen does not pursue them. Perhaps a model of more or less continuous attunement is applicable to the surface meaning of discourse but needs substantial modification for its deeper levels.

It should be noted that Gwendolen's problem in connecting with Grandcourt has what might be called a sociological component. She is dealing with a member of another class: she is from a middle-class background; he is an aristocrat. Since this is her first direct encounter with an aristocrat, she must translate not only across male and female cultures but also from aristocratic culture to that of the middle class. She must decide how much of his untoward behavior is merely a manifestation of upper-class mores and how much is expressive of his own character. Perhaps, she might say to herself, this is only the way upper-class males are supposed to act in public; in private he might be quite another person. This question points to a larger problem of attunement than is being considered here, which concerns attunement between persons. At the societal level, there is also a problem of attunement between groups, which will be taken up in chapter 5.

A final point concerns the extent of Gwendolen's imaginative activity during pauses in the conversation. I have already suggested that the length of these pauses, as indicated by the reach of her thoughts, implies arrogance and discourtesy on the part of Grandcourt. There also may be a second implication about the rapidity of internal search. As far as I know, there have been no studies of the exact duration of pauses in conversation. In my own earlier studies of actual interviews, I found that a pause of longer than two seconds led to feelings of discomfort in myself and the raters in the studies. Although five seconds may be considered a very brief time in the abstract, to a participant in a conversation, an unexplained pause of that duration might seem an eternity.

The question of the absolute duration of pauses is relevant to the passage from Eliot's novel. If we assume that Grandcourt's delays in responding, insupportable as they might have seemed to Gwendolen, are only five or six seconds long, we then must give some consideration to the lightning-like rapidity with which internal search must take place. Even allowing for considerable exaggeration by Eliot for comic effect, the extraordinary extent of Gwendolen's reflections leads in this direction. Testimony by persons in crises to the effect that their whole lives flashed before their eyes also makes this point. Finally, this possibility is supported by current work on problem solving in cognitive psychology. For example, in Anderson's (1983) model, he posits that internal events of one millisecond (one thousandth of a second) duration make up problem-solving sequences.

The question of the rapidity of external and internal search is an extremely important one for any model of interpretive understanding; it relates directly to micro-macro linkages in social action. I will return to this issue in subsequent chapters. In the next chapter, models of internal search will be described. Because of the ambiguity of expression, it seems necessary that internal search be so rapid that it must occur as many parallel processes. The argument developed in this chapter and the next leads to a discussion of social action in chapter 6, the relationship between individual action and social structure.

4

Studies of Problem Solving and of Conversation: A Critique and a Proposal

To understand the speed, breadth, and flexibility of interpretive process, we need studies which deal with both inner and outer search, in complex domains like those in real life. This critique is applied to the models of problem solving in artificial intelligence (AI) and cognitive science (CS), on the one hand, and to conversation analysis (CA), on the other. Although the problem-solving studies provide models of inner process, they have been generated by and tested in closed domains which lack ecological validity.

Conversation analysis faces the opposite problem: these studies of naturally occurring conversations concern open domains and have ecological validity. But without investigation of inner search, the results gloss the very process ethnomethodology sought to uncover: interpretation which leads to contextual understanding. In its stead, the results can be seen as descriptions of the micro-rules of conversation.

A problem that CA shares with the problem-solving models in AI and CS is the use of a single type of mental connection, one based on the principle of similarity (classification). Although classification is a part of interpretive process, it is not the only one: it can be considered one of many types of association. I call mental process which involves both similarity and contiguity *total* association.

To provide an example of the kinds of studies which seem to be needed, I describe two guessing games: Password and charades. These games provide a lifelike open domain, allowing research access to both inner and outer search. Outer search could be observed in videotape records, and interviews might allow for the partial reconstruction of inner search sequences.

Interpretation and Search

In the last chapter, the issue of the rapidity and breadth of internal search was raised. While managing to understand and respond to Grandcourt when he spoke, Gwendolen still is able to conduct a vast amount of inner business while awaiting his response. Her experience probably rings true with most readers. Like her, they too may range over what seems to be half the world during their own conversations.

Eliot's description of the dialogue between Gwendolen and Grandcourt illustrates a very general problem. If all human expression is only indexical, if the references of words and gestures are always ambiguous, how do we solve the problem of understanding others as well as we do? Although there are certainly many mistakes, we often manage to understand not just the surface meaning of words, as in the case of Gwendolen, but also more hidden implications of words and gestures, feelings, motives, and intentions. As Eliot seems to suggest, Gwendolen's failure to understand Grandcourt in this latter area may have not been due to lack of ability, but lack of desire: she is pictured in the novel as self-deceiving.

As already indicated, even the observable, public aspects of expression, the words and gestures, pose a complex problem of interpretation. As difficult a problem as words and gestures pose, the feelings, motives, and intentions are still more difficult since they are not directly observable, often have no conventional definition, and may be actively disguised by the bearer. Perhaps for these reasons, there is probably much less understanding and more misunderstanding of feelings, motives, and intentions than of words.

Yet in ordinary life there is considerable understanding, not only of outer expression but also of the inner experience of others. Since accurate understanding at both levels may occur in a few seconds, any model of problem solving would have to admit the extraordinary speed, intricacy, and flexibility of the human capacity to solve problems. Before discussing such models, I need to say more about the evidential status of feelings, motives, and intentions.

In many areas of philosophy and the human sciences, there is a tendency to assign a dubious status to inner experience. Since words and actions are directly observable, contemporary research has focused largely on the outer world. If inner experience is discussed at all, it is treated in an unsystematic manner or discounted as unreliable. In philosophy, the problem of "other minds" is framed and treated in such a way as to suggest that one can never really know another's experience. Similarly, most discussions of intentionality in modern philosophy seem to suggest that intentions, like motives and feelings, do not have the same status in reality as do words and actions. A similar current can be found in the human sciences: behaviorist, structuralist, and most other approaches ignore or discount inner experience. As suggested in the discussion below, this tendency is also found in discourse and conversation analysis.

One way of understanding the tendency to ignore or discount inner experience is to consider it as a special attitude that has grown up in one institutional sector of modern society—the academy. Since this institution is dominated by the image of science and system, an ideology has formed which downgrades inner experience. This tendency can be seen more clearly if a comparison is made with the status of inner experience in other sectors of society.

To illustrate the point, I refer only to intentionality, although motives and feelings share a similar fate. Intentionality plays a particularly crucial role in interpretive understanding because it involves a prediction that can be tested empirically. If we are told that we are to be paid a sum of money on a certain date, on that same date we are able to ascertain whether or not we correctly understood the other's intention to pay. Banks and other businesses, indeed nations and empires, are built upon structures of intentions. Without them, society would be little more than a vast junkyard.

Legal institutions also have no difficulty with the concept of intentions and with systematic investigation and documentation of actual, specific intentions held by specific persons. The whole structure of criminal law rests on the concept of *mens rea,* criminal intent. To convict a defendant of a crime, the state must gather evidence which demonstrates, beyond a reasonable doubt, not only that the defendant committed an act but also that he or she intended to do so. To make such a case, the state usually gathers evidence composed both of verbal testimony and of physical evidence to reconstruct actions and intentions.

When the stakes are high enough, similar procedures are used in civil suits. In an automobile accident which involves substantial injury, the opposing sides go to great expense to reconstruct events as they actually happened, including the inner states of the drivers. These states are inferred not only from testimony but also from physical evidence, such as skid marks. Judges and jurors are expected to understand intentions by abducting, to use Peirce's term, from testimony about inner events and reports of outer gestures and events. In such suits, the watchwords of an earlier tradition of historiography, *wie es wirklich gewesen war* (history as it actually happened), are being continually realized. Historical events are reconstructed down to second-by-second actions and intentions.

How does it happen that such reconstructions have not taken place in the academy, that structures of intention are taken for granted only in other sectors of a society? Perhaps it is a matter of the valuation involved. In banking and judicial transactions, issues of great moment are involved. The investigators may give intentions a status equal to outer actions because they agree that it is supremely important to do so. Since there is no such immediate pressure in the academy, researchers seem to have agreed to discount inner experience. This reasoning is greatly oversimplified, but it could account for one of the origins of behavioral and structuralist ideologies.

Perhaps the first step in constructing models of problem solving is to promote inner experience to a status equal to outer action. Such a step would require a massive shift of attitude and attention: very little is known about intentions, motives, and feelings. There are exceptions, of course. The work in cognitive science and artificial intelligence is a resource that will be discussed below. Another resource is the microscopic, second-by-second readings of words and gestures in conversations, such as those by Pittenger et al. (1960), Lewis (1971), and Labov and Fanshel (1977), which could provide an empirical basis for systematic study of intentions and feelings. At a conceptual level, the meshed intrachain sequences (MIS) model of events occurring both between and within interactants, devised by Kelley and his associates (1983), seems a promising beginning. (These studies will be further discussed in subsequent chapters.) In the absence of a body of knowledge, the close examination of literary and factual discourse could provide an initial framework.

The Mead-Schutz theory of interpretive understanding suggests the need for an additional step, the study of the process of search—both outer and inner search. An extremely rapid and complex process of outer search is postulated in Mead's treatment of "role taking," since the observation of outer signs of inner activity is exactly half of the role-taking process. Although there is a considerable literature on rapid eye movements (REMs) during sleep and dreaming, there seems to be no studies of REMs during interpretive activity. Such studies would be necessary to test the validity of the theory that is being proposed.

Similarly, inner search would also need to be studied systematically. As already indicated, there is now a large literature on one kind of inner search: cognitive problem solving. To indicate its relevance to my argument, I need to refer to the formula for interpretation in chapter 3. This process was formulated in terms of the function, F, which transforms a collection of signs, S, into an interpretation, I, such that $I = F(S)$. In this formulation, finding the function, F, is only half of the problem; the other half is considering the goodness of fit between the actual signs, S, and the predictions generated by F, which I call S'.

In the study of problem solving in artificial intelligence and in cognitive science, there is a body of discussion and research which attempts to model the function, F, and, to test the goodness of fit, the degree of correspondence between S and S'. In AI, this line of investigation started with the work of Simon and Newell, who devised a computer program which they called the General Problem Solver (GPS). The GPS was also one of the sources of the study of problem solving in CS, but that study also had wider sources in the traditional approaches to mental process.

As it turned out, the GPS proved to be anything but general: it functioned only in extremely tiny and restricted domains. That is, GPS and similar models can solve problems posed by relatively simple games such as tick-tack-toe and checkers and problems involving abstract mathematical or logical symbols. These models also do well with more complex games, such as chess, although there appear to be limitations (Dreyfus and Dreyfus 1986). But such programs have failed in areas depending upon large or complex bodies of knowledge, such as those involved in most human problem solving (Fahlman 1981).

Since there is controversy about the effectiveness of chess-playing programs, I will briefly consider that issue and use it to introduce the idea of "ecological validity" and the distinction between open and closed domains. The mass media have suggested that chess programs have been able to beat all but the greatest chess masters. As Dreyfus and Dreyfus (1986) propose, this claim is exaggerated. I refer to only one of their observations: a skilled player is likely to be defeated only if he plays the game without exploiting the program's weaknesses, for example, long-range strategy. Even a player unaware of these weaknesses is likely to discover them in the course of play.

The promotion of AI in chess programs has depended on several victories over skilled chess players in only one round of play. In more than one round, as would occur in chess tournaments, chess programs usually fare poorly. For example, in 1984 a relatively low-ranked chess master (rated as approximately the thousandth player in the world), who was also a computer enthusiast, decisively (4–0) defeated the state-of-the-art chess program. Even though his opponent was only a machine, the chessmaster's evaluation of the match seems somewhat gratuitous: "The nature of the struggle was such that the machine didn't understand what was going on" (Dreyfus and Dreyfus 1986, 114). Perhaps the player should have been more respectful. Undoubtedly as computer speed and size increase, the programs will go deeper into future moves, becoming more proficient. However, as will be suggested below, proficiency at chess does not solve the problem of open domains.

The dispute over the effectiveness of chess programs illustrates the problem of ecological validity, a crucial issue not only in AI but also in social and behavioral sciences. To establish the validity of their claims, the promoters of chess programs chose single games against skilled chess players, most of whom apparently had no familiarity with computers. On the basis of these tightly restricted encounters, they have claimed a near equity between chess programs and human masters. To show ecological validity, however, they need to enter chess tournaments, which involve repeated matches, since this is the way chess skill is determined in the human world. Under such conditions, apparently, their claims would be discredited. Matching a chess program against another program, or against isolated players in single games, gives a misleading impression of the power of these "expert systems."

The issue of ecological validity comes up in a more subtle form in the evaluation of the goodness of fit of models of problem solving in CS. Like the programs in AI, these models make explicit the interpretive function, F, and test its goodness of fit, the degree of correspondence between S and S'. Unlike the AI programs, however, models such as those of Anderson (1983) and Wye and Krull (1986) do not limit themselves to games and puzzles in testing goodness of fit but use a much wider variety of studies of various types of problem-solving behavior. From the point of view of the problem of interpretation being discussed here, however, the range of these studies is still much too restricted. Since all the studies are laboratory experiments, it has been argued that (like the tests in AI) they also lack ecological validity (Winkler and Murphy 1973; cf. Einhorn and Hogarth 1981).

The general issue of the ecological validity of laboratory experiments is so complex that it can be touched on here only briefly. Some of the criticism of the validity of experiments has been very specific. Neisser (1982) has criticized the choice of topics that are studied in the typical experiment on memory, which are often nonsense syllables. Since nonsense syllables are virtually never memorized in real life, he has argued that most of the findings in the experimental study of memory lack ecological validity and are therefore irrelevant. This criticism seems also to be applicable to the studies of problem solving in CS. The problems that are posed to subjects are apt to be of a certain type, that is, computations, or deal with very small, truncated units, such as words and sentences, rather than with more complete units of meaning that would figure in social transactions (e.g., a letter or a phone conversation).

Although it is seldom made explicit, there is also a sense in the critical literature of a more basic limitation to the validity of experiments with human subjects. The possibility is suggested that subjects in the laboratory behave as they do because of the particular setting. The criticisms of the Milgram experiments have sounded this note especially. To draw a crude analogy: perhaps the laboratory behavior of humans, like that of animals in captivity, is usually quite unrepresentative of their behavior when in their natural, free-ranging state.

This criticism touches on what seems to be, from the point of view of a general model of interpretation, a very basic limitation of the scope of the studies in AI and CS. To return to the chess illustration: even if programs were devised which could defeat all human opponents, such programs would still be very far from being general problem solvers. The distinction between open and closed domains is useful in understanding this point. As complex as chess is, it is still a closed domain. That is, every component of the game of chess is uniquely defined; there is no ambiguity whatever about the nature of the moves, the pieces, and the outcomes of encounters between them. Like mathematics, another closed domain, all ambiguity has been removed.

As already pointed out, in social encounter, since it is based on the game of natural language, the amount of ambiguity is staggering because each word and gesture may have more than one conventional meaning or even an unconventional meaning. This point becomes obvious when dealing with computers: in programming, computers balk at the slightest ambiguity, even a missing comma. As indicated, research in automated translation has shown that no program has been devised which can accurately translate a single sentence of natural language without human assistance.

There are indications that the same issues arise in all experiments and sample surveys but in a more subtle form. The ambiguities in social encounter are less obvious because they seldom cause the experiment or interview to come to a complete halt. Instead, they are glossed by either the researcher or the subject, or both. Garfinkel's (1967) discussion of the tactics of the coders in one of his studies provides an example. No matter how precise the instructions, they never covered all the actual decisions which arose in coding. For this reason, the coders practiced what Garfinkel calls "ad hocing," making their own decisions in instances of ambiguity. Later work by Garfinkel and his students (reviewed in Heritage 1984) suggests that the same thing happens in physical science. Results from different labs may be different, they suggest, because the exact procedures used are not even acknowledged, much less written down.

It has been customary in science to view the ambiguity of natural language only as a weakness or fault that must be removed from procedures and from thought. It has long been supposed that the only clear thinking is analytical thinking, where ambiguity has been removed, as in mathematical logic. It seems likely, however, that the clearest thinking is that which takes place in natural, rather than artificial, language. An open domain is characterized not merely by a large number of elements, but elements which are multivalued. As will be suggested below, the power of natural language is that it makes an enormous vista of connections almost instantaneously available. It is this feature, I believe, that gives rise to what is called *intuition,* the virtually instantaneous and unlabored solution to problems insoluble in an analytic mode. Indeed, natural language connects the native user not only with a panoply of possible worlds but also with the actual worlds of society and of nature.

Mathematical and analytic thought has its uses, but it is a weak reeds when compared with the awesome power of natural language. Using one's mother tongue, the speaker must continuously unravel ambiguities of meaning by recourse to perception of the outer world and the inner: feeling, memory, and imagination. In the course of such swift search, one is in touch with one's own history and the history of society. Natural language carries history disguised within it. I will return to this issue below in the discussion of associative thought.

From the point of view of a general model of interpretation, the great failing of the existing models in AI and in CS is that they are oriented toward closed domains. The computer-oriented models in AI deal with games, puzzles, and mathematical logic; the problem-solving models in CS with small conceptual tasks in a laboratory setting. Neither models deal with rapid problem solving, the "ad hocing" that takes place in social encounter, as it occurs in natural language. But for my purpose, this is the very problem that needs to be solved.

I have already proposed two steps toward resolving this impasse: the incorporation of inner experience into models of interpretation and the empirical study of external search process as it occurs in social interaction. Finally, I propose a third step, which involves broadening the image of inner process to include primitive types of association in addition to the classificatory processes on which the existing models are built. A close look at AI shows that although alternative types of association may be mentioned, they never are built into the actual model. These models all deal with cognition composed of concepts, that is, classes. Although classification is certainly an important part of the problem-solving process, it is much too narrow a base to generate rapid and flexible solutions of the kind required.

Contiguity and Similarity

To introduce this section, I quote a description of mental problem solving by a great savant, George Steiner (1975, 289–90):

> Introspectively, one draws pictures. Thus one describes oneself as "looking for" a word. Whenever it is baffled or momentarily vacuous, the search, the act of scanning, suggests circuitry. The relevant sensation or, more cogently, the vulgarized images we make up of what are subliminal processes, leave one with a compelling notion of nervous probes "trying this or that connection," recoiling where the wire is blocked or broken and seeking alternative channels until the right contact is made. The sensation of a "near-miss" can be tactile. The sought word or phrase is a "micro-millimeter away from" the scanner; it is poised obstinately at the edge of retrieval. One's focus becomes excited and insistent. It seems to press against a material impediment. The "muscles" of attention ache. Then comes the breach in the dam, the looked-for word or phrase flashing into consciousness. We know nothing of the relevant kinetics, but the implication of a correct location, of a "slotting into place" is forceful, if only because of the muted but unmistakable impression of release, of a calming click which accompanies the instant of recall. When the right word is found, compression gives, and a deep-breathing currency—in the dual sense of "flow" and "integrated routine"—resumes. In contrast, under the spur of stimulants or histrionic occasion, or in the strange weightless tension of tiredness of mind, resistance seems to diminish in the verbal circuits and synapses multiply. Every bell chimes. Homonyms, paronomasia, acoustic and semantic cognates, synec-dochic sets, analogies, associative strings proliferate, undulating at extreme speed, sometimes with incongruous but pointed logic, across the surfaces of consciousness. The acrostic or cross-word yields faster than our pencil can follow. We seem to know even more than we had forgotten, as if central sediments of memory or reserves normally unrecorded, because lightly imprinted or laid down without deliberate marking, had been galvanized.

This description suggests the flavor of effective mental problem solving, which appears helter-skelter yet may be astonishingly penetrating. Of particular interest is the set of differing types of mental connections which Steiner offers: "Homonyms, paronomasia, acoustic and semantic cognates, synechdochic sets, analogies, [and] associative strings." This list turns out to be types of connection other than similarity, that is, connections not dependent on classification (concepts).

The first three types—homonyms, paronomasia, and acoustic and semantic cognates—all involve wordplay, such as punning. Synechdoche and analogy involve connections still looser and more arbitrary, for example, when "The White House" is made to stand for the government of the United States. All these types defy the logic of classification. They all describe connections made on the basis of "mere" association. What Steiner seems to be saying is that rapid and effective mental processing suggests that such thought occurs in an open domain rather than a closed one.

What is most interesting about Steiner's list of types of mental connections is not what it contains but what is missing, that is, any type of logical classification. His last type, associative strings, is not simply another type of connection but a summary name for all the types that he seems to be implying. His list leaves out the only type of connection that is used in current modeling of problem solving in AI and CS and contains five types which are not used, suggesting the weakness of current models.

Concepts (classifications) involve a powerful relationship among items in a knowledge base: membership in groups. This membership may be based on similarity or merely on convention, as when historians group all the events that occurred in the nineteenth century. Although this method of connecting items is broad, it has severe limits on inclusion, that is, actual or conventional similarity. The principle of association knows no such limits: any two items may be connected, at least momentarily, on the basis of what might seem to be the merest pretext: sound, spelling, or contiguity in space or time, either of the items themselves or the occasion on which the person associating first learned of the items.

There is one particular type of contiguous connection which is never even mentioned in the discussion of problem-solving models, much less built into the models themselves—connection by feeling. Yet champion problem solvers, whether they be chess masters or physicists, virtually always mention this kind of connection. Freud's idea that emotions have a signal function, although developed in a different context, seems relevant to this issue. Emotional reactions often seem to follow a logic that is independent of conscious reasoning yet call our attention to features of a problem which we might otherwise overlook. Since these reactions are virtually instantaneous, it is plausible that they could also be an important element in problem-solving activity.

The type of mental connections suggested by this discussion can be arbitrary, inventive, and playful, but such connections also may be based on strict classificational logic. Since there seems to be no conventional term which covers both types of connections, I will refer to it as *total* association. It is important to distinguish between this idea and Freud's, which he referred to as *free* association. He taught his patients to develop the skill of using only contiguous mental connections, specifically excluding analytic logic. Perhaps the most successful problem solving alternates between the two modes. It seems necessary to stress this principle in order to assemble a workable model of interpretive procedures since it will require a vast knowledge base and seemingly instantaneous access to almost all of it. The size of the problem has been described by workers in AI: "What is needed is a switching network capable of connecting millions of link-wires to millions of specific nodes, all at once: a sort of huge telephone switching network, capable of handling millions of calls at once" (Fahlman 1981, 157–58). In attempting to describe parallel processes in the brain, Hinton and Anderson (1981) uses similar language. These images of complex processes stand in stark contrast to those prevalent in AI and CS. Simon (1977, 1187), in an expansive mood, provides an exemplary statement: "No longer accepting the geocentric view of the universe, [humankind is now beginning to learn] that mind, too, is a phenomenon of nature, explainable in terms of *simple* mechanisms" (emphasis added).

The classificatory principle, similarity, is powerful but not broad enough to deal with a million-voiced switchboard. The process of connection by inherent or conventional similarity is necessarily serial and therefore much too slow for what is needed. To decide what items belong in a class, one has to proceed item by item, comparing similarities and differences with the criteria of class inclusion. This is not to say that similarity is not an important basis of association in thought. It may be the most important single type of association. But my point is that it is only one among many types, perhaps one among hundreds of types. For this reason, the attempts to model parallel processes in problem solving which are organized around classification as the basic mental connection (Hinton and Anderson 1981) may never succeed.

The principle of total association, on the other hand, may be what is needed to envision a switchboard capable of handling a million calls at once, since most of the connections may be impromptu, for the purpose immediately at hand. If each item in the knowledge base involved, on the average, a hundred associations, then associative strings would proliferate exponentially from a single item. With an exponent of one hundred, it would require only three associative steps to access a million items in the knowledge base. In the first association, there would be a hundred items; in the second, ten thousand (one hundred multiplied by one hundred); and in the third, a million (one hundred multiplied by ten thousand).

Total association allows not only for the speed needed in the model of problem solving but also for the breadth. The example above, positing a hundred associations with the typical item in the knowledge base, automatically gives rise to a model of parallel processes, a hundred for each associative step. That is, each step of total association, again assuming a hundred associations for the average item of knowledge, produces a hundred parallel processes since each of the new associations produces associations in turn.

The concept of total association may be used as a way of understanding the intuitive, asystematic side of creative thinking. (The issue of the two components of creative problem solving, intuition and system, is taken up in greater detail in chapter 8.) *Total association makes it possible to get the right answer for the wrong reasons.* Using the hundreds of chains of association which are merely contiguous may lead the thinker to envision the problem in a new way, a way that would have been difficult or even impossible within the limits of logical connections. A dramatic example of this process, to be discussed in chapter 8, is Kepler's solution to the transit of Mars. His discovery of the correct solution to the problem was based on a premise which was spectacularly erroneous. Since he was meticulous about keeping a daily log of these thoughts, and most other creators are not, perhaps Kepler's process of discovery is much more common than has been thought.

Research Sites for the Study of Problem Solving

The most severe test of a model of mental process is that of flexibility: Can the proposed model conceivably encompass the feats of creativity observable in human actions? It is possible that cues from empirical studies will be needed in order to develop a model. The strategy adopted by many of the researchers in AI (e.g., Hinton and Anderson 1981) in programming parallel processes is to attempt to use the brain as model, seeking to envision the structure of storage of information in matrices of symbols.

Although constructing models of the structure of the brain may ultimately prove important, it might not be the most fruitful starting place. As an analogy, it would be like studying the organization of libraries in order to understand science and scholarship. To be sure, a good researcher could probably derive some shrewd insights into the nature of science or scholarship by careful study of libraries. But a more direct route might be to study the activities of researchers in the round, and not just their equipment. (The idea of studying social and mental processes rather than hypothetical structures is in the spirit of the work by Rommetveit and Blakar [1979].)

The research site needed for studying mental problem solving should have ecological validity (it should mirror real-life mental processes), should be accessible to the researcher, and should accentuate the central features required in a model of interpretive procedures: breadth, speed, and flexibility. One possible site is social guessing games, such as Password or charades. In Password, the players are required to guess the reference word (the password) from a series of cue words that are provided. The team wins that needs the fewest cues.

Charades is a guessing game on a broader scale. The hidden reference in this game is a phrase (such as the name of a poem) or a sentence (such as an epigram or saying). The signs which are used to signal the hidden reference are not words, which are forbidden, but gestures; the player mimes the hidden reference in a silent drama. The skillful play of charades, more than Password, accentuates the feature of problem solving I have emphasized here—inventive and unconventional mental connections. The mimes on the winning team use, and their team understands, the wildest, most arbitrary connections between the signs and what they signify.

Detailed study of problem-solving sequences in charades might provide a rich source for the development of a model of interpretive process. A videotape record of play might provide data for understanding external search, particularly if cameras were focused on eye movements. In interviews after the fact, the sequence of events which led to correct guesses might be at least partially reconstructed. Videotape and interviews would allow a unified assessment of outer and inner events, rather than separate them into separate studies, as is usually done. Perhaps such a study could pave the way for constructing a new model.

On a more modest scale, the reader can try a small study of the effectiveness of total association compared with classification, using the game of Password. All that is required is teams composed of members who do not know the game. Two steps are required: first, matching the teams to be as nearly equal as possible and, second, giving the teams different instructions. The first team is to be told that the clue words must be selected on the basis of similarity. this team will proceed to provide clues that are synonyms or at least class members. The second team is told that they can use any kind of association, not just similarity. For example, for the password "white," the first team might give the clue word "colorless," the second team "sheet."

My experience is that the second team always win, and wins by wide margins. Furthermore, the players on the first team usually complain that the game is dull and lifeless. Classification alone seems to be too restrictive a principle to allow swift, accurate, and entertaining guessing to occur. Perhaps a model of problem solving based on total association, rather than one based on classification, might resolve some of the current impasses in the field.

Conversation Analysis

The basic problem faced by conversation analysis is opposite to that of the problem-solving studies in AI and CS. Studies in CA, since they deal only with naturally occurring conversation in real-world settings, all concern open domains and have ecological validity. However, unlike the problem-solving models, there is little attempt in CA to deal with inner search. The strategy adopted in CA is to restrict the data collected and most of the analysis to outer behavior, that is, words and gestures. To understand the consequences of this strategy, one must review the origins of CA and some of its principal findings. For both purposes, the summary by Heritage (1984) has been invaluable.

The program of research in CA originally intended to find empirical evidence to support the Schutz-Garfinkel approach (chapter 3), that all human expression is indexical. This approach was a reaction against the reigning paradigm in American social science, the theory of the social system, that is, Parson's. Both Schutz and Garfinkel protested that Parsons's analysis was less an objective description than an affirmation of the status quo under study. They argued that Parsons's whole approach rested on the assumption that social action arose out of members' conforming to a set of norms, that social behavior is organized and bound by social rules.

In the Schutz-Garfinkel approach, however, there is an important step prior to the evocation of the appropriate rule, the construction of context. This is the same step referred to in symbolic interaction terms as "defining the situation" (Blumer, 1969). Prior to deciding whether to conform to a rule, the interactants must decide *which* rule is relevant. The Parsonian approach, it is argued, since it glosses this first step, converts the members from active agents into passive automatons. In the Schutzian perspective, there is a complex relation between members' actions and social structure, one of reciprocal causation: social action causes and is caused by the normative structure. In the Parsonian scheme, the relationship is a simple one: social action is caused by normative structure.

The Parsonian scheme leads to several difficulties. Since it glosses the search for the relevant rule, it generates explanations of social action which are ex post facto. It is also profoundly conservative: in explaining behavior normatively, the observer must engage in "ad hocing" in the same way as the interactants, assuming, and thereby reaffirming, the interpretive practices that were applied rather than describing and investigating them. By the same token, the approach seems to reify the status quo since it invokes a set of causal agents, the social norms that make up the normative structure, which have not been defined independently of the behavior that they are said to explain. (For a brilliant critique of Parson's *Social System,* see Mills, 1959.)

Conversational analysts intended to gather empirical evidence in support of the Schutz-Garfinkel framework. I will argue, however, that a methodological decision made a priori led to results which actually support the Parsonian perspective. In CA, the major focus is on outer behavior, words and gestures; there is little attempt to construct complex inferences about inner experience.

Even without explicit reference to inner experience, CA has already made an important contribution to understanding social encounter by demonstrating the importance of sequencing (turn taking) in conversation. The studies suggest the possibility that sequence signals are pancultural universals, a significant achievement. These findings suggest that cooperative activity in conversation, the fluid taking of turns, is achieved through an unnoticed but nevertheless vital feature of conversation, the linguistic and paralinguistic markers in a sentence which indicate whether a speaker will stop at the end of the sentence or continue. Since these markers are an unarticulated aspect of all social encounter, the interactants must take them into account in their construction of the social context. (The issue of turn taking is discussed in greater detail in chapter 6.)

In order to realize CA's full potential, however, the analysis of the status quo in social interaction, one may need to explore not only words and gestures, but also inner and outer search which allows us to construct the meaning of the words and gestures in context. The contextual meaning of expressions must be determined anew in each moment; this is the thrust of the Schutz-Garfinkel approach. Unless the interactant's inner and outer search is subject to investigation, the researcher must either assume that expressions have meaning that is context free or ad hoc the meanings just as the subjects themselves do. Some of the findings in CA suggest these elements.

One of the directions in CA studies has been the discovery of "adjacency pairs," patterns of utterance by one speaker followed immediately by the response of the other: questions and answers, invitations and responses (accepting or declining the invitation), for example. I refer only to the pair "questions and answers" since the findings with respect to the other types of pairs are parallel.

The findings can be summarized as follows: (1) If one is asked a question, one is expected to provide an answer. (2) If an answer is not provided, one is expected to give an account of why it is not. (3) Since solidary responses are preferred, mitigation and repair are expected if no answer is provided or if the answer is not acquiescent. Although the first and second steps are not surprising, they form the foundation for the third, which leads the researchers into some complex and hitherto little understood features of social encounter. The same is true of the other pairs which have been reported.

As useful as this formulation is, note how easily it is accommodated in a conventional normative account: the first step concerns a basic rule, the second a qualification of that rule, and the third a qualification of the qualification. The explanation of the responses to a question seems to be linear and serial: given the basic rule, the responder is seen as proceeding through a series of decisions based on subrules. This approach, which uses Schutzian language, fits exactly into a normative explanation: the findings consist of a set of "microrules" which are invoked as explanations of the responders' behavior in the situation in which a question has been asked.

To illustrate some of the analytic problems with the CA approach, I use one of the passages quoted in Heritage (1984, 257) from a study by Terasaki (1976):

MOM: Do you know who's going to that meeting?
KID: Who.
MOM: I don't know!
KID: Ou::h prob'ly: Mr. Murphy an' Dad said prob'ly
        Mrs. Timpte an' some o' the teachers.

Interest in the article from which this passage was taken was centered on the "Mom's" second response, correcting the misunderstanding by "Kid" of her first response. Mom's second response is referred to in CA as a "repair," a correction of one speaker's misunderstanding by another. Heritage (258) makes an important point about repairs:

. . . after any "second action" the producer of the first has a systematically given opportunity to repair any misunderstanding of the first action that may have been displayed in the second. Given the generic availability of this procedure, any second speaker may look to a third action to see whether this opportunity was taken and, if it was not, conclude that the analysis and treatment of the first action that was displayed in his or her second was adequate. Any "third" action, therefore, which implements some "normal" onward development or trajectory for a sequence, tacitly confirms the displayed understandings in the sequence so far. By means of this framework, speakers are released from what would otherwise be an endless task of confirming and reconfirming their understandings of each other's actions.

As Heritage realizes, the analysis of the process of repair, that is, of either its presence or its absence in a conversation, constitutes an analysis of the inner experience of the participants. In the absence of a repair by the first speaker, the second can conclude that he or she has correctly understood the first speaker's meaning. Conversation analysis has developed a systematic approach to the study of intersubjective understanding by analyzing the relationship between outer behavior (words and gestures) and inner experience (understanding or misunderstanding).

It is important to note, however, that although the analysis of repair process is a great achievement, it is by no means a complete analysis of intersubjectivity. It omits a step which might be considered prior to repair, the process through which the second speaker, in this case Kid, "analyzes" the first speaker's utterance. As it happens in this instance, he concludes, incorrectly, that Mom's statement is not really a request for information but a kind of throat clearing before announcing the answer herself. (Schegloff [1984] has noted the basic ambiguity of the question format in conversations but does not attempt to describe how the ambiguity is resolved.) Kid makes this mistake even though Mom's first utterance sounds like it is a real question. (In CA usage, the question mark signifies a rising pitch of the last syllable, the conventional paralinguistic marker for a question.)

Kid's error raises a question about the extended context of the game of questions and answers between Kid and Mom. Is this Mom in the habit of drumming up an appreciative response from Kid by prefacing announcements with fake questions? (Terasaki [1976] calls them "pre-announcements.") One can imagine Mom's fake questions as delivered in a breathless, high-pitched style, in the manner of one of Bruner's (1983) moms: * "Can you see the pretty DOLLY?" Instead of saying * "Of course I know who's going to that meeting, do you think I'm an idiot?" as an adult might, Kid goes along with what he might see as the same old game. Adroit questioning of Kid, or a comparison of the paralanguage of Mom's questions which result in errors by Kid with those that do not, might test this conjecture.

It is not yet known how much repair occurs in ordinary conversations, but it seems safe to guess that it is relatively infrequent. That is to say that most intersubjective understanding, perhaps a hundred instances to one, is based not on repair but on tacit analysis, on what I have called inner search. Although Mom fooled Kid this time, he probably makes very few such errors.

I dwell on this example at some length because it points to a subtle issue in Heritage's comment and, by implication, in the entire CA approach. When he says that "speakers are released from what would otherwise be an endless task of confirming and reconfirming their understandings of each other's actions," he is speaking only of outer behavior. WHAT HE DOES NOT SAY IS THAT THERE IS NO RELEASE, EVER, FROM THE INNER SEARCH FOR THE MEANING OF EXPRESSIONS. Each time Mom poses what might be a real question, Kid has to decide whether it is or not. Although Heritage does not use the term "automatically," his words come very close: "systematically," "generic," and "normal." His words and imagery obscure what is to me the central feature of discourse, the endless task of the participants—the contexual understanding of meaning.

The "systematic," "generic," and "normal" aspects of discourse would seem to refer to its polished outer surface. By attending only to the surface of discourse, one may easily see human behavior as rule bound. In most conversations, everyone behaves him- or herself. As Labov and Fanshel's (1977) analysis of a therapy session with an anorexic suggests, even persons who are enraged may obey most of the rules of polite society: their anger occur beneath the surface of polite conversation.

By focusing only on outer observables, CA is in danger of repeating the Parsonian fallacy of confounding a status quo with the social order. Members of a society who are emeshed with the status quo find its standards compelling, as if they were absolute and eternal. But more objective observers realize that any given status quo is only one of many possible forms of social order. As suggested in the last chapter, CA, like most other social research, is utopian in some ways, but it is mostly ideological, accepting most of the background suppositions of the host culture.

The a priori decision in CA to devote most of the effort to outer behavior gives a misleading impression since it ignores the inner maelstrom of activity, what Fahlman (1981) has in mind when he refers to a switchboard's handling a million calls at once. To provide an evidential basis for a science of interpretation, we need equal attention to inner and outer experience. The next chapter proposes a theory and method for the study of one aspect of inner experience: emotion.

Part 3

Implicature and Emotion in Discourse

5

Shame and Conformity: The Deference-Emotion System

This chapter continues my discussion of Durkheim's approach. As a first step toward specifying the causal sequence implied by his theory, I outline a model of social influence, how it is experienced as *exterior* and *constraining*. The emotions of pride and shame play a key role in the model: pride signals an intact social bond; shame, a threatened one.

I show that Darwin, McDougall, and especially Cooley were shame theorists, each proposing the same context for pride and shame: *self's perception of the evaluation of self by other(s)*. Their work, as well as that of Mead and Dewey, suggests that social monitoring of self is virtually continuous. This assumption gives rise to a puzzle: If social monitoring is all but ubiquitous, and if it gives rise to either pride or shame, how is it that so few manifestations of either emotion are visible in our lives? One answer would be to predicate that *either pride or shame is occurring almost continuously but has low visibility*.

It remained for Helen B. Lewis (1971), a research psychologist, to confirm the theoretically derived hypothesis. In her analysis of over a hundred clinical interviews, she demonstrated the existence of "unacknowledged" shame. Neither the patient nor the therapist referred to it or, indeed, seemed to be aware of it, though it was present, in varying degrees, in every session. She is the discoverer of low-visibility shame. Her work implies a general theory of human behavior, a model which specifies causal sequences and empirical markers of abstract concepts.

Drawing upon Lewis, and Goffman's analysis of the relation between deference and embarrassment, I describe a *deference-emotion system*. Members experience this system as compelling conformity to norms exterior to self by informal but pervasive rewards (outer deference and its reciprocal, inner pride) and punishments (lack of deference, and the normal shame that is its reciprocal). I show how Asch's (1956) study of conformity illustrates the role of shame in compelling conformity. The theory points to *pathological* (as distinct from normal) shame as the causal agent in excessive or rigid conformity.

I am indebted to Suzanne Retzinger and to T. D. Kemper for comments on an earlier draft, presented in the Section on the Sociology of Emotions, at the annual meeting of the American Sociological Association, Chicago, August 1987, and published in the *American Sociological Review* 53 (1988): 395–406.

I propose modifications of Asch's design in order to elaborate the theory further. It provides a unitary explanation for conformity, the central problem in social science.

Durkheim's Paradigm

As indicated earlier, Durkheim is the central figure in modern sociology. He established the majority stance of contemporary sociologists. He showed that Protestant populations had consistently higher rates of suicide than Catholic ones, and that among Protestant groups, the pietistic sects, for example, the Calvinists, had consistently higher rates than the other groups. He interpreted these differences in terms of cultural differences between religious groups: individualism was greatest in the pietistic sects, less in the nonpietistic Protestant groups, and least prevalent among Catholics. As the individual becomes less solidary with the group, the likelihood of suicide increases.

He reasoned that there was need for a new discipline which tracked social influences of this kind, influences which he demonstrated to be separable from psychological, political, and economic factors. Social influence, he argued, constituted an independent system in its own right. The dominant methodology in current sociology grew out of this one study: teasing out differences among groups on the basis of statistical aggregates.

Durkheim's Legacy: Methods

There are two aspects of Durkheim's methodology which have important implications but which go unremarked. First, as mentioned earlier, although the differences in suicide rates were consistent, they were also very small. In statistical parlance, they were statistically significant; that is, it is quite unlikely that they represented mere sampling errors. On the other hand, knowing the religion of an individual is not an efficient predictor of suicide; there are many other factors as highly correlated with suicide as religion.

A second difficulty concerns the understanding of causation. Durkheim's interpretations of the statistical differences he found were speculative and abstract; they were not based on intimate knowledge of causal sequences. He was not able to show the intervening steps which led from religious belief to suicide; he simply speculated. He developed no explicit model which specified the detailed linkage between cause and effect. These two difficulties, the small size of effects and the inability to specify causal sequences, continue to haunt modern sociology.

My primary emphasis is this chapter will be not on methods but on theory. The issue of method comes up incidentally in my reinterpretation of Asch's study and, more directly, in my proposals for follow-up studies. The approach advocated here is intended not to replace statistics but to complement them. I show the usefulness of analyzing single events, in addition to aggregates, by looking at concrete instances of social interaction. Perhaps a blend of extensive and intensive research could lead to a new methodology. Intensive research may be just as necessary for generating hypotheses as extensive research is for testing them.

Durkheim's Legacy: Theory

In addition to the method of statistical aggregates, Durkheim also bequeathed a theoretical building block, the idea that social influence is experienced by individuals as exterior and constraining. He argued that the individual experiences social influence as coming from the outside, a force exterior to self, and that this force seems absolutely compelling. As in his interpretations of suicide rates, however, nowhere does he spell out the causal sequence implied. What are the steps involved such that individuals experience social control as exterior and constraining? This is an important question because the exterior constraint idea has become a basic premise for modern sociologists: we feel it in our bones, so to speak. Yet an adequate model of this idea has never been formulated on the conceptual level, much less proposed in an operationally definable way. Durkheim's theory remains a "black box"; no wiring diagram has been drawn.

As already suggested, Durkheim introduced the idea of social solidarity as the fundamental sociological concept. But he never specified the content of this very abstract idea. Rather than exploring it, he differentiated two types of solidarity—the mechanical and the organic. Almost all his exposition about solidarity in *The Division of Labor* concerns the two types rather than the nature of social solidarity as such. Like most social theorists, he assumed social connectedness, that there is a *binding force* which holds groups together, without examining his assumption.

The Division of Labor also hints at a second assumption, that the binding force involved in organic solidarity is stronger than that in traditional societies, that is, mechanical society. My argument suggests that this assumption was in error. The deference-emotion models suggest the opposite, that communal solidarity is the strongest force in human affairs and that the absence of such a force plays a central role in social conflict and turmoil.

One of the ways Durkheim formulated the process of social influence was in terms of "collective representations" (1906, 18,21): "Collective representations are exterior to individual minds . . . they do not derive from them as such, but from the association of minds, which is a very different thing." "Once a basic number of representations has been thus created, they become . . . partially autonomous realities, with their own way of life." I complained earlier about the vagueness of this formulation (Scheff 1967, 36): "Durkheim insists that collective consciousness is more than the sum of individual consciousnesses, that it has a life of its own, yet he gives no explanation of how individual consciousnesses (in "association") become group consciousness. Durkheim leaves us not with a theory but an enigma." In that same article, I proposed a model of consensus: collective representations involve not just agreement in a group but an infinite series of reciprocating understandings. That is, I not only agree with my neighbor that God exists, but I also know that she agrees, and she knows that I agree, and I know that she knows that I agree, and so on, up the ladder of reciprocating attributions. In the article, I showed that my model paralleled many theoretical statements and that it seemed to be supported by empirical findings. A subsequent article suggested that the same model might solve puzzles in an unexpected quarter, experimental studies of mixed-motive games, such as the Prisoner's Dilemma (Scheff 1967a).

Because of new ideas and findings during the ensuing twenty years, however, I now feel that my earlier model was incomplete. It was entirely *cognitive,* since it concerned only beliefs and perceptions of beliefs. It omitted entirely a component which is easily as important as beliefs and perceptions and may even predominate over them when there is conflict: *emotions.*[1] The earlier cognitive model may be adequate to explain how social influence is experienced as *exterior* but not how it could be experienced as *constraining.* The accurate perception of our neighbors' beliefs and expectations does not compel us to conform to them. What is the process which leads us to conform, even when we do not wish to?

Conformity is encouraged by a system of sanctions, that is, rewards and punishments: we usually conform because we are likely to be rewarded when we do so and punished when we do not. However, conformity usually occurs even in the absence of obvious sanctions. It is to the ubiquity of conformity that Durkheim's formulation refers. The reward of public acclaim and the punishment of public disgrace rarely occur, yet the social system marches on. Formal sanctions are slow, unwieldy, and expensive. In addition to the formal system, there must be a highly efficient system of informal sanctions, a system which is almost invisible.

A clue to this puzzle can be found in Goffman's treatment of interaction ritual (1967). He noted that the emotion of embarrassment or anticipation of embarrassment plays a prominent role in all social encounter. In presenting ourselves to others, we risk rejection. The form rejection takes may be flagrant, but much more frequently it is quite subtle, perhaps only a missed beat in the rhythm of conversation. Depending upon its intensity and obviousness, rejection usually leads to the painful emotion of embarrassment, shame, or humiliation (shame is used as the generic class name for a whole family of emotions, including embarrassment and humiliation). By the same token,

---

1. There is a parallel omission in my treatment of residual deviance, at about the same time (Scheff 1966, 1984). My concept of the symptoms of mental illness as residual deviance is entirely cognitive. Fortunately, Thoits (1985) provides the analysis of the emotional components that mine omitted.

when we are accepted as we present ourselves, we usually feel rewarded by the pleasant emotion of pride and fellow feeling.

The degree and type of deference, and the attendant emotions of pride and shame, make up a subtle system of social sanctions. This is the system that leads to experiencing social influence as constraining. Our thoughts and perceptions of social expectations only set the stage for social control. We experience it as so compelling because of emotions: specifically, the pleasure of pride and fellow feeling, on the one hand, and the punishment of embarrassment, shame, or humiliation, on the other.

The deference-emotion system may take formal and public forms: the ceremony for awarding the Congressional Medal of Honor illustrates the conferring of the highest degree of deference, and may be assumed to arouse pride in the recipient. At the other extreme, an impeachment proceeding takes away deference and presumably would arouse shame in the defendant. The idea of disgrace seems to assume both public and private sides: outer demotion and inner shame.

But formal rewards and punishments are infrequent, even rare. The deference-emotion system functions virtually continuously, even when we are alone, since we can imagine and anticipate its movements in vivid detail. The documentation of this system has so far escaped the net of systematic research; it is too subtle to be caught by the laboratory experiment or the social survey. Since it often functions outside the awareness of interactants, field workers have also missed it.

Unlike the system of formal sanctions, the deference-emotion system is virtually instantaneous and invisible, and cheap as dirt. Its lack of visibility makes for difficulties in describing its features since it is so taken for granted. Although shame and pride are implied in Durkheim's writing about social influence, they are never mentioned by name.

Even Goffman, whose analysis of the role of embarrassment, a shame variant, is a tour de force, falls short of a complete analysis. As suggested in chapter 1, he pointed to the ubiquity of embarrassment in social encounter, but he restricted his purview to the *social* aspects of embarrassment, to what is going on *between* interactants. He intentionally excluded the *within* part of emotions (1967, 108):

> In every social system, however, there are times and places where audience segregation regularly breaks down and where individuals confront one another with selves incompatible with the ones they extend to each other on other occasions. At such times, embarrassment, especially the mild kind, clearly shows itself to be located not in the individual but in the social system wherein he has his several selves.

This early statement is very qualified in excluding inner feelings, since it seems to limit the analysis to a particular situation, the breakdown of audience segregation, and to mild embarrassment. A later statement, however, is completely unqualified; emotion occurs *between* persons (Goffman 1974, 573): "Incapacity to perfectly contrive expression is not an inheritance of our animal or divine nature but the obligatory limits definitionally associated with a particular frame—in this case, the frame of everyday behavior." The tactic of limiting his analysis to outer behavior in the social domain paid rich dividends in certain areas, for example, the contagion of embarrassment between interactants. As Ricks (1984) recognized, Goffman's treatment of social embarrassment is subtle and evocative.

Since Goffman (1967) did not attempt to describe the interaction between outer and inner processes, he was unable to convey the explosive force of the deference-emotion system. One difficulty is that he separates his analysis of embarrassment ("The Social Organization of Embarrassment") from his analysis of anger and hostility, "character contests" such as duels and vendettas ("Where the Action Is").

A vivid contrast is provided by Lewis's (1971) treatment of shame. She treats only the inner process. In analogy to his use of the metaphor of contagion between persons, she points to what she calls a *feeling trap,* or inner contagion. In Goffman's analysis, one becomes ashamed that the other is ashamed, who in turn becomes ashamed, which increases the first person's shame, and so on—an *interpersonal* feeling trap. For Lewis, one becomes ashamed that one is ashamed, an inner loop which feeds on itself—an *intrapersonal* trap. Unlike Goffman, however, she does not separate her analysis of shame and anger. She postulates an affinity between the two emotions, with shame usually followed by anger. This loop, which can go on indefinitely, is usually experienced as a single affect, "helpless anger," or, in a more intense form, "humiliated fury."

By combining Goffman's social analysis with Lewis's psychological one, one can convey the extraordinary force of the deference-emotion system. This system occurs both *between* and *within* interactants. Ordinarily it functions so efficiently and invisibly that it guarantees the alignment of the thoughts, feelings, and actions of individuals. As already indicated, the German word *gleichaltung* captures this idea (in mechanical engineering, cogs which are aligned so perfectly that there is virtually no friction). Mutual conformity and respect lead to pride and fellow feeling, which lead to further conformity, which leads to further positive feeling, and so on.

However, when there is a real or imagined rejection on one or both sides (withdrawal, criticism, insult, defeat, etc.), and the resulting emotions are not acknowledged, the deference-emotion system may show a malign form, a *chain reaction* of shame and anger between and within the interactants. This explosion usually is very brief, perhaps a few seconds. But it can also take the form of bitter hatred lasting a lifetime. It can occur not only between individuals but also between groups, even very large groups, like nations. I have referred to such explosions as *triple spirals* of shame and anger (one spiral within each party, and one between them [Scheff 1987]). A chain reaction of this kind between groups can last longer than a lifetime since it can be handed down from generation to generation.

For all its brilliance, Goffman's analysis of interaction ritual, of the moral dimensions of interaction, leads one to conclude that such matters may be fateful, at most, only to individuals but not in larger arenas. Embarrassment, he seems to imply, can be exquisitely painful, but it is personal and transitory and not directly relevant to large and mighty social institutions. His tactic of behavioral analysis, which excludes the psychological domain, and of separating embarrassment from anger, is so specialized that it misses the larger implications of his vision.

Lewis's specialization, equal and opposite to Goffman's, also precludes drawing out the social implications of her work. Although she was aware that her concept of the feeling trap had implications beyond neurosis, there was little development in this direction in her written work. Only by combining the two partial analyses can the larger implications be seen.

Because of the ubiquity of shame and shame/anger sequences, *all* social and societal interaction can instantly become what Goffman called a character contest. When chain reactions of shame or shame/anger occur between and within interacting persons or groups, there is no natural limit to the intensity and duration of arousal. The unlimited furor of painful emotions in a triple spiral may explain why social influence is experienced as compelling. The emotion-deference system, as represented in the sequence of honor, insult, and revenge, may decide the fate of individuals and of nations, civilizations, and, indeed, in the current state of the world, of the human species as a whole.

Shame/Anger Sequences in Collective Behavior

By microscopic analysis of sequences of interaction ritual in concrete episodes, it may be possible to enlarge upon the beginning that Durkheim made in his investigation of suicide. In chapter 7, I outline a model of the way in which a class-based insult led to suicide in a classic work of fiction. In a study of Franco-German relations, 1871–1945 (Scheff 1989b), I explain the bizarre and highly self-destructive behavior of two nations in terms of the interaction ritual within and between them. To show the flavor, I summarize some aspects of the study here.

It appears that the French nation as a whole experienced its defeat by Germany in 1871 as a humiliation. Although it never appeared in official documents, *revanche* (revenge) was the watchword in French politics and diplomacy in the years 1871–1919 (Weber 1968). French political and military behavior during this period was extremely irrational and may be understood as dedicated to revenge even at the risk of self-destruction.

Social scientists have long been suspicious of applying concepts derived from individual behavior to the behavior of groups. This suspicion is amply justified by many earlier studies, for example, of so-called national character. My purpose, however, is only to provide a model that might be tested rather than to assume automatic applicability. The model of the triple spiral of shame/rage seems to clarify the otherwise baffling behavior of nations which led to the onset of World War I. Whether this model will survive empirical testing must await future investigations.

For brevity, three examples will suggest the flavor. It now appears that although Germany was involved, France was also an instigator of World War I. Through relentless secret diplomacy with England and especially with Russia, the president, Poincaré, followed a course which ensured an incident like the one that occurred at Sarajevo, which would lead to war (Goodspeed 1977). Apparently Poincaré was dedicated to the return of the French province of Alsace-Lorraine, which was ceded to the Germans as a result of the defeat in 1871. The return of this province seems to have symbolized for the French the revenge for their humiliation. Like many of his compatriots, he seemed to fear that time was running out because of the "Germanization" of Alsace.

The second example is closely related to the first. In 1914, the French army, instead of devoting itself to defending Paris against the German sledge-hammer blow that everyone else knew was coming through Belgium, occupied Alsace-Lorraine with a large force. From any conceivable point of view, this was a colossal blunder. It served no military purpose and, more important diverted a vast army to eastern France, far from the defense of Paris. This blunder very nearly brought French defeat in the first month. As sometimes happens in human affairs, monumental irrationality on this scale is so surprising that the blunderers are not called on to pay the price of their failure. The German army was unprepared for the swiftness of their conquest of northern France and perhaps suspicious of the inadequacy of the French defense. They hesitated to make good their advantage just long enough for English and French reserves to arrive.

The third example concerns the Allied blockade of Germany, which was continued for ten months after the German surrender. Although England participated in the blockade, it now appears that the instigation came almost entirely from the French. The German feeling of betrayal by the Allies in defeat had many components, but in the case of the continuing blockade, it was completely justified. This one act alone would probably have guaranteed that the Germans would experience their defeat as a humiliation and that they, in turn, like the French after 1871, would want a rematch.

Although there is controversy among experts over the first example, the role of France in instigating World War I, there is little about the other two. Nor is there any controversy about the role of revenge in leading to the rise of Hitler (Scheff 1989c). Just as revenge was the open secret of French politics 1871–1919, it became the open secret of German politics 1919–33. In the Weimar period, all the politicians vowed revenge. Because Hitler was the most extreme and fanatical in his adherence to this doctrine, he gained support because his followers felt that he was the most likely to take action, as indeed he did. For Hitler, *Lebensraum* (living space) served the same purpose as Alsace-Lorraine for Poincaré, a tangible object to symbolize an intangible emotion—humiliated fury, rage bound by shame. The irrationality of Franco-German conflict in this whole era perhaps can be best understood in terms of the functioning of the deference-emotion system.

The Sources of Shame: Biological and Social

In modern societies it is taken for granted that shame is a rare emotion among adults, prevalent only among small children (e.g., "Shamey, shamey," and the odd gesture of pointing the index finger of one hand at the victim while stroking it with the other index finger). This belief is reflected in the division made in anthropology between shame cultures and guilt cultures, with traditional societies relying on shame for social control; and modern societies, guilt. A similar premise is found in orthodox psychoanalytic theory, which places almost total emphasis on guilt as the adult emotion of self-control, with shame thought of as "regressive," that is, as childish. (An early attempt to break away from both premises can be found in Piers and Singer [1953].)

For many years, however, there has been a literature suggesting that shame is the primary social emotion in that it is generated by the virtually constant monitoring of the self in relation to others. Such monitoring, as already suggested, is not rare but almost continuous in social interaction and, more covertly, in solitary thought. If this line of thought is correct, shame would be the most frequent and possibly the most important of emotions, even though it is usually invisible. This thread can be found in Darwin (1872), Cooley (1922), McDougall (1908), and, more recently, in Lynd (1958), Lewis (1971), Braithwaite (1989), and, as already indicated, in Goffman (1967).

Lewis (1976) has made a suggestion about shame that links it to my earlier discussion of social solidarity and the social bond. Drawing upon recent studies of infant-caretaker interaction, she argues first that humans are genetically programmed to be social and cooperative. The infant-caretaker studies show, with a wealth of detail, that very young infants do not need to learn to be socially responsive. One example is the ability to take turns, a basic building block for cooperative activity. Very young infants quickly show the rhythm of looking into the caretaker's eyes then away. The precise rhythm of periods of mutual gaze, alternating with first one then the other party looking away, appears to be crucial in the development of a strong bond. The studies point to the management of turn taking as necessary to the development of mutual delight and love. As Yeats suggested, love comes in at the eyes. When a secure bond has been formed, both parties feel pride. Social solidarity begins in the nursery.

In the second step of her argument, Lewis proposes that shame is the most important of the social emotions because it arises when there is a threat to the social bond. In her scheme, shame has a signal function, alerting one to threats to the bond. Just as feelings of pride signal a secure bond, feelings of shame signal a threatened bond. These two conjectures can serve as a foundation for a structure/process theory of social solidarity. Before proceeding further with such a theory, I first review earlier discussions of pride and shame.

In his *Expression of Emotions in Men and Animals* (1872), Darwin devotes a whole chapter, the last substantive one, to "Self-Attention—Shame—Shyness—Modesty: Blushing." As his punctuation suggests, his primary interest is the phenomenom of blushing: What evolutionary function could it serve? He proposes that blushing may be universal in the human species, even among the darkest skinned people, and, in passing, by way of comment on the blushing of Australian aborigines, that blushing is caused by shame.

Under the section heading "The Nature of the Mental States Which Induce Blushing," he states his thesis: "These consist of shyness, shame, and modesty, the essential element in all being self-attention." For my purposes, the most essential proposition comes next, where he explains what he means by "self-attention": "It is not the simple act of reflecting on our own appearance, but the *thinking what others think of us, which excites a blush*" (325). His preliminary discussion suggest that blushing may be caused by perceptions of evaluation of the self, whether positive or negative. The bulk of the complete discussion suggests, however, that more frequently than not, the social perceptions of self which cause blushing are negative. Consider, for example, his summary statement: "Blushing, whether due to shyness, to shame for a real crime . . . or a breach of the laws of etiquette . . . or humility . . . depends in all cases on . . . a sensitive regard for the opinion, more particularly the *depreciation* of others" (335).

Darwin's argument about the relationship between blushing, emotions, and "self-attention" can be restated as two propositions connecting blushing with emotions, on the one hand, and social perception, on the other. First: Blushing is caused by shame. "Shyness" and "modesty," Darwin's two other "mental states" which induce blushing, can be considered to be shame variants.[2] Second, and more important for my purposes here, shame is caused by the perception of negative evaluations of the self. As will be suggested below, blushing is only one of several visible markers of overt shame and therefore is not a primary concept for a theory of social influence. The second statement, however, contains the basic proposition for the whole theory: shame is *the* social emotion, arising as it does out the monitoring of one's own actions by viewing one's self from the standpoint of others.

---

2. Lewis (1971) uses the term "variants"; Wurmser (1981), "cognates." "Variants" seems to be the more appropriate word; the various terms refer to states that are similar in that they all involve shame but vary in other ways. Embarrassment, for example, refers to a shame state of less intensity than humiliation or mortification.

Shame as a crucial emotion for adults is prominent in the thought of William McDougall (1908). He considered shame as one of what he called the "self-regarding sentiments," the most important one: "Shame is the emotion second to none in the extent of its influence upon social behavior" (124). Like Darwin, he seems to have understood that it arose as a result of self-monitoring, although he was not as precise on this point as Darwin or Cooley: "The conduct which excites our shame is that which lowers us in the *eyes of our fellows,* so that we feel it to be impossible for our positive self-feeling to attain satisfaction" (127; emphasis added). He seems clear on one important point: although shame undoubtedly has a biological basis that we share with the higher mammals, the human emotion of shame in adults is considerably more elaborate and complex (56).

We next turn to Cooley (1922), whom I regard, because of the clarity and forcefulness of his views, as the prophet of the role of shame in human behavior. He considered pride and shame as examples of what he called "social self-feelings," a conception very close to McDougall's "self-regarding sentiments." At some points in his discussion he seems to regard as a self-feeling *any* feeling that self directs toward itself, as if pride and shame had no particular prominence in this large group. This passage about the extraordinary importance of the self-feelings in human behavior, at first glance, would seem to be in this key: "With all normal . . . people, [social self-feeling] remains, in one form or another, the *mainspring of endeavor and a chief interest of the imagination throughout life* (208; emphasis added). Cooley continues:

> As is the case with other feelings, we do not think much of it
> [that is, of social self-feeling] so long as it is moderately and regu-
> larly gratified. Many people of balanced mind and congenial ac-
> tivity scarcely know that they care what others think of them, and
> will deny, perhaps with indignation, that such care is an important
> factor in what they are and do. But this is illusion. If failure or
> disgrace arrives, if one suddenly finds that the faces of men show
> coldness or contempt instead of the kindliness and deference that he
> is used to, he will perceive from the shock, the fear, the sense of
> being outcast and helpless, that he was living in the minds of others
> without knowing it, just as we daily walk the solid ground without
> thinking how it bears us up.

Although neither pride nor shame is mentioned by name in this passage, they are implied, especially the almost continuous presence of low-visibility pride in ordinary discourse. Moreover, the two examples he gives to illustrate his point are rich in implication:

> This fact is so familiar in literature, especially in modern novels,
> that it ought to be obvious enough. The works of George Eliot are
> particularly strong in the exposition of it. In most of her novels
> there is some character like Mr. Bulstrode in *Middlemarch* or Mr.

Jermyn in *Felix Holt,* whose respectable and long-established social image of himself is shattered by the coming to light of hidden truth.

Both examples, Bulstrode and Jermyn, involve the coming the light of shameful truths, truths which result in immediate public disgrace. In stressing the central importance of social self-feelings in this passage, Cooley may have been thinking primarily of pride and shame.

This possibility is confirmed when we examine his concept of "the looking-glass self," his description of the social nature of the self. He saw self-monitoring in terms of three steps (184): "A self-idea of this sort seems to have three principal elements: the imagination of our appearance to the other person; the imagination of his judgment of that appearance, and some sort of self-feeling, such as pride or mortification." In this passage he restricts self-feelings to the two which he seems to think are the most significant—pride and shame (considering "mortification" to be a shame variant). To make sure we understand this point, he mentions shame three more times in the passage that follows (184–85; emphasis added):

> The comparison with a looking-glass hardly suggests the second
> element, the imagined judgment, which is quite essential. The thing
> that moves us to *pride or shame* is not the mere mechanical reflec-
> tion of ourselves, but an imputed sentiment, the imagined effect of
> this reflection upon another's mind. This is evident from the fact
> that the character and weight of that other, in whose mind we see
> ourselves, makes all the difference with our feeling. We are *ashamed*
> to seem evasive in the presence of a straightforward man, cowardly
> in the presence of a brave one, gross in the eyes of a refined one,
> and so on. We always imagine, and in imagining share, the judg-
> ments of the other mind. A man will boast to one person of an
> action—say some sharp transaction in trade—which he would be
> *ashamed* to own to another.

Cooley's analysis of the social nature of the self can be summarized in terms of two propositions: (1*a*) In adults, social monitoring of self is virtually continuous, even in solitude. (We are, as he put it, "living in the minds of others without knowing it" [208].) (1*b*) Social monitoring always has an evaluative component and gives rise, therefore, to either pride or shame.

These two propositions, when taken together, suggest a puzzle. If social monitoring of self is almost continuous, and if it gives rise to pride or shame, why is it that we see so few manifestations of either emotion in adults? Among the possible answers to this question, one would be that pride/shame is ubiquitous but of a kind that has such low visibility that we do not notice it, giving rise to a third proposition: (1*c*) Adults are virtually always in a state of either pride or shame, usually of a quite unostentatious kind.

In his discussion of grief (he calls it distress-anguish), Tomkins observes a parallel puzzle (1963, 56): "The reader must be puzzled at our earlier affirmation that distress is suffered daily by all human beings. Nothing seems less common than to see an adult cry. And yet we are persuaded that the cry, and the awareness of the cry, as distress and suffering, is ubiquitous." His answer also parallels the one I have suggested for pride and shame (56): "The adult has learned to cry as an adult. It is a brief cry, or a muted cry, or a part of a cry or a miniature cry, or a substitute cry, or an active defense against the cry, that we see in place of the infant's cry for help." He goes on to an extended discussion of various substitutes for, or defenses against, crying. For example, an adult suffering in the dental chair might, instead of crying, substitute muscular contractions: clamping the jaws, tightly contracting the muscles in the abdomen, and rigidly gripping the arms of the chair with his hands (59). As an example of defending against the cry, Tomkins suggests masking the expression of sadness with one of anger by becoming angry as well as sad (64–67). It may be observed that most men in our society use this transformation, but many woman do the opposite, masking anger with grief.

One way of summarizing the various gambits that adults use when they are suffering loss is to say that in adults, most grief would be of a type that has low visibility because its manifestations have been disguised or ignored.

The finding of what they call "miserable" smiles by Ekman and Friesen (1982) can be seen as partially supporting Tomkins's conjecture. They found that most smiles were not indicative of joy but were either "false" or "miserable." That is, most smiles are voluntarily enacted rather than spontaneously express joy. Miserable smiles occur when a smile is used to disguise a negative emotion, such as grief.

Proposition 1c, the positing of almost continuous low-visibility pride or shame in adults, parallels Tomkins's conjecture about grief. Both Tomkins and Cooley imply the virtually continuous presence of low-visibility emotion.

The most dramatic of Cooley's views on shame, and the one which brings him closest to the position taken here, is his example of the power of what he calls "social fear," that is, the anticipation of shame (291; emphasis added):

> Social fear, of a sort perhaps somewhat morbid, is vividly depicted by Rousseau in the passage of his *Confessions* where he describes the feeling that led him falsely to accuse a maid-servant of a theft which he had himself committed. "When she appeared my heart was agonized, but the presence of so many people was more powerful than my compunction. I did not fear punishment, but I dreaded *shame:* I dreaded it more than death, more than the crime, more than all the world. I would have buried, hid myself in the center of the earth; invincible *shame* bore down every other sentiment; *shame* alone caused all my impudence, and in proportion as I became criminal the fear of discovery rendered me intrepid. I felt no dread but that of being detected, of being publicly and to my face declared a thief, liar, and calumniator.

Rousseau's phrase "invincible shame" will stand us in good stead in the reinterpretation of the Asch study undertaken below. Notice also that Cooley suggests this instance as an example of "morbid" (i.e., pathological), rather than normal, shame. I make a similar distinction in my discussion below.

Cooley's analysis of self-monitoring posits pride and shame as the basic social emotions. At this point intellectual history takes a somewhat surprising turn. G. H. Mead and John Dewey based their entire social psychology upon the process of role taking: the ability of humans to monitor themselves continuously from the point of view of others. Yet neither Mead nor Dewey ever mentions what was so obvious to Darwin, McDougall, and Cooley, that social monitoring usually gives rise to feelings of pride or shame. Mead and Dewey treat role taking, their basic building block of human behavior, as entirely a cognitive process. Neither has anything to say about pride and shame, as if Darwin, McDougall, and Cooley never existed. Social psychology has yet to recover from this oversight.[3]

In modern societies, adults seem to be "uncomfortable" about manifesting either pride and shame. This is to say that the emotions of shame and pride often seem themselves to arouse shame. (This proposition explains Darwin's observation that both positive and negative evaluations can give rise to blushing.) It seems likely, as both Darwin and McDougall suggest, that shame has a biological basis, that it is genetically programmed, not just in humans, but in the higher mammals. It may also be true, as recent infant-caretaker studies suggest, that for infants and very young children, the arousal of shame is largely biological.

For adults, however, it seems equally true that shame is not only a biological process but also, overwhelmingly, a social and cultural phenomenon. The discussion so far has suggested that adult shame is doubly social: shame arises in social monitoring of the self, and shame itself often becomes a further source of shame, depending upon the particular situation and the normative structure of the culture.

The second social aspect of shame, its recursiveness, can give rise to *pathological* shame, a potentially limitless spiral, as I already suggested. Although most of my discussion here refers only to normal shame, I suggest below that the concept of pathological shame may be the key to understanding the results of the Asch experiment, and that it may play a key role in all excessive or rigid conformity.

Low-Visibility Shame

If, as suggested, shame has as strongly recursive character in modern societies, then we would expect that most shame and pride would have low

---

3. An earlier attempt to rectify Mead and Dewey's oversight can be found in Shibutani (1961), particularly chapter 13, "Self-Esteem and Social Control," which anticipates, in part, the thesis of this chapter.

visibility. Even if shame and pride were widespread, persons who were proud or ashamed would be ashamed of their state and attempt to hide it from others and from themselves. How can one study pride and shame if they are usually hidden from view?

I know of no systematic studies of pride, but a beginning method for locating low-visibility shame was developed by Gottschalk and Gleser in their manual for rating emotion in verbal texts (1969). Although primarily oriented toward detecting hostility and anxiety, the manual also includes a section on typical sentences which they take to contain words that are shame markers. (In keeping with the psychoanalytic practice of considering all covert emotions to be related to anxiety, they call it "shame-anxiety.") These sentences are listed under five categories (I provide a few examples under each category [see Gottschalk and Gleser 1969, 49–52].)

1. Shame, embarrassment:
   I was so ashamed . . .
   I feel funny . . .
   I felt myself blushing.
   . . . I had behaved improperly. . . .

(Other sentences refer to the self with such words as "disconcerting, self-conscious, degrading, nonsense, shy, disreputable, discreditable, or unworthy.")

2. Humiliation:
   I don't know what was wrong with me, letting myself go like that.

(Other sentences involve such terms as "humbling, degrading, or little self-respect.")

3. Ridicule:
   He twitted me about being fat.
   I really feel utterly ridiculous in a situation like that.
   They stared at me and laughed.
   I'm being silly.
4. Inadequacy:
   I want to help myself but I don't know how to do it.
   Where was I when brains were passed out?
   I never do as well as I think I should.
   I feel stupid . . .
   My mind is a complete blank.
5. Overexposure of deficiencies or private details:
   I don't even know how to wipe my ass.
   I didn't want to talk about such personal things.

Although Gottschalk and Gleser do not discuss the matter, or refer to any of the shame theorists discussed above, only a few of the sentences contain explicit references to shame, embarrassment, or humiliation. Instead, most of their examples assume what the shame theorists posited to be the basic context for shame, a perception of negative evaluation of the self by self or others. Nor do the authors attempt to include markers of shame which are nonverbal. Their scale deals with both direct and indirect verbal markers, but not with nonverbal ones.

In her pioneering analysis of clinical dialogues, Lewis (1971) takes up the issue of shame markers more explicitly and more broadly than Gottschalk and Gleser. Her work is both theoretical and empirical, since she ties broad concepts and hypotheses to concrete episodes of behavior. In this respect she is the inheritor of Darwin, McDougall, and Cooley. She advances our knowledge of shame, however, because unlike the original theorists or the more recent advocates Lynd (1958), Tomkins (1963), Goffman (1967), Kohut (1979), and Ricks (1984), who use examples only in an illustrative way, she conducted an exhaustive analysis of shame content in complete episodes of real social interaction, entire clinical sessions. Her patient analysis of these sessions, word for word, led her to the discovery of "unacknowledged" shame, the low-visibility shame predicated here.

Lewis prepared the foundation for her analysis by distinguishing acknowledged and unacknowledged shame. She shows that in the clinical sessions she examined, most of the shame episodes that occurred were virtually invisible to the participants; they were acknowledged by neither the patient nor the therapist. She divided these episodes into two basic types: *overt, undifferentiated* shame and *bypassed* shame.

For Lewis, overt, undifferentiated shame involves painful feelings which are not identified as shame by the person experiencing them. Rather these feelings are named by using a variety of terms, all of which serve to disguise the shame experience: feeling foolish, stupid, ridiculous, inadequate, defective, incompetent, low self-esteem, awkward, exposed, vulnerable, insecure, and so on. All the terms used by Gottschalk and Gleser fall into this category.

Lewis classified the undifferentiated terms as shame markers because they occurred in conjunction with two other central events: (1) contexts in which the patient appeared to perceive self as negatively evaluated, either by self or other(s), the central context for shame, and (2) a change in the patient's *manner,* characterized by nonverbal markers such as speech disruption (stammering, repetition of words, speech "static" like "well," "uhhhh," long pauses, etc.), lowered or averted gaze, blushing, and, especially noticeable, a sharp drop in the loudness of speech, sometimes to the point of inaudibility.

Note that both the verbal and nonverbal markers of overt shame can be characterized as forms of "hiding" behavior (Scheff and Retzinger 1991): the verbal terms hide shame under a disguising label; the nonverbal forms manifest suggestions of physical hiding: averting or lowering the gaze to escape the gaze of the other, and speech disruption and oversoft speech to hide the content of one's speech and thoughts.

To summarize: overt, undifferentiated shame occurs when the patient

(1) feels the self negatively evaluated, either by self or other, (2) shows non-verbal indication of shame (speech disruption, lowered or averted gaze, blushing, or oversoft speech), and (3) labels or associates the painful feeling with undifferentiated terms such as those listed above. In these instances the negative evaluation of self appears to cause so much pain as to produce fluster, to slow down or interfere with the fluent production of thought or speech. But the pain is mislabeled.

In addition to the overt, undifferentiated pattern, Lewis described a second pattern of unacknowledged shame, *bypassed* shame. Like the overt pattern, bypassed shame always begins with a perception of the negative evaluation of self. Where the markers of undifferentiated shame are flagrant and overt, however, those of bypassed shame are subtle and covert. Although thought and speech are not obviously disrupted, they take on a *speeded up* but repetitive quality which Lewis refers to as *obsessive*.

Typically, a patient repeats a story or series of stories, talking rapidly, but not quite to the point. The patient is intellectually active but appears to be unable to make decisions, each involving seemingly balanced pros and cons, which Lewis refers to as "the insoluble dilemma." Frequently a patient complains of the endless internal replaying of a scene in which she felt unfairly or critically judged or in which she made an error. Upon being questioned, she may report that when she first realized the error, she winced or groaned, then immediately began obsessing about the incident. The patient often complains of feeling ineffectual. The patient's mind seems to be taken up with the unresolved scene to the point that she is unable to become effectively involved in events in the present even though there is no obvious disruption. She is subtly distracted.

The two patterns of shame appear, on the surface, to involve opposite responses. In overt, undifferentiated shame, the victim feels emotional pain to the point that it obviously retards or disrupts thought and speech. He seems to be trying to hide the painful state from self as well as from others. In bypassed shame, the victim appears to *avoid* the pain before it can be completely experienced, through rapid thought, speech, or actions. These two types correspond to my own distinction between under- and overdistanced emotion (Scheff 1979). Overt, undifferentiated shame is underdistanced since the intense pain of embarrassment or humiliation is experienced. What Mead called the "I" phase of the self, the "biologic individual," predominates in consciousness. Bypassed shame is overdistanced. One avoids the pain by stepping outside self into the "me" phase of the self, as if the pain were not happening.

Both the slowed-down pattern of overt shame and the speeded-up pattern of bypassed shame are disruptive, however, since both involve the victim in rigid and distorted reactions to reality. Both kinds of shame are equally hidden since one is misnamed, the other avoided. These two basic patterns explain how shame might be ubiquitous yet usually escape notice.

Adler's (1956) theory of human development anticipated Lewis's discovery

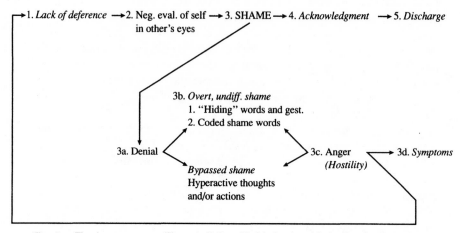

Fig. 1.—The shame construct. The underlining of 1, 3*b*, 3*c*, 4, and 5 signifies that these phrases usually produce visible cues.

of the two basic types of unacknowledged shame. Although he did not use the term, what he called "the feeling of inferiority," that is, shame, played a central role in his theory. He argued that developing children's greatest desire is for a secure bond. If that bond is not available at crucial points, the child's personality proceeds along one of two paths. Either it develops "inferiority complexes," that is, it becomes prone to overt, undifferentiated shame, or it compensates by seeking power, that is, it avoids feeling shame by bypassing it, using rapid thought, speech, or actions for this purpose.

Although Lewis's distinction parallels Adler's, her work is an enormous advance over his. Adler's theory, true to the psychoanalytic genre, uses concepts that are static, abstract, and imprecise. For this reason his ideas, although they are provocative, are untestable. Neither he nor anyone else has stated the observable markers for his concepts or specified the causal process which connects them.

By contrast, Lewis's formulations provide the foundation for a testable theory since they imply observable markers for the major concepts and for the events in the causal chain that connect them. Her theory is dynamic, precise, and testable, where Adler's is structural, vague, and untestable. (See fig. 1 for my representation of the shame construct as a flow chart.)

The work of Tomkins and of Lewis supports Freud's early work on *repression* but extends it. In his first book (1895), with Breuer, he argued that hysteria was caused by repressed *emotion*—"Strangulated affect," as he called it. He based his conjecture on the observation that patients improved when they expressed hitherto forgotten emotions, for example, by crying or with heated words, a rudimentary theory of catharsis (Scheff 1979). His theory was based on successful therapy rather than on systematic research.

Tomkins (1963) approached repression from a different direction, through deduction about the fate of grief which did not result in catharsis (crying). This approach led him to describe the outer signs of low-visibility grief, an affect which overlaps but is not identical with that of repressed grief. For example, some low-visibility grief is a result of conscious masking or avoidance.

Lewis extended the concept of repression both theoretically and empirically. She laid the groundwork for the shame construct, the description of the context and cues for unacknowledged shame, and its role in the genesis and maintenance of neurotic symptoms. Most of the shame episodes she found were not only outside, but also not available to, awareness. Her work therefore not only confirms part of Cooley's conjecture (the part about shame) but also confirms and expands upon Freud's (1895) original hypothesis that neurosis is caused by strangulated affect. I now turn to the reanalysis of a study which points to the role of shame in rigid or excessive conformity, a much more widely prevalent form of pathological behavior than psychopathology.

The Asch Study

To illustrate the way in which emotions lead to social control, I review a study (Asch 1956) of conformity to group decisions, one of many such studies in social psychology. In this classic laboratory study, the experiment was designed in such a way that single subjects found themselves alone, facing what seemed to be a unified majority. Since the task was a simple comparison of lengths of lines, subjects must have been baffled by the completely erroneous responses of other "subjects." Unknown to the naive subject, the others were confederates of the investigator, instructed to give erroneous responses. The design of the study resulted in a high proportion of conforming behavior: three-quarters of the subjects were swayed by the majority responses; only one-quarter remained independent.

Asch followed the inductive design which characterizes modern experimental social psychology; he did not test a hypothesis derived from theory. In retrospect, however, the study can be seen as relevant to a basic element in Durkheimian theory, holding constant one element in social influence, exteriority, while allowing the other element, constraint, to vary. All the naive subjects perceived the judgment of the majority to be different from, and therefore exterior to, their own judgments. (Asch demonstrated the exteriority of group standards by showing that naive subjects who made judgments alone, in the absence of an erring majority, made no errors whatsoever.)

The study can be seen as testing the hypothesis that given the kind of task demanded, *a majority of the subjects will find group standards compelling even though they are exterior and contradictory to their own individual standards.* This formulation suggests a key question: What is the difference between those subjects who maintained their independence from the group and those who yielded? My analysis suggests that the answer to this question involves emotions: subjects who yielded to the majority were those who attempted to avoid the embarrassment (shame) of appearing different from the group.

Although Asch did not design the study in order to show the effects of emotion, or ask questions about emotions, many of the poststudy interviews suggest that they played an important role. It is clear both from Asch's observations and from the subject's responses that many of them found the experience of being in the minority extremely painful. Asch reports that as the clear division between the majority and the individual continued, the individual became tense, flustered, nervous, or anxious. A reaction which occurred both in independent and yielding subjects, he reports, was the fear that they were suffering from a defect and that the study would disclose this defect (1956, 31).

> I felt like a silly fool.
>
> A question of being a misfit. They agreed—the idea that they'd think I was queer.
>
> It made me seem weak-eyed or weak-headed, like a blacksheep.

Many of the comments show the negative viewing of self from the point of view of the others:

> You have the idea that the attention of the group is focused on you.
>
> I didn't want to seem different.
>
> I didn't want to seem an imbecile.
>
> They might feel I was just trying to be out of the ordinary . . .
>
> They probably think I'm crazy or something.

These comments are all indicative of overt shame. Asch makes an important point, however, in differentiating the poststudy interview responses of those who remained independent from those who yielded to the majority. He notes, first, that both independent and yielding subjects were troubled by disagreeing with the majority:

> As the disagreement persisted many began to wonder whether it signified a defect in themselves. They found it painful to be (as they imagined) the focus of attention, in addition to which they feared exposure of their weakness which they suspected the group would disapprove. [32]

Asch points out that though these feelings were all but universal, not everyone who experienced them yielded. Those who maintained their independence responded to their own perceptions of the lines despite their strong feelings. Asch characterizes the responses of those who yielded in a different way:

> They were *dominated* by their exclusion from the group which they took to be a reflection on themselves. Essentially they were *unable* to face a conflict which threatened, in some undefined way, to expose a deficiency in themselves. They were consequently trying to

merge in the group in order not to feel peculiar. [45; emphasis added]

There are several key ideas in this passage. First, there are two markers of overt, undifferentiated shame. In the last sentence, Asch suggests that the yielding subjects conformed so that they would not "feel peculiar," and in the sentence before that, that maintaining their independence of judgment might "exposure a deficiency in themselves" rather than errors by the majority.

A third basic idea is not stated explicitly but implied by the first sentence: the subjects' perception of "exclusion from the group" which they took to be a "reflection on themselves" rather than on the group. Since the group took no action to exclude the naive subjects, the perception of exclusion must have been solely in the imagination. This movement implies the basic shame context: perceiving one's self as negatively evaluated.

Finally, the entire passage can be summarized by translating it into the language of emotions: the subjects who yielded to the group were those who felt overt shame and whose perceptions, cognitions, or actions were controlled by the attempt to avoid shame. Conversely, the subjects who maintained independence from the group appeared to feel conflict, that is, overt shame, but elected to respond in spite of this feeling.

So far the discussion of the role of emotion in compelling conformity has been entirely in terms of overt, undifferentiated shame. There is also scattered evidence in the remarks of the subjects, and in Asch's summaries of these remarks, of the presence of bypassed shame as a causal element in compelling conformity. In the summary by Asch cited above, he is referring to those subjects who acknowledged conflict between themselves and the group. There is another group of subjects, however, all of whom yielded to the influence of the group, in which there is little or no acknowledgment of conflict and no markers of overt shame. The emotion cue in this group suggest bypassed shame.

After stating that the interview responses of the independent subjects were apt to be frank and forthright, he notes that those of the yielding subjects had a different quality (33):

> [Their] reactions were more often evasive and shallow, and some revealed a lack of appreciation of the situation and of the possible significance of their action. . . . When asked to describe his experiences at the outset of the interview, one subject (who yielded completely) inquired: "Exactly what do you mean by experiences?" Another remarked: "I didn't have any experiences, I felt normal."

These two responses, especially the second, suggest a complete denial of conflict and of the feelings resulting from that conflict. The comments of two other yielding subjects also suggest denial, but in a different form, by reducing their whole experience of the study to a ponderous or obfuscating generalization: "People perceive things differently . . ." and "How do we know who is right?"

Another group of yielding subjects, according to Asch (42), "granted to the majority the power to see correctly . . . allowed themselves to become confused, and at the critical point adopted the majority judgments *without permitting themselves to know of their activity.*" This is a very strong statement involving avoidance of conflict, denial of feelings, and self-deception. Asch found among the yielding subjects another frequent form of self-deception: underestimation of the number of times each had yielded. He showed that the amount of underestimation was proportional to the amount of yielding (the greater the yielding, the greater the underestimation [34–35]). Many of these subjects acted as if there were only a few such incidents, even those who had yielded at every opportunity. By denying reality, perhaps they sought to avoid painful feelings.

One of Asch's summaries of the interview responses emphasizes both types of shame responses, the conflict of overt shame and the obsessive quality of bypassed shame (51):

> Our observations suggest that independence requires the capacity to accept the fact of opposition without a lowered sense of personal worth. The independent person has to organize his overt actions on the basis of experience for which he finds no support; this he can do only if he respects his experiences and is capable of claiming respect for them. The compliant person cannot face this ordeal because he translates social opposition into a reflection of his personal worth. Because he does so the social conflict plunges him into pervasive and incapacitating doubt.

Most of this passage is commensurate with both forms of shame, but the last sentence seems to focus on the obsessive form, the insoluble dilemma characteristic of bypassed shame. On the whole, Asch's report inadvertently suggests that unacknowledged shame plays a central role in causing subjects to yield to group influence.

To conclude this section, I return to a still unresolved issue. Recall that Asch reported that the subjects who remained independent, as well as some of those who yielded, manifested markers of overt, undifferentiated shame. (All those who showed bypassed shame had yielded.) Apparently, in this case, the presence of bypassed shame gives an adequate causal explanation of yielding, but overt, undifferentiated shame does not since it was present in both those who yielded and those who did not. For this latter group, a further explanation is needed.

One possible formulation would be in terms of "self-esteem." The subjects who remained independent, although they experienced shame, had sufficiently high self-esteem such that they acted on their judgments despite their feelings of shame. Those who yielded had low self-esteem; they sought to avoid further feelings of shame by acting contrary to their own judgments. This explanation is very similar to the one suggested by Asch; indeed, he comes very close to stating it in these terms. Such a formulation, a causal explanation based on the personalities of the subjects, could be subjected to verification in future studies.

Although this formulation might mark an advance in understanding, it might be slight. The concept of low self-esteem can be seen as a gloss, implying a person who habitually feels shame rather than pride. Perhaps the concept of pathological shame, as already indicated, would specify the causal process more precisely. Low self-esteem might be conceptualized as a tendency toward endlessly recursive shame, spirals of potentially limitless intensity and duration. As suggested in my earlier article (1987), in such persons, shame alone, or in combination with other emotions such as anger, might be recursive to the point of *chain reaction*. Such a dynamic sequence could be used to explain explosive episodes of acute panic (a shame-fear alternation), resentment (shame-anger alternation, with the anger directed out), and guilt (shame-anger sequences, with the anger directed in).

Under this model, persons with high self-esteem would be those with the experience of managing shame such that it was acknowledged and discharged. Although shame is a painful emotion for them, as for everyone else, it is not overwhelming. Persons with low-self esteem are unable to manage shame in a way that leads to acknowledgement and discharge. For such persons, a situation which threatened shame would be overwhelmingly painful since it would be likely to involve them in an unending spiral of shame. Such a person might do *anything* to avoid pain, to "turn the world upside down, rather than turn themselves inside out," to use Helen Lewis's phrases. Obsession with revenge, leading to vendetta or war, might be explained in this way.

Lewis's phrases recall the episode in which Rousseau's conscience lost the battle with what he called "invincible" shame. It also might explain a baffling comment that one of the yielding subjects made to Asch, that he voted for Dewey even though he preferred Truman because he thought that Dewey would win and that he was preferred by most (48). It appears that shame, when it is unacknowledged, may be not only invincible, but insidious. If we were able to observe such persons in a shaming situation, we might be able to detect markers of spiraling shame, which would differentiate them from persons with high self-esteem. The format of such a study will be discussed below.

This formulation does not imply that social control is dependent entirely on individual personality, only that individuals have differing susceptibilities to shame. The situational component in conformity is equally important in the deference-emotion model, the deference awarded to individuals in a situation. The Asch experiment is diabolical with respect to shame since it is arranged to rob the individual of his or her own view of reality but in a covert way. As the deference-emotion model suggests, conformity results from the interaction of *individual* and *situational* components. This interaction can also be seen as a cultural phenomenon since status arrangements consist, at the microscopic level of analysis, of the mix of awarding and withholding status. (For an earlier formulation which suggests a link between status and emotion, see Kemper [1978].)

Further Studies

All the interpretations of the Asch study made here have been indirect. How could they be tested directly in future studies? One possible direction would be to vary the experimental format that Asch used but in a way that includes the emotion-deference system as part of the design. One obvious modification would be to conduct a test of self-esteem before the experiment to see how well it could predict who would yield and who would not. Such a modification would probably be the most direct check of the part played by personality in social control.

As already indicated, it would probably also be desirable to know the effect that external sanctions have, since such sanctions play a prominent role in social influence in real life. Having the experimenter or the confederates praise or criticize some of the naive subject's responses could be used to investigate the interaction between internal emotions and external sanctions. Having real as well as imagined sanctions would also open a further possibility, gauging the effect of acknowledging or discharging shame on the degree of social control. If we read between the lines of the original study, the social scene in which the experiment was conducted seems to have been stiff, formal, awkward, and uncomfortable, that is, shaming. The author's descriptions, the subjects' remarks (and the photographs in the article in *Scientific American*), all suggest strain and tension as the dominant mood of the experiment. Seemingly live interaction between the naive subjects and the confederates would allow the effect of mood to become itself an object of study. For example, saying that the study involved "playing a judgment game" and encouraging the naive subjects to express feelings by having some of the confederates stage "playful" behavior (as in the "joy" condition of the Schachter and Singer study) might give rise to laughter and other forms of the relief of tension.

However, before one recommends *extensive* studies of this kind, which compare responses of many subjects, it might be helpful to begin with *intensive* studies of single subjects' responses. Perhaps we know too little about the specific processes through which emotions compel conformity. The discussion of the postinterview findings indicates that the specific ways in which shame influences perception, thought, and action are still unclear. As suggested by my remarks on pathological shame, preliminary studies which made moment-by-moment analyses of only a few subjects might increase our understanding of the causal process and pave the way, therefore, for more sophisticated studies in the experimental format.

One approach would be to use the standard Asch design to select individual subjects, each of whom clearly manifests one of three types of response: the completely independent subject, the yielding subject whose shame responses clearly fall into the overt, undifferentiated type, and the yielding subject whose responses clearly indicate bypassed shame. By making a videotaped record of their behavior during the study and the poststudy interview, one could establish a basis for moment-by-moment analysis of causal sequences. In addition to the standard Asch postinterview questions, however, a further interview could be designed to study their thoughts and feelings. For example, stop frames of each subject, taken during the study and the poststudy interview, could be shown to the subjects to help them remember inner responses which they might otherwise ignore or forget.

An intensive analysis of the videotape record could yield new information about the shame process in its relationship to thought and behavior. For example, the disruption of speech and the visual markers of overt shame have already been documented (Lewis 1971; Retzinger 1985, 1987a). But the speeding up of speech and thought and the distortion of reality characteristic of bypassed shame have not; this type of response is based mostly on clinical impressions (Lewis 1971). A careful analysis of rates of speech and interview questions about rates of thought might help clarify this matter.

Summary

In this chapter I have proposed that Durkheim's analysis of social influence implies a deference-emotion system in which conformity to exterior norms is rewarded by deference and the feeling of pride, and nonconformity is punished by lack of deference and feelings of shame. In this analysis, social control involves a biosocial system which functions silently, continuously, and virtually invisibly, occurring within and between interactants. I have shown how Asch's study of independence and conformity may be reinterpreted in these terms and suggested future studies. If the deference-emotion system is universal in all cultures, the theory would provide a unitary explanation of conforming behavior, the central problem of social science.

Addendum to second printing: In his brilliant analysis of advice manuals over five hundred years of European history, Elias (1978) anticipated my argument about the rise of unacknowledged shame in western societies. Carefully and rapidly moving between verbatim excerpts and interpretations, his method also resembles the part/whole approach I describe here. For further discussion, see Scheff and Retzinger (1991).

6

Microlinguistics: A Theory of Social Action

The last chapter proposed a mechanism for social control: the deference-emotion system. In this chapter, I connect emotion and cognition in a theory of social action.[1] The problem of social action concerns the linking of individual behavior to social structure. I describe a model of attunement, the process through which interactants achieve (or fail to achieve) joint attention and feeling, and a methodology appropriate for studying it. Two separate but interrelated systems are involved—a system of communication which can lead to joint attention and a system of deference which can lead to the sharing of feeling. I draw upon the theoretical work of Goffman and Lewis and the microlinguistic work of Pittenger et al. which points to processes which occur both *between* and *within* interactants.

Through prospective-retrospective and counterfactual methods, interactants appear to use the resources of an entire society in each encounter. Their ability to understand any given moment in reference to the *extended context* in which it occurs provides the link between the individual and social structure. Society is based on the minute and unexplicated events which make up the microworld underlying ordinary discourse. I suggest that research on human action involves reference to this world and requires methods similar to those the interactants use, as well as systematic methods.

Social Action and Natural Language

How are the actions of individuals translated into recurring patterns of collective behavior? How is social structure realized in the actions of individuals? These questions pose an obvious conceptual problem for the social sciences since they involve the basic model of social behavior. Less obviously, also implicated is the methodology of social science. All empirical research implies a model of social action since it is ultimately dependent on observations of individual behavior. In the absence of an explicit theory, each researcher is forced to improvise a theory for the case at hand.

In this chapter I outline a rudimentary theory of social action and a meth-

1. For an earlier version, see Scheff (1986a). I am indebted in writing this chapter to conversations with Ursula Mahlendorf and Suzanne Retzinger.

odology appropriate to it. In order to do so, I bridge areas that are usually kept separate: micro- and macroworlds, inner and outer, thought and feeling. I claim that the basic human *bond* involves mental and emotional connectedness, that social organization requires what Stern et al. (1984) have called *attunement* between individuals, the sharing of thoughts and feelings. Society is possible to the extent that its members are able to connect with each other in this way. Society is endangered by anarchy to the extent that interacting members fail to find attunment, lack connectedness, as in the excerpt below. I illustrate this model with findings from recent research and with a concrete episode of social interaction.

My starting point is an empirical finding from work on artificial intelligence. In the past twenty years an important discovery has been made by attempts at automated interlanguage translation. No algorithm has been found that is sophisticated enough to translate sentences from one natural language to another. Put in a slightly different way, computers have been unable to understand natural language sentences and are unlikely to do so in the foreseeable future (Winograd 1984).

As indicated earlier, the words in natural languages have more than one meaning. Consider the sentence "The box is in the pen." Is pen to be understood as an enclosure or as a writing instrument? The computer faced with this decision has recourse only to a dictionary. The native speaker has encyclopedic knowledge of the meaning of pen and also recourse to the contextual knowledge of the sentence involved. Considerations of the usual sizes, shapes, and uses of pens and boxes might lead the native speaker to prefer enclosure as the meaning in this case. Even though this is a relatively simple problem (compared with highly metaphoric sentences), it would be extremely tedious to make the speaker's decision process explicit for just this one sentence.

Even at this elementary level, verbal sentences appear to involve *open,* rather than *closed,* domains. As already indicated, the latter involve a finite number of objects, choices, and rules, each of which is uniquely defined. The game of tick-tack-toe provides a simple example: there are only two objects, X and O, and, on the first move, nine choices. The rules are uniquely defined so that there is no possibility of ambiguity. Most branches of mathematics involve closed domains (e.g., algebra, calculus).

An open domain involves a very large number of objects and rules, none of which are uniquely defined. The ability to function in an open domain like natural language now appears to be based on extraordinarily complex skills, which are executed with lightning-like rapidity. If we move from the arena of sentences composed of words to those that are spoken, with their accompaniment of nonverbal gestures, we may appreciate the complexity. The amount of information carried by digital language is small compared with that carried by gestures both seen and heard. These gestures are not digital but continuous; they signal vastly more information.

Recent findings from conversation and discourse analysis suggest the im-

portance of nonverbal gestures in social interaction (Sacks, Schegloff, and
Jefferson 1974; Atkinson and Heritage 1984). To summarize many studies
and extrapolate to expected future findings: it would appear that every sentence uttered contains sequencing signals which allow the listener to determine whether the speaker will continue to speak, or will stop at the end of the
sentence. Although some of this information is conveyed verbally, most is
nonverbal. Particularly important is the intonation contour of the sentence: the
relative speed, loudness, and pitch of the syllables which make it up.

Sequencing signals allow for rapid and seemingly effortless coordination of
speech between speakers, a turn-taking system. This finding may constitute
the first universal, pancultural regularity in language use. As indicated in the
last chapter, turn taking also appears to occur virtually at birth in the interaction between caretaker and infant (Stern et al. 1984; Tronick et al. 1982).
For this reason, it is plausible that the motive and some of the ability to take
turns are genetically inherited.

It would appear that sequencing signals are only a minute part of the socially relevant information packed into a spoken sentence. In the last chapter,
I discussed the deference-emotion system. Turn taking makes up only one
small aspect of this larger system. Coordinating turns at speaking is only in
part a mechanical problem of avoiding interruption. It also involves a moral
issue, the signaling of status.

In order to show respect, the listener must avoid speaking before the speaker
has finished. There must also be a decent pause (perhaps one or two seconds)
before the listener begins, showing that speech has been registered, considered. Even if the listener's response has no overlap with the last sentence spoken, the absence of the requisite pause will usually be heard as
disrespectful.

The listener must also avoid too lengthy a pause. A silence of more than
three or four seconds will usually be heard as implying disagreement or confusion and therefore as possibly disrespectful. The rhythm of spoken speech is
freighted with deference signals. Speaker and listener must both be involved.

In the role of listener, the interactant must take care to detect and honor
sequencing signals. In the role of speaker, the signaling task is much greater.
Not only sequencing must be signaled but also the status of the speaker and
the listener(s). For example, speaking too rapidly or with too little intonation
may be understood as signaling lack of interest or respect. Similarly, speaking
too slowly and with too much emphasis and gesticulation may also be taken as
disrespectful of the listener's ability to understand.

The rhythm of speech is only one of many avenues for awarding or withholding deference. Goffman (1967, 33) proposed that every sentence—its
words, paralanguage, and gestures—implies an evaluation of the social and
interpersonal status of the interactants:

> The human tendency to use signs and symbols means that evidence
> of social worth and of mutual evaluations will be conveyed by very

minor things, and these things will be witnessed, as will the fact
that they have been witnessed. An unguarded glance, a momentary
change in tone of voice, an ecological position taken or not taken,
can drench a talk with judgemental significance. Therefore, just as
there is no occasion of talk in which improper impressions could
not intentionally or unintentionally arise, so there is no occasion of
talk so trivial as to require each participant to show serious concern
with the way in which he handles himself and the others present.

Goffman argued, furthermore, that all interactants are exquisitely sensitive
to the exact amount of deference they are being awarded. As suggested in the
last chapter, if they believe they are receiving too much or, much more frequently, too little, they will be embarrassed. His argument concerning embarrassment introduces us to the *realm of feeling*. Before discussing this realm, I
once again refer to a second system with which the deference system is
entangled.

Goffman's analysis of social interaction also implies another extremely intricate system—the system of communication which enables interactants to
understand each other. Although misunderstanding also occurs, it is clear that
interactants, at times, can understand each other. We are certain that we have
understood another when we learn that we have correctly predicted her intentions, and she ours.

For example, an appointment is set up on one occasion for dinner on a later
one. When one's partner arrives at the right time and place, dressed as expected, and in the expected frame of mind, it is clear that interpretive understanding occurred on the earlier occasion. One has correctly understood the
other's intent, an inner phenomenon, by noting outer markers. One has understood not only the spoken words but also the inner intent to which the words
referred; as expected, the other was not lying or joking. As suggested in the
analysis of the excerpt below, the same process of prediction and confirmation
can also take place *continuously* within any given episode.

Although interpretive understanding is so frequent that we take it for granted,
it is by no means clear how one "reads another's mind." Goffman carefully
describes the conditions under which successful mind reading is most likely to
occur (1967, 34; emphasis added):

> An understanding will prevail as to when and where it will be per-
> missible to initiate talk, among whom, and by means of what topics
> of conversation. A set of significant gestures is employed to initiate
> a spate of communication and as a means for the persons concerned
> to accredit each other as *legitimate* participants. When this process
> of *reciprocal ratification* occurs, the persons so ratified are in what
> might be called "a state of talk"—that is, they have declared them-
> selves officially open to one another for purposes of spoken commu-
> nication and guarantee together to maintain a flow of words. . . . A
> *single focus of thought and visual attention,* and a single flow of

talk, tends to be maintained and to be legitimated as officially representative of the encounter.

This is a detailed description of the situation in which the "mystic union" of successful communication is likely to occur. The concept of legitimacy which Goffman introduces in this passage serves to bridge the two different systems, deference and communication. Communication occurs most effectively if the interactants "reciprocally ratify" each other as legitimate partners in the communication enterprise. Such ratification is signaled by the virtually continuous awarding and registering of markers of deference. (Bruner [1983], in his analysis of the child's acquisition of language, treats the communication system in a way very similar to that of Goffman, as the achievement of joint attention, but makes no reference to the deference system.)

It would appear that each uttered sentence is a dynamic package, loaded with an extraordinary amount of information. It may be considered to be analogous to the cell in a living organism, the smallest system. As Goethe suggested in his discussion of morphogenesis, it may be necessary to understand the structure of the cell in order to understand the organism, and the structure of the organism in order to understand the cell. In the proposed model, society continues to exist so long as its members are able to achieve attunement, the sharing of meanings and feelings.

Example of Interaction Ritual: The Opening Exchange in a Conversation

Goffman's analysis is so dense and abstract that it is difficult to know whether we understand his meaning. In this section I show, in a concrete example, the markers of deference and communication which suggest the existence of two distinct but interrelated systems. The analysis of this example will be used to describe exchanges of feeling and the methods interactants (and researchers) use when they are interpreting events.

The passage comes from a widely known psychiatric interview (Gill, Newman, and Redlich 1954). It was the basis for a subsequent study (Pittenger et al. 1960). Because the original work was accompanied by a long-playing record, Pittenger and his colleagues were able to conduct a microscopic study of the verbal and nonverbal events in the first five minutes of the interview. My analysis of the opening exchange is based upon, and further develops, that of Pittenger et al. In particular, I use techniques implied in their work and that of Labov and Fanshel (1977) and Lewis (1971) to interpret the *message stack*. That is, I use the words in the transcript and the nonverbal sounds in the recording to infer the unstated implications (the *implicature*) and *feelings* which underlay the dialogue (for a more comprehensive discussion of this session, see Scheff 1989)

(Therapist [T] and patient [P] enter interviewing room)
T1:   Will you sit there. *(Softly)*

P1:   (*Sits down*)
T2:   (*Closes doors*) What brings you here? (*Sits down*)
P2:   (*Sighs*) Everything's wrong I guess. Irritable, tense, de-
       pressed. (*Sighs*) Jus' . . . just everything and everybody gets
       on my nerves.
T3:   Nyeah.
P3:   I don't feel like talking right now.
T4:   You don't? (*Short pause*) Do you sometimes?
P4:   That's the trouble. I get too wound up. If I get started I'm all
       right.
T5:   Nyeah? Well perhaps you will.

A close reading of this passage suggests several puzzles. For example, a pause of eight seconds occurs in T4. As already noted, a pause of more than two seconds is likely to make interactants uncomfortable. In seeking to understand why the patient did not respond to the first part of T4, we notice her preceding comment (P3): "I don't feel like talking right now." Why would the patient not feel like talking when less than a minute has elapsed in the interview? I suggest an answer to this question to illustrate Pittenger et al.'s methods and findings and my elaboration of them.

Pittenger et al.'s analysis of the language and paralanguage in this passage suggests that failure of attunement occurred during the first three exchanges, resulting in a crisis after T4*a*. (lower-case letters refer to sections of responses that are separated by periods). This crisis seems rectified after T4*b*. Their analysis of the rest of the first five minutes, however, and mine of the rest of the interview, suggests that the crisis was averted only temporarily; the interactants are inadequately attuned for most of the interview. My analysis will be used to illustrate the interdependence of the systems of communication and deference. In this instance, the crisis involved both misunderstanding and an exchange of painful feelings.

Pittenger et al. suggest that a misunderstanding occurred at T4*a* because of T's choice of words and intonations in his first three utterances. Almost all the words chosen are "pronominals," blank checks, and the intonations are "opaque," that is, flat. They say that P must have heard these utterances as indicative of detachment, boredom, and uninterest: * "Here we go again! How many times have I heard this kind of thing!" [2] Although unstated, these sentences are implied by the choice of words and intonations, part of the structure of communication which I refer to as implicature.

The authors go on to argue that P has misunderstood at least T's intent, if not his actual behavior. They say that he did not intend to signal detachment but neutrality: * "You can tell me anything without fear of condemnation." The authors argue that during the silence after T4*a*, T must have realized that P had heard him as cold and detached, because in T4*b*, for the first time, he

---

2. As indicated earlier, the asterisk is used in linguistics to signal a statement that did not actually occur, a "counterfactual."

uses "normal" intonations; that is, he signals warmth and interest. (Perhaps he also leans forward slightly in his chair, and for the first time, smiles.)

The understanding of T of P's mental state is apparently confirmed by P4: she resumes talking. To appreciate the significance of P4, we need to refer again to the rhythm of turn taking: P responds to T4 ("You don't?") with an eight-second silence. She does not say, * "No, I don't," or its equivalent, signaling that she is still involved. Her silence suggests, rather, that she has withdrawn. Conversation is like a ping-pong game: P has put her paddle down on the table, seated herself, and folded her arms. * "If you want me to play this game, Buster, you better show me something different from what I have seen so far."

In T4b, T gets the message and is rewarded with P4. In T5a, however, "Nyeah?" he seems to forget what he just learned, since it is delivered without intonation. This time, however, a silence from P of only 1.8 seconds is necessary to remind him: T5b is delivered with normal intonation.

Another confirmation of the authors' interpretation is suggested by their analysis of the paralanguage of P3 and P4. They say that P seems upset in P3 but not upset in P4. Since the issue of emotional upset will be crucial for my argument, I review and elaborate upon their comments.

Embarrassment and Anger: The Feeling Trap of Shame-Rage

Pittenger et al. (30) interpret the paralanguage of P3 as indicative of *embarrassment* on the patient's part:

> This is a momentary withdrawal of P from the situation into embarrassment with overtones of childishness . . . [as signaled by] the slight oversoft, the breathiness, the sloppiness of articulation, and the incipient embarrassed giggle on the first syllable of *talking*.

Pittenger et al. frequently infer embarrassment in P's utterances, as well as irritation, annoyance, or exasperation. As was the case with the therapist, however, these phenomena do not figure prominently in their concerns but are mentioned only in passing.

The same thing is true of the analysis of emotion that occurs in Labov and Fanshel (1977), even though their analysis is much more sophisticated; for example, they note signs of the compound emotion "helpless anger" appear very frequently in the patient's paralanguage. Since no explicit theory of the role of emotions in behavior was available to them, these authors made little use of their findings concerning the emotional states of their subjects.

In my analysis, however, their references to emotional states will play a central role. As indicated in earlier chapters, I draw upon the work of Goffman and Lewis to understand the exchanges of feeling that seem to take place in this interview. I will also call upon a graphic depiction of social and psychological process. Kelley et al. (1983) offer a flow chart of processes which take place both within and between interactants, which they call meshed intrachain sequences (MIS). The MIS diagram (fig. 2) may prove helpful in visualizing the process I describe. This model can be used to depict a theory of social action. The basic human bond involves both communication and deference, exchanges of thoughts and feelings. It will encompass understanding and misunderstanding, on the one hand, and love and hatred, on the other.

Interpretive understanding (*verstehen*) involves a process between and within interactants which was referred to by G. H. Mead (1934) as role taking, as indicated in earlier chapters. He suggested that each party can, under ideal conditions, come very close to sharing the inner experience of the other party. By cycling between *observing* the outer behavior of the other and *imagining* the other's inner experience, a process of successive approximation, people can reach intersubjective understanding. As already suggested, Peirce used the term "abduction" when describing a similar process in scientists. Scientific discovery, he argued, involves not induction (observation) nor deduction (imagination) alone, but a very rapid shuttling between the two. This shuttling process is depicted in the Kelley et al. model.

Like Goffman's analysis, the formulations concerning *verstehen* by Dilthey, Mead, Peirce, and others have been so abstract and dense that it is difficult to find out whether they are useful or not. Because they offer no applications to concrete episodes, their ideas have remained mysterious.

Bruner's (1983) work on the acquisition of language is much more concrete. He does not invoke the concept of *verstehen* but refers rather to "joint attention." His examples of instances in which the mother teaches the baby the meaning of a word suggests the origins of intersubjectivity. The mother places an object (such as a doll) in the baby's line of gaze, shakes it to make sure of the baby's attention, and says, "See the pretty *dolly.*" The mother intends only to teach the name of the doll, but, in doing so, she also teaches the baby shared attention. I will illustrate shared attention with the incident already cited. Before I do so, it is necessary to outline a model of exchanges of feeling.

Goffman's analysis of interaction ritual suggests that embarrassment and anticipation of embarrassment are pervasive in social interaction and, particularly, that they are exchanged *between* the interactants. Lewis's analysis outlines the process of *inner* sequences, how one may be ashamed of being angry and angry about being ashamed, for example. The Kelley et al. model allows us to envision the joint occurrence of emotional processes between and within—how love and hate are both psychological and social processes.

Recent studies of infant-caretaker interaction, particularly that of Stern et al. (1984), provide a picture of the elemental love relationship. Beginning very early in the infant's life, perhaps even on the first day, the infant and caretaker initiate a process which might be described as falling in love. It seems to begin with taking turns at gazing into the other's eyes. This process rapidly leads to mutual eye gaze, mutual smiling, and what Stern calls mutual

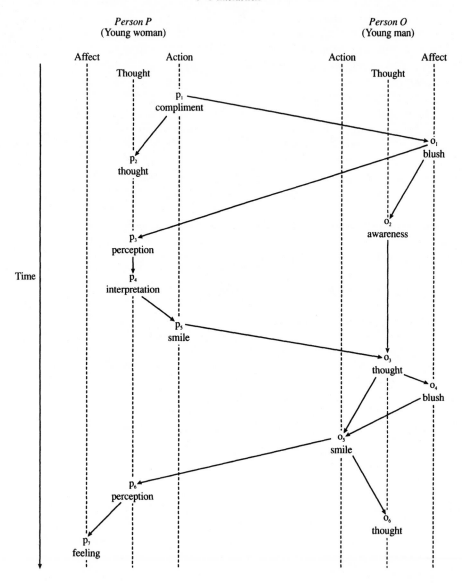

P-O Interaction

Person P
(Young woman)

Person O
(Young man)

Affect   Action   Action   Affect

Thought   Thought

p_1
compliment

o_1
blush

p_2
thought

o_2
awareness

p_3
perception

Time

p_4
interpretation

p_5
smile

o_3
thought

o_4
blush

o_5
smile

p_6
perception

o_6
thought

p_7
feeling

Fig. 2.—Brief portion of interaction between a young woman and man. The events in each person's chain of affect, thought, and action tend to produce further effects within that chain (shown by the *p*-to-*p* and *o*-to-*o* causal connections) and effects in the other person's chain (shown by the *p*-to-*o* and *o*-to-*p* causal connections). (Source: Kelley et al. 1983, fig. 2.2.)

delight. Love can be visualized as occurring between and within the mother and child, involving meshed intrachain sequences. The perception of the mother's smile causes the baby to feel delight, which leads it to smile, which causes the mother to feel delight, which leads to a further smile, and so on, a "virtuous" circle.

The hate relationship can also be delineated by using Lewis's concept of the feeling trap. A combination of anger and shame snowballs between and within the interactants, leading to extraordinarily intense, long-term relationship of hatred. In the kind of hatred that occurs between avowed enemies, the shame component in the exchange of feelings is not acknowledged, but the anger is overt. The vendetta provides a model for this kind of bond, involving insult to honor (shaming), vengeance in order to remove the stain on honor, and mutual hatred and interminable conflict, as suggested in the last chapter. As in the love relationship, there is a snowballing of emotional reactions between and within the antagonists: an action of one party that is perceived as hostile by the other leads that other to feel ashamed and angry, which leads to a hostile action which causes the same cycle in the other party, and so on, a vicious circle. In relationships between intimates, elements of both love and hate often seem to be involved, as suggested by Bowlby's studies of attachment (see chap. 2, above).

> I hate while I love; would you ask how I do it?
> My case proves it true; that's all there is to it.
>   —Catullus

To point out some of the ingredients of this mixture, I return to the exchange which was discussed above.

In this interview there are several instances of attunement between the therapist and the patient. As already indicated, even though they got off to a bad start, between T4*b* and the end of T5*b* one such moment occurred. The therapist, in the silence after T4*a*, seems to have accurately sensed the cause of P's embarrassed withdrawal and corrected for it. In T4*b* he offers the sympathy and respect missing from his initial manner. The patient responds appreciatively, relieved of her embarrassment. Such moments recur in the interview but infrequently. For the most part, the interview is characterized by misunderstandings and feelings like those in the initial crisis at T3–T4*a*. Since there is little direct hostility or anger expressed, the interview is not an open quarrel but involves many impasses.

The causes of impasse can be inferred from Pittenger et al.'s analysis. They do not attempt to characterize the mood of the interview as a whole, but they point to recurring elements in the manner of the two interactants. They repeatedly remark on the therapist's tone: "cold, remote, and detached." They also point repeatedly to the emotionality of the patient. For example, about P6, "I'm a nurse, but my husband won't let me work," they say (50–51; emphasis added): "The narrowed register, overlow, scattered squeeze, and the rasp on 'work,' together with the [lack of] intonation on the last phrase, mark P6 as a real complaint, invested with *real annoyance, misery, and resentment.*" The authors also note frequent instances of embarrassment in the patient's manner (e.g., 70, 101*b*). Finally, they note several instances of what they call "whining," "fishwifely raucousness" (82, 83*b*), or a "fishwifely whine" (158). (These particular comments seem to slur the patient's gender, social class, and emotionality.) In summarizing the therapist's tactics, the authors suggest that one of the therapist's primary goals is to get the patient to reduce her level of emotionality in the session.

The paralanguage which the authors say accompanies the patient's "annoyance," "resentment," "raucousness," and "whining" is very similar to what Labov and Fanshel (1977) take to be the signs of "helpless anger," that is, shame-anger. At the beginning of the interview, the patient is surprised, puzzled, and very soon insulted by the therapist's manner. Although there are moments of reprieve, the patient seems to remain in that state for most of the interview. Since neither the patient nor the therapist acknowledges her emotional state, the interview turns into a polite but nevertheless baffling impasse, a mixture of understanding and misunderstanding, acceptance and rejection, love and hate.

So far the excerpt from the interview has been used to show the entanglement of communication and deference systems, how in this case, misunderstanding and exchanges of embarrassment and anger go hand in hand. The next step is to show how attunement of thought and feeling, or its absence, is related to social structure.

Interpretation and Context

Before I continue with the example, it is necessary to outline what I consider to be innovative aspects of Pittenger et al.'s methodology: (1) the emphasis on paralanguage, (2) the separation of inferences from observations, (3) the prospective-retrospective method of understanding, and (4) the use of counterfactual variants. The decision of the authors to attempt a virtually complete phonemic and phonetic analysis of every word of a text is a marked departure not only from the practice of everyday life but also from the practice of research on human behavior. The intensity of their description of the characteristics of the utterances and of their analysis and interpretation of these characteristics gives their work a microscopic quality. They deal not just with the nuances of communication but with the nuances of nuances.

The intensity of their analysis in itself results in a somewhat unexpected finding: if one forces oneself to pay as much attention to the paralanguage of a message as to the language, the extraordinary richness and complexity of human actions springs to life off the printed page. The sensation of reading the authors' descriptions and interpretations is like looking at a drop of water under a microscope: one is shocked by the seemingly infinite variety of life that suddenly appears below the smooth surface of ordinary experience.

The authors' method of intensive, rather than extensive, investigation may hold a lesson for contemporary social science and psychology. Perhaps we have put too much emphasis on generalization, on extensive knowledge, without adequate understanding of a single instance. Perhaps the single case, sufficiently understood, could generate hypotheses that would be worth testing. As William Blake had said: "To see a world in a grain of sand."

The second of the authors' methods concerns strict separation between their *observations* of utterances and the *inferences* they make on the basis of these observations. This principle is made explicit by the authors: they strongly urge research discipline. The researcher must be continually aware, and wary, that interpretations are inferential only and therefore have a different status from observations, raw facts in the recorded transaction.

At first glance, this method does not seem at all innovative: it merely repeats one of the accepted tenets of science. However, their attempt to honor this tenet turned out to be fruitful because they were unable to carry it out completely. By considering their analysis to be part of the text that I am investigating (along with the recorded transcript), I make deductions about the *authors'* process of understanding, the process that enabled them to arrive at many of their interpretations.

The authors show varying degrees of tentativeness or confidence in their interpretations. The most tentative are those made at the beginning of their analysis. In their first interpretation of the therapist's utterances, T2 and T3, they use the device of reporting the response of only one of the authors, how these two utterances were heard as cold and detached. This is their most cautious mode. Later, with respect to T16, they provide an interpretation that is less tentative, but still restrained, when they state that by this point, all three authors "came to have the feeling" that although there was some variation in T's style, it was basically, "cold, detached, and remote."

This latter statement is typical of their usual style of interpretation. The implication is that they are only reporting an inference which could easily be in error. With conventional scientific caution, these statements invite the reader to make his or her own interpretations for the sake of comparison.

There is another style which the authors occasionally use, however, which seems to be a lapse from scientific prudence. These are the occasions in which they state that some matter is obvious, clear, or, in one instance, "unmistakeable." These matters are almost always inferences about what one of the interactants understands or intends. Although the authors do not acknowledge it, they are implying, with complete confidence, that they have been able to penetrate into the minds of the persons whose speech they have studied.

In order to illustrate these lapses from their stated rule, I present the evidence they cite for their most unguarded imputation:

P2*b* shows unmistakable signs of "rehearsal." In anticipating the interview, P has planned certain things that she is going to say, and now simply reads this one off from memory. (Many therapists put a premium on spontaneity of patient's response during therapy; we must therefore make it clear that in the present context we imply no adverse judgment of P.) The pause with glottal closure after *so,* and then the spacing-out of the three adjectives, the first two with non-final intonations and the third with a distinctly final one, are reminiscent of "dramatic reading," and not characteristic of ordinary informal conversation. The wording—particularly the non-use of *and between the second and third adjectives—also contributes to the impression.

A sort of pedantic itemization, of which P's rehearsed statement is reminiscent, is customary in schools and in certain other situations where a student or junior is addressing a teacher or other senior. This style is perhaps especially emphasized by doctors. We learn later that P is a nurse. Her experience as a nurse may have reinforced earlier school experience to supply the basis for the pedantic itemizing style; one need only think of a nurse delivering a report on a patient, partly from written notes (*The patient was sleepless, uncomfortable, . . .*). P knows, and has known in advance, that this interview is with a doctor, and knows from experience that the "nurse's report" style is one of the appropriate ways to address a doctor.

Is this evidence strong enough to warrant the authors' disregard for their own methodological principle? After listening to P2*b* several times, I found their argument compelling. However, the reader is not required to accept my judgment on faith. Since the record of this interview is available in most university libraries (Gill et al. 1954), the interested reader can make his or her own judgment. For this reason, all the authors' inferences are directly falsifiable, which gives their study a strong evidential status. Perhaps the raw data can serve as a warrant for the *validity* of the findings. Their ready availability stands in stark contrast to quantitative studies. I return to this issue below when I consider an appropriate methodology for testing the theory that is offered here.

If we accept the authors' assertion about this utterance, then we are confronting an important issue. The authors are claiming that not only are they able to share the conscious experience of the person being studied, as they do many times in their analysis, but, in this instance, they are also able to understand what the patient was thinking before she even arrived on the scene. They attribute to her what Mead called "imaginative rehearsal." Moreover, they are so confident of the validity of their imputation that they seem to forget their own rule of rigorously separating inference from observation.

Another example of their unguarded style of inference occurs in their analysis of T4: "In either case, *it is clear that P does not understand T,* and the only obvious factor that may possibly be responsible is his intended opaque intonation" (emphasis added in this and the following passage). In the next sentence they also make an impetuous inference with respect to T's experience: "After a silence of eight seconds (which is quite a long time), this [the authors are referring to P's not understanding T3] *becomes obvious to T,* and he tries again." In an unself-conscious way, the authors infer, with great confidence, the inner experience of the interactants at this moment in the session.

Except for these and a few similar lapses, the book is a model of scientific rigor and probity. How can they be explained? To understand the source of these errors, we need to consider the two further methods that the authors used to interpret the text they studied.

The third of the authors' methods is the prospective-retrospective method of understanding (Schutz 1962). In interpreting the significance of the utterance being considered, the authors do not limit themselves to the immediate context but range far and wide, backward and forward.

For example, in their analysis of P2, quoted above, the inference that it is rehearsed is based on their knowledge that later in the interview P reveals that she is a nurse. The authors use this piece of information, which is prospective, in a retrospective way: she may have been accustomed, as a nurse, to reporting to doctors in the "pedantic" style they hear in P2. Thus the rehearsal inference is based not merely on the authors' knowledge of events in the text but also on their imagining P's experiences even before she began this transaction. In interaction, as well as in research on interaction, to understand the significance of an utterance, one must consider what is happening at the moment, what has happened before, and what might happen in the future.

Although the authors never name this method, it is a vital element in their analysis. They use it in all their more extensive interpretations. I have just described one of their many uses to infer a moment of the patient's inner experience. They also use it, again only implicitly, to explain the basis of their own understanding of the text.

For example, they state that by the therapist's sixteenth utterance, all three "came to have the feeling" that T's manner to this point in the text was usually "cold, detached, and remote." They explain that it was only at this point in the analysis "that we finally realized that all of us had been registering a certain reaction to T's speech." In retrospect, they had understood they had been having reactions to most of his earlier utterances similar to those they were having to T16. Although not mentioned, their knowledge of T's manner after T16 was probably also involved. The interpretation of T's intonation in T16 used, it would seem, the prospective-retrospective method.

They also use this method with their analysis of T16 in a much more wide-ranging way. They state that their "impression of relative coldness is based on a comparison of his interview style with styles of everyday conversation. Perhaps relative to the interview styles of other therapists, T's manner in this interview would be felt as warm" (134). In the first sentence, they seem to be saying that they each actually carried out, in their own minds, a comparison of T's style with what they thought of as the style of intonation of the average everyday conversation. In the second sentence, they suggest that they did not actually carry out a comparison of T's style with the other therapists that they knew, but if they had, his might have turned out warmer.

Although it is only implicit, I believe that the authors used these two inferences throughout their analysis in imputing understandings to the two interactants. That is, they used the first inference to imply that the patient must also have heard T's intonations as cold and detached since her standard of comparison would be not other therapists but ordinary conversations. (We learn toward the end of the interview that P had seen a psychiatrist only once before the present interview.) They use the second inference to imply that T, on the contrary, might have been hearing his intonation relative to other therapists. This point is hinted at in the authors' analysis of T3 and of T16 ("the special sub-culture of the psychiatric interview").

One might consider these two inferences to be couched in the authors' most completely guarded style of inferential statements since they are never actually stated (my single jest in these sober pages). Nevertheless, these inferences overshadow the authors' whole analysis: the two interactants have a misunderstanding about the meaning of T's intonations since they bring to the transaction two different sets of earlier experiences. The method of prospective-retrospective understanding can be seen as a powerful tool for interpretive understanding.

The fourth and final of the authors' methods they refer to as the "working principle of reasonable alternatives." I prefer to call it the method of *counterfactual variants* in order to relate it to earlier developments in philosophy and social theory. Counterfactuality concerns what might have happened in a given instance, but did not. In human experience, the imagining of what might have happened often seems to be at least as important as what actually happened.

Although Mead (1934) did not use this term, his theory provides a disciplined analysis of the origins of counterfactual imagination in the development of the self and its importance in social interaction. The movement from the game stage to the stage of the *generalized other* is the basis for the human ability to escape from outer stimuli. It lays the foundation for the ability to construct imaginary standpoints, which is necessary for reflective intelligence and the construction of a self. Vaihinger's philosophy of "as if" (1924) explores some of the implications of the ability to live in worlds which are subjunctive, contingent, or conditional.

By far the most comprehensive exploration of this issue can be found in the work of George Steiner, in his magnum opus, *After Babel* (1975). Although focused on the problems involved in translation from one language to another, Steiner also establishes that all understanding involves translation, translation from one mind to another. Every understanding involves "translation" from the personal idiom and cultural background of one person to the personal idiom and cultural background of another, from one imagined world to another. His discussion of the all but insuperable impediments to communication between men and women, ethnic groups, and social classes exactly parallels his illustrations of the limitless chances for error in interlingual translation.

Counterfactuality is also of fundamental importance in physical and social sciences, but is virtually undiscussed. Peirce's concept of abduction implies the critical importance of counterfactuals. Peirce seems to be saying that if the scientist is to come up with an original and important hypothesis, he or she must be just as aware of what is not occurring as of what is. One does not observe events passively but within a framework, a framework which includes counterfactual conditions or expectations.

The prevailing mood in modern science is inductive: one makes discoveries by passively observing nature. According to this view, systematic observation gives rise to generalizations about recurring sequences of events. As suggested, Mead and other theorists of counterfactuality indicated that all human understanding, including scientific understanding, depends upon the imagination, as well as on accurate observations. As suggested, Pittenger and his colleagues not only reacted to the actual utterances they could hear on the tape; they seem to have understood what was said by placing it in the context of what could have been said but was not. A brief and somewhat begrudging acknowledgment of the importance of counterfactuality in physical science can be found in Hofstadter (1980, 634–40, 641–44).

Pittenger et al. frequently employ the method of counterfactual variants. As already indicated, in their first analysis of an utterance by T (T2) they note that three of the four words in "What brings you here?" are "substitutes," words with no determinate references. In order to understand the significance of T2 as uttered, they contrast it with five alternatives which were not uttered: "what *troubles, what *problems, what *difficulties," and, instead of "here," T might have said, *"to a psychiatrist" or *"to this clinic." Similarly, in my own comparison of what the authors might have done had they noticed that most of the words in T1 were also substitutes, they might have tried out a sentence like: *"Will you please sit there, Mrs. Johnson, where it will be convenient and comfortable for you?" as a counterfactual alternative to T1. (This is an actual initial sentence used by another therapist, FD2's therapist, in Lewis [1971].)

As they did the prospective-retrospective method, the authors use the method of counterfactual variants in every one of their major interpretations at least once. In the case of T2, they use it twice. The first use, quoted above, was to try alternatives involving words which were not substitutes. The second use of the method on T2 was much more elaborate, trying out five variant stress patterns in the sentence, with the greatest stress on "what" for the first variant, on "brings" for the second, and so on. Since T's actual utterance con-

tained a complex pattern of stresses, with ties between two words and a crucial change in stress from the beginning of the last word to its end, the authors
could have tried out many more than five variants.

At first glance, it might seem that the method of counterfactual variants, as
used by the authors, is laborious beyond any conceivable value it might have.
Since I am going to claim that, if anything, the authors were too timid rather
than too bold, I will draw out some of the implications of their analysis of T2
(and of mine of T1) for an understanding of the emotional exchange between
T and P during the first moments of the session.

With respect to T2, the authors make the case that the words used are
mostly substitutes and that they have an opaque intonation. Later in their
analysis, they imply that P has misunderstood the meaning that T intended for
his intonations, as part of their interpretation of the effect of T's style on P
throughout the first five minutes. This is the only use they make of their
lengthy analysis of T2. They never refer to the significance of T's use of
substitutes.

If we wish to understand the emotional components of the exchanges between T and P, we can make further use of the authors' analysis of T2 joining
it with my comments on the similarity between the words used in T1 and T2;
most of the words in both sentences were substitutes. Supppose we extend the
method of counterfactual variants beyond its uses by the authors. They limit
themselves to imagining words or sentences alternative to those that were used
by the therapist (whom I will call Dr. Noland) and the patient (whom I already
referred to as Mrs. Johnson).

Suppose that instead of Mrs. Frank Johnson, the patient had been Mrs.
Lyndon Johnson. Is it conceivable that T could have greeted her with these
two blank check sentences? ("Will you sit there?" and "What brings you
here?")? We know that the second sentence was intoned opaquely. Even if we
allowed that the intonation of T1 might have been more normal than T2, since
Gill et al. tells us that it was spoken softly, the conclusion still seems ines-
capable, to take on the authors' most impetuous style of inferential statement.
Mrs. Lyndon Johnson would have found these two utterances insufferably
rude and would probably have said so and perhaps even bid Dr. Noland a
heated farewell. The counterfactual of Mrs. Lyndon Johnson suggests that
Mrs. Martha Johnson may also have been insulted by T's manner.

I have drawn upon the authors' analysis of the verbal and nonverbal elements in the early parts of the session to solve the problem of the patient's
withdrawal at P3 and the therapist's response to her withdrawal. Their analysis, and my extension of it, suggests that P heard the therapist's first two utterances as cold and detached to the point of rudeness. She became confused and
"hurt" by this treatment to the point of withdrawing.

Turning now to their analysis of the therapist's experience of P3, and P's
silence after T4a, we see that the authors infer that he must have understood
her hearing of his initial utterances as detached because he changes his manner of intonation in T4b ("Do you sometimes?"). It becomes much more

suggestive of interest and concern, as in ordinary, as opposed to therapy, conversations. Furthermore, they argue, the patient's response in P4 seems to confirm these inferences; she ends her withdrawal, resuming her part in the conversation. Using the authors' analysis and my own, we can arrive at an understanding of a crisis and its resolution.

It should be noted that the second two of the four methods used by the authors differ in character from the first two. The prospective-retrospective and counterfactual methods are intuitive and freewheeling; they draw upon the resources of the entire culture. In order to understand a particular utterance, Pittenger et al. do not limit themselves to the immediate context but range far and wide in their imaginations over what could have happened before, during, or after the utterance.

The first two methods, the exhaustive analysis of the text and the separation of observation and inference, are, by contrast, not intuitive but analytical. These methods are used to control and discipline the flight of the imagination. The continuous shuttling back and forth between imaginative and analytic methods, between intuition and observation, implied in their narrative illustrates what Peirce meant by the method of abduction. If one interprets a text that is publicly available, as Peirce did not, the interpretation may be as verifiable as in any other method in science.

Implicature, Context, and Social Structure

In this section I suggest a model of the process which links individual behavior to social structure, using the Pittenger et al. study as an example. Since their narrative provides a report not only of their methods and findings but also of their inner experiences, it can be used to envision the complex process of social action. The key concepts in the proposed model are the *message stack*, on the one hand, and the *extended context,* on the other.

The authors understood the intentions of the interactants because they did not limit themselves to observing their actual utterances but also imagined their inner experiences. In order to accomplish this feat, the authors referred to the interactants' words and nonverbal gestures, to their feelings, and to the "implicature," the unstated implications of their words and gestures.

An example of implicature is the authors' comments on the therapist's choice of pronominals in T3 and the flatness of intonation: * "Here we go again! How many times have I heard this kind of thing before!" This sentence was never uttered. It is the meaning which the authors imagine the patient attributed to the words and gestures in T3. The authors constructed this counterfactual implication by shuttling back and forth between the words and gestures they observed before, during, and after this moment, imagining what these words and gestures might have implied to the patient. This is the informal process of testing inferences about inner experience by checking their implications against observable outer signs, the process of role taking.

Although the authors are extremely energetic in pursuit of the unstated implications of the words and gestures, they are much less so with respect to the fourth component of the message stack, the feelings. Like Labov and Fanshel (1977), they limit themselves to the inductive method with respect to feelings. They note the occurrence of signs of anger and embarrassment but do not construct complex inferences about them, as they do with the implicature. Because no theories of emotional process were available to them, both sets of authors emphasize the cognitive components of the interaction they observed.

Lewis's work on feeling traps, together with the Kelley et al. model, provides a way of integrating all four components of the message stack. The observables, the words and gestures, provide data for making inferences about the inner experiences of the interactants—the thoughts and feelings.

The method of inferring implicature plays a crucial role since it serves as a bridge between observables and inner feelings. If the interactants *stated* the implications of their actual words and gestures, rather than being silent about them, they could probably understand why such intense emotions are aroused by them. Since the interactants do not state them, however, and seldom investigate them, they ignore or are puzzled by the intense feelings engendered.

My analysis of the components of the message stack in the interview suggests that the therapist and the patient are seldom attuned because they are emeshed in a feeling trap. Mutual resentment, puzzlement, and misunderstanding occur because of chain reactions of shame and anger within and between them. The signs of a shame-rage spiral are clear in the patient, her embarrassment and exasperation. They are less obvious in the therapist, however. To clarify this point, we need to return to Lewis's distinction between bypassed and overt, undifferentiated emotion.

My interpretation of the patient's emotional state is that from T3 onward, she is frequently involved in a spiral of *overt,* undifferentiated shame and anger. She is grossly insulted by the therapist's manner. Although she tries to hide her feelings, they can be inferred from her words and gestures, as Pittenger et al. show.

Bypassed emotion does not cause disruption of behavior and speech, as the overt, undifferentiated type does. Rather it disrupts the fine-tuning of thought necessary for effective action in problematic situations. Since one's inner resources are given over to emotional arousal and to the attempt to hide it, one can not devote full attention to problem solving. At best, while obsessing because of unacknowledged shame and anger, one may go into a holding pattern, repeating stereotyped behavior sequences.

In the present instance, the therapist does not respond constructively to the impasse between him and the patient. As Pittenger et al. indicate, his agenda appears to be to discourage the patient from her repeated emotional complaints about her husband. Like the patient, he simply repeats the same sequence over and over, even though it is ineffective. He does not attempt to negotiate about their respective agendas: * "I notice that you keep complaining about your husband. Could you get away from him a while, and talk more about yourself?" Similarly, the patient does not say, * "I notice that every time I express emotion, you respond by ignoring it and asking me a question about some irrelevant fact. I am puzzled and offended because you seem to be condemning my feelings just like my husband does. What are you doing?" Since their conflicting agendas are never discussed, they butt heads for the entire interview.

It is possible that the therapist is ineffective because the patient's behavior touches off his own shame-anger sequence. He may have experienced the patient's balking and emotionality as insulting to his authority or, more subtly, to his competence as a therapist. In order to test this hypothesis, we would need to investigate this same therapist's behavior in a different setting, one in which he was acting effectively, to highlight the subtle signs of bypassed shame and rage in the present interview (Scheff 1987).

The inference of emeshment of the two interactants leads to the last issue to be discussed. In what way are the exchanges of feeling and innuendo that are discussed here related to social structure? The spontaneous use of prospective-retrospective and counterfactual methods by the interactants, and by Pittenger et al. and by Labov and Fanshel, who use very similar methods in their study, suggests an answer to this question.

These methods suggest that for an understanding of the meaning of even a single utterance, it may be necessary to invoke not just the immediate *context* but also the *extended* context, that is, all that has happened before or after, retrospectively and prospectively, and all that might have happened instead, counterfactually. Each interpretation of meaning presupposes both the history of the whole relationship and the history of the whole society insofar as it is known to the interactants. Effective communication implies a social structure shared between the interactants. Insofar as interaction takes place in an open domain such as natural language, and insofar as the interactants are experts in that domain, then each exchange depends upon, and helps maintain, the social structure.

I have argued that that there is a microworld underlying all social interaction. This microworld connects individuals in shared meanings and feelings and also connects them to the social structure of their society. I have given an example of analysis of the microworld involved in a single brief exchange between a therapist and his patient. In this example, following Pittenger et al., I examined the message stack of words, gestures, implicature, and feelings that occurred at several particular moments during the exchange. By interpreting these stacks, we can understand the thoughts and feelings of the interactants.

According to the theory outlined here, social interaction involves an open domain. In order to understand any given utterance, the interactants must have access to the extended context of the utterance, all events which took place or could have taken place before, during, and after the particular moment. The micromomentary actions of the interactants in relating the moment to the extended context connect them with the social structure. Paradoxically, understanding social structure involves examination of the minute events in the microworld.

The methodology appropriate to testing such a theory requires painstaking analysis of recorded instances of social interaction: the repeated playing of film or audiotape allows the researcher to use the same intuitive interpretation of the message stack that is used by the interactants. I have argued, in another place, that the reporting of this kind of study would require that the texts be appended so that the readers could also use their own intuitive understanding in assessing the validity of the findings (Scheff 1986). A method like this would bridge the present gap between the proponents of objective measurement and those who uphold intuitive methods, perhaps helping to resolve what are usually thought of as irreconcilable differences.

In the next chapter, I apply this approach to another genre—not an audiotape but a dialogue in a novel. I argue that a novel, by supplying the extended context, may compensate for the absence of nonverbal cues. The novel offers a life in context rather than bits and pieces. Perhaps the "lifeworld" can be reconstructed if either the extended context or the dense cloud of nonverbal cues is available. I use Goethe's novel *Werther* for this purpose.

7

Emotion and Suicide: Analysis of an Incident from *Werther*

This chapter describes the way in which emotion can lead to false consciousness by analyzing an incident in a novel. I trace a sequence of events which occur after the hero is humiliated in public, using Lewis's theory of shame dynamics. I argue that such an analysis may lead toward models of causality in social science. My interpretation of class idealization in the mass media, myths, and legends and of class shaming in humor suggests that social differentiation between sacred and profane persons may have an emotional basis.

Art and Science

It is customary to distinguish between art and science in terms of levels of abstraction. Scientific work employs abstract, general concepts which are used to describe classes of events. Art, on the other hand, provides extremely detailed descriptions of a single concrete event or moment. The idea that science is abstract will probably be readily acceptable to most readers; that art is correspondingly concrete may be less so. For this reason, I provide several examples to illustrate it.

Art critics often comment on the singularity of the portraits by great painters, the *Mona Lisa* or any of Rembrandt's self-portraits. The point is not just that the person represented is portrayed in such detail that he or she is unique. The complex facial expression that Rembrandt caught in each of his self-portraits establishes his unique individuality and the uniqueness of a particular moment in his life. Artistic representations of persons portray both unique individuals and unique moments.

The singularity of the moment caught by art has been suggested by many critics:

> In the Fitzwilliam Museum at Cambridge, there is a painting by
> Ruisdael, a view of Amsterdam from the river Amstel. It expresses
> not a single afternoon hundreds of years ago, but a particular, se-
> lected moment in that afternoon. It has been raining—the fields
> glisten with rain in the pallid light—and it will rain again. The

An earlier version of this chapter, published in *Theory, Culture and Society* 5 (1988): 57–80, was written in collaboration with Ursula Mahlendorf.

> tender and sallow sun, streaming through a sky patched with black cloud and cineraria blue, touches a few sails on the river: soon they will be shadowed again. It is an interim between storms. [Johnson 1971, 195]

The point that Johnson is making is that this painting is not a generalization; it represents a *particular moment* between storms. To carry her point a bit further, suppose that in looking carefully at this painting, we noted a single leaf of one of the trees by the river; we see on the tip of that leaf, about to fall, a single drop of rain. This shockingly minute detail would testify that this scene depicts a unique moment.

The power of science is that, unlike art, it is equally at home with a particular item and an abstract class of items. The universal law of gravitation applies as exactly to the apple that fell on Newton's head (as legend would have it) as it does to the class of objects that make up the heavenly bodies in the universe.

In contemporary social science, the connection between abstract generalizations and particular moments is often ignored. There is a vague but powerful sentiment abroad that generalizations are ends in themselves even though they cannot be applied to particular instances. There are no agreed-upon operational definitions for the most important concepts in social science. For this reason, it has not been possible to test any of the major theoretical systems or to formulate, even hypothetically, a program of testing. The divorce between abstract theory and concrete instance is virtually complete.

The approach in this chapter bridges the gap between the concrete and the abstract. It involves the microscopic analysis of a single episode, a detailed interpretation of a brief sequence of events, in order to advance our understanding of what Marx called "false consciousness."

As indicated in chapter 2, Max Weber (1947), among many others, warned against the reification of concepts, the forgetting that social facts, no matter how imposing, are created in the actions of living human beings. Although Weber clearly stated that we must deal with particular instances, in his own work he never got down to this level of concreteness. His studies concern whole historical eras, seldom individual actors, much less particular moments in their lives. In this respect he is like other theorists: they apply abstract concepts such as "Protestant ethic" or "false consciousness" to classes of persons in such a casual way that it is never clear what these concepts mean or how well they fit. Attempting to apply a concept or hypothesis to a concrete instance leads toward more valid, precise, and testable theories by generating detailed models of causation.

What kind of single instance would be ideal for such work? It would be a sequence which was appropriate to the concept or hypothesis that was being applied and which was accurately recorded so that it could be reviewed repeatedly. Verbatim recording allows for the analysis of features of a transaction which an observer or a participant might miss, as indicated in chapter 5.

Although verbatim records are useful, they have limitations. They are in limited supply, even for scheduled events, such as psychiatric interviews. Transcripts relevant to many kinds of social or political transactions simply are not available. Furthermore, there is always the possibility that the recording of the transaction interfered with or changed it in some way. Verbatim records also omit an entire dimension of the transactions they represent, the inner experience of the participants. Even transactions which are focused on inner experience, such as psychoanalytic sessions, probably tap only a small part of inner experience, and this small part is for only one of the interactants, the patient. Novels supply another element missing in mechanical recordings, the extended context, the mass of biographical detail which frames each event.

One way of obtaining texts that involve both inner and outer experiences and biographical detail is to resort to art and artists. At first glance one might think that the autobiographies and letters of the great artists, such as Goethe, Keats, or George Eliot, might provide a resource. Although these materials are of social psychological interest, they are not sufficiently microscopic to provide what is needed here. Where they do represent an actual sequence of events, they seldom record the subjective experience of even one of the participants.

When we turn to the fiction of the great novelists, we find what seems to be needed: extremely detailed renderings of episodes of interaction, which report both outer behavior and inner experience. The novels of Proust, George Eliot, and Goethe are particularly rich in this regard. There are many scenes in *Middlemarch* and *Daniel Deronda* in which George Eliot describes, moment by moment, the "minute particulars" (Blake) of the inner and outer experiences of the characters. One example has already been discussed in chapter 3. Another example is a different scene in *Daniel Deronda*, where Eliot describes what Gwendolen thought and felt in the few seconds before replying to a comment of her husband's: the lengthy sequence of Gwendolen's thoughts and feelings while she is trying to decide whether or not her husband's comment was insulting. Eliot had a genius, like the other writers mentioned, that enabled her to observe her own inner experiences and tap them in writing fiction.

Although the descriptions of interaction in great novels include subjective experience, they introduce another difficulty. To what extent are these descriptions actually autobiographical rather than purely fictional?

This is an extraordinarily complex question, the mirroring of nature in art. It has been the subject of many a disquisition in the past and undoubtedly will be in the future. We must be satisfied to make only two points here: First, although autobiography can be extremely rewarding for the researcher, it does not guarantee facticity. The contrary may often be true, that fiction is more unguarded and therefore more revealing of the truth. In the case of Goethe, his autobiography, written in his old age, is largely concerned with intellectual issues of art and philosophy. It reveals very little of Goethe's inner life. What it does reveal seems to be in part, at least, mythologized. In this connection, the title he chose is of interest. He called it *Dichtung und Wahrheit,* which literally means "Poetry and Truth" but might be better translated as "Fiction and Fact." Great artists like Goethe and Proust had a penchant for secreting fact in their fiction, and fiction in their lives.

My second point: As is the case with most important questions concerning human experience, there seems to be no direct way of assessing the facticity of a novel like *Werther* at the present time. The most that can be said is that the descriptions contained in it suggest a new way of modeling causal process between and within persons. A novel suggests how an artist constructs social scenes which ring true to readers and therefore depicts basic elements in the construction of the lifeworld. The validity of the novelistic descriptions can be decided only by the usefulness of the models that result from them.

With reference to the novel *Werther* (1774) we can infer from Goethe's remarks and from his life that it is at least in part autobiographical. In one of his most general statements on this issue, he said that all his works were "fragments of a great confession." We also know that Goethe, in his youth, like his hero, was a young middle-class man of culture, sensitivity, and talent, looking for a niche for himself in a society which was dominated by a hereditary aristocracy. In a later, clearly autobiographical novel, *The Apprenticeship of Wilhelm Meister,* there are many scenes which portray the frustration and humiliations a middle-class man encounters in dealing with the aristocrats who control the society (Eissler 1963, 512).

Unlike his hero, Werther, however, Goethe found a niche in his society. He not only was recognized as an artist, scientist, and scholar but also held the highest administrative posts in government. (He ultimately became the first minister of the independent state of Weimar.) Unlike Werther, Goethe was a genius, with the brilliance, energy, and resourcefulness that enabled him to overcome the class discrimination he faced.

Perhaps *Werther* was a thought experiment by Goethe: "What would have happened to me if I had been an ordinary young middle-class man of talent, and not a genius? Perhaps I would have been overwhelmed by the injustice of the way in which I was treated." We assume that *Werther* is partially autobiographical in order to use it to delineate a model of the relation between thought, feeling, and behavior.

False Consciousness and Emotion

Marx used the concept of false consciousness in an attempt to understand a puzzling phenomenon, the acquiescence of subordinate classes to systems of stratification which are patently unjust and, in the usual case, also extremely ineffectual. Marx included in his purview not only class but also systems based on slavery, serfdom, and caste. In my discussion, I will further expand the field to include racial and gender stratification. Why does the disadvantaged class, race, or sex tolerate a system which is unfair and ineffectual?

One answer that Marx provided was that the ruling elite used physical force to coerce the lower classes into acquiescence. But he recognized that this explanation was not sufficient. Although force or the threat of force may be a partial explanation, it does not seem complete. The survival of the caste system in India is a notorious example. The subordination of women in modern societies is another, more subtle but perhaps even more compelling. Although the threat of force may be an element in women's acceptance of discrimination, it seems unlikely that it is the only or even the major cause.

To explain the elements other than force which lead to the submission of disadvantaged classes, Marx used the idea of false consciousness. That is, he used a term that *describes*, rather than *explains*, the situation in which a ruled class acquiesces to a social system which is not in its best interests. Marx did not address the question of what social and psychological process might give rise to false consciousness.

The possibility that acceptance of unjust rule had an emotional base was voiced by Nietzsche (1867) in his discussion of what he called "slave morality." With what now seems to us considerable foresight, Nietzsche focused upon resentment and guilt as the basis for the acceptance of oppression. Like those of other theorists, however, Nietzsche's analysis was abstract; he did not describe particular instances.

It remained for twentieth-century literature to offer examples: victims of oppression who suffer from a crushing sense of guilt even when they are in fact quite innocent. This idea is expressed in Koestler's treatment of the Moscow purge trials in the 1930s, *Darkness at Noon* (1951). Its most forceful expression, however, is found in the work of Kafka. Almost all his characters are victims of injustice, yet they are paralyzed by a haunting sense of shame and guilt. Although Marx stated that members of the subordinate classes might experience feelings of alienation and impotence, these statements are extremely abstract. They do not evoke the nightmare reality of Koestler and Kafka.

In this chapter, I describe emotional bases of false consciousness by tracing a sequence of emotions in a passage from *Werther.* My analysis leads to a reconsideration of a powerful idea suggested by Durkheim (1915) concerning the differentiation in a society between the sacred and the profane. Before beginning my analysis of *Werther,* however, I need to review once again recent developments in the analysis of shame.

As indicated in earlier chapters, Lewis's (1971) empirical study of the manifestations of shame and guilt in psychotherapy sessions suggests the outlines of a theory of feeling traps. One part of the theory, particularly relevant to the situation of ruled groups, concerns the origins of shame in social monitoring of self. Both forms of unacknowledged shame, the overt and bypassed, may be generated in the internal theater of viewing one's self through the eyes of others.

Shame may be produced by events in the real world: lack of deference or respect, public errors or mistakes, criticism or insult. However, shame may also be aroused by purely internal events. Perhaps the most common sequence involves seeing one's self from the point of view of another who is critical or scornful. A person feels proud when imagining the self from the point of view of another who is laudatory toward self. But if the person is imagined to be judgmental or rejecting, then one may feel deeply ashamed, even when there is no factual basis for the scorn that is imagined.

Members of subordinate groups or classes may have a particularly difficult time with shame because it is generated both by outer scorn or ridicule and by interior events. Low-status persons must not only face lack of deference in the outer world. In order to get through each day, they must very often take the view of the dominant group and thus view themselves through the eyes of a scornful other, a powerful source of self-generated shame. Faced with both internally and externally generated shame, low-status persons may be particularly susceptible to shame-rage feeling traps. The model of the feeling trap will be applied to a specific incident in order to illustrate some of its features.

Tracing Sequences of Evoked Shame: The Case of *Werther*

Goethe's novel created a sensation in its day, at the end of the eighteenth century. It was one of the first international best-sellers. Its hero, a sensitive and talented young man from the middle class, falls in love with a woman already promised to another. In a sequence of increasingly emotional letters to a friend, Werther portrays his despair; the novel ends with his suicide.

Because Werther's love for Lotte plays a central part in the letters, many critics have responded to the novel as if it were only a love story. Since the young Goethe also suffered many stormy episodes of unrequited love, the same critics often emphasize the similarities between the author and the character. My analysis will suggest that Werther's unrequited love for Lotte is only one of a series of defeats that he experienced.

For example, Werther is defeated in his desire to be an artist. He describes in great detail the beauties of nature that he wishes to paint but never once even attempts to paint a single scene. In this respect, as in many others, he is quite unlike his creator, Goethe. Although both the character and the author were hampered in a society dominated by an aristocracy, Goethe was able to express himself artistically from an early age to the end of his life.

Another great difference between the author and the character is of central concern. As already indicated, both the character and his author were middle-class young men trying to make their ways in a society dominated by an aristocracy. Because of Goethe's extraordinary talents as an artist, scientist, and administrator, he was able to create a place for himself in his society. During his lifetime, he received recognition for his talents and employment at increasingly higher levels in government. At the beginning of his career, however, he must have suffered many embarrassments, to say the least, at the hands of gentry infinitely less able than himself.

I will interpret the novel as Goethe's attempt to envision the situation of the ordinary man of the middle class, someone without Goethe's genius, trying to survive in a rigidly stratified society. The only alternatives for such a man appeared to be groveling before the aristocrats for a status lower than he deserved in terms of his talents or being a social outcast, withdrawing into a cultivation of private sensibility. Three reactions to these possibilities are presented in *Werther*. One of the minor characters becomes insane; another, an uneducated man, commits murder. Although Werther thinks of murder, this way is ruled out because of his conception of himself as a man of sensitivity and culture. Instead he kills himself.

In my interpretation, the scene describing Werther's humiliation at the embassy (in the passages to be quoted below) is the pivotal point in the novel. By this point Werther has already realized that his love for Lotte is hopeless. The Count is Werther's last chance for a meaningful place in his (Werther's) society. The Count's friendship and, by implication, his sponsor- and mentorship are his last hope.

Goethe made the crucial nature of this incident quite explicit in a passage in the first edition (1774). As purported editor of Werther's letters (the novel is in epistolary form), Goethe placed this statement near the end of the book:

> Werther couldn't forget the upset which he experienced at the Embassy. He rarely mentioned it, but even if he merely hinted at it, one could sense that he felt his *honor* had been irrevocably impugned. This event had given him a disinclination toward all business and political activity. Because of this incident, he gave himself over totally to the strange way of thinking and feeling which we know from his letters. He gave himself over to a limitless passion that eventually drained away all of his strength. [Emphasis added]

The crucial word in this passage is "honor." In case the reader might have missed the point, Goethe also placed a further hint at the very end of the novel. Among Werther's effects in the room where he killed himself, Goethe had his friends find a book lying open on the table, *Emilia Galotti* (Lessing 1772). As most contemporary readers would have known, this play concerned a young middle-class woman who felt that her honor had been impugned by a prince's advances and so had her father kill her. In his prescient way, Goethe suggested the link between gender and class oppression, which I discuss below.

The passage quoted above, which points to the crucial role of the incident at the embassy, was removed by Goethe from the second (1786) and subsequent editions. He replaced it with a passage which diminished the importance of the embassy incident and increased the importance of Werther's unrequited love for Lotte:

> Everything disagreeable that had ever happened to him in his active life, his grievance against the embassy, every failure that hurt him,

now ran rampant through his tortured mind . . . lost . . . in a sad
intercourse with the gracious and beloved creature whose inner re-
pose he disturbed. [76]

Goethe's mentor, Herder, a spokesman for what was to become the right
wing of the romantic movement, objected both to the original passage and to
the embassy scene to which it referred. Like much of the public for this novel,
he preferred to think of it as a love story and objected, therefore, to the political content. In his sly artist's way, Goethe yielded, in part, to his critics. He
changed the offending editor's commentary on the embassy incident but left in
the incident itself and the disguised commentary that is suggested by *Emilia
Galotti*. Like Galileo, and all great scientists and artists before and after him,
he reaffirmed allegiance to the truth of his vision even in the act of seeming to
abandon it.

The incident in the embassy did not go unnoticed by another of Werther's
readers, Napoleon, who claimed to have read the novel seven times. According to Lukács (1953) Napoleon carried it into battle with him (in the Egyptian
campaign). When he and Goethe met at Erfurt in 1808, both were at the
height of their considerable powers. (The issues of precedence even in arrang-
ing this meeting stagger the imagination. Perhaps each of the two august per-
sonages simply granted the other an audience.)

Napoleon's complaint was similar to Herder's: Why sully a beautiful love
story with the ugly incident at the embassy? Like Archimides with Alexander,
Goethe seemed little awed by the grandeur of the imperial fan. In rebuttal, in
fact, he lodged a countercomplaint against Napoleon as reader: "He ironized
Napoleon's critique, saying that he [Napoleon] had studied Werther like a
criminal judge studies his legal document" (Lukács 1953, 46).

Herder and Napoleon were two of the most powerful voices of reaction in
Europe, reaction against the forces unleashed by the French Revolution. Why
should they both object to a few pages of a popular novel? A proper answer to
this question is beyond the scope of this chapter but will be addressed in an
article concerning the history of the critiques of *Werther* (Mahlendorf and
Scheff, n.d.). I believe that shame dynamics provide a hidden link between
Werther's infatuation with Lotte and his idealization of the Count, between
private life and public issues (Mills, 1959), as will be discussed below.

The Incident at the Embassy

The text concerning this incident will be presented in two parts: first the
description of the incident itself, then the aftermath.

March 15, 1772
1 | Count von C—— likes me, singles me out, you know that—I've
2   told you so a hundred times. | Well, I was at his house for dinner
         yesterday, the very day on which the aristocratic ladies and gentle-
3   men gather at his place in the evening. | I hadn't remembered this,

and it never occurred to me that we of the lower ranks don't be-
4   long there. | Well, I dine at the Count's, and after dinner we are
walking up and down in the great hall, I'm talking to him, and
to Colonel B—— who joins us, and so the hour of the soirée ap-
5   proaches. | Heaven knows, I suspect nothing, when in comes
supergracious Lady von S—— with Her Consort and Her well-
hatched little goose of a daughter with the flat chest and the dainty,
laced bodice, *en passant* they turn up their highly aristocratic eyes
6   and nostrils in the usual manner. | I heartily detest the whole breed
and was on the point of taking my leave, only waiting till the Count
had freed himself from the dreadful chatter, when my Fräulein von
7   B—— came in. | As I always feel cheered when I see her, I simply
stayed on, stood behind her chair and noticed only after a while that
she was talking to me with less than her usual frankness, in fact,
8, 9   with some embarrassment. | I was perplexed by this. | Is she, too,
10   like all the others? I thought. | I was nettled and wanted to go but
stayed nevertheless because I wanted to find excuses for her, and
couldn't believe it, and still hoped for a kind word from her and—
11   anything you please. | Meanwhile, the rest of the company ar-
12   rives. | There is Baron F——, dressed entirely in clothes dating
from the coronation of Emperor Francis I, Count Councillor R——
(here called Herr von R—— *in qualitate*) with his deaf wife, etc.,
not to forget the shabbily dressed J——, who repairs the holes in
13   his old-fashioned wardrobe with modern patches. | They come in
droves, and I talked with some people I know, all of whom were
14   very laconic. | I thought—and paid attention only to my Fräulein
15   von B——. | I didn't notice that the women were whispering to
each other at the end of the drawing room, that the whispering was
taken up by the men, that Frau von S—— was talking to the Count
(all this I learned later from Fräulein von B——), until finally the
16   Count came up to me and led me to a window. | "You know our
strange ways," he said, "the company, I notice, is not happy about
17, 18 seeing you here. | I would not, for anything in the world. . . ." |
"Your Excellency, I beg a thousand pardons," I interrupted, "I
ought to have thought of it sooner, and I know you will forgive
19   me my untoward behavior. | I meant to leave some time ago, but an
evil genius kept me here," I added with a smile, and bowed to
20   him. | —The Count pressed both my hands with a depth of feeling
21   which spoke eloquently. | I quietly slipped away from the distin-
guished company, took my seat in a cabriolet and drove to M——
to watch the sun set there from the hilltop, and to read that glorious
canto in Homer in which Ulysses is entertained by the excellent
22   swineherd. | It was a satisfying experience.

The incident on first reading seems simple enough. Werther committed a faux
pas by staying after dinner, to which he was invited, to join a reception, to
which he was not. When the Count, his host and supposed friend, begins to
call his attention to his error, Werther apologizes and leaves quickly. He
departs without causing any kind of scene, nor does he describe any painful

emotion. Indeed, the one emotional response described in the passage is a positive one. In the last sentence he says, "It was a satisfying experience." He seems to be referring to his actions of quietly leaving the reception and reading a passage in Homer while watching the sunset. He is satisfied with the way he managed what might have been an upsetting incident.

Before proceeding, note an element in this last part of the quoted passage which suggests covert emotional response, a response so disguised that it seems to be hidden even from Werther himself. The episode in Homer he refers to concerns Ulysses finding more courteous treatment from a swineherd than from the noble suitors. In the context, reading this particular passage suggests covert revenge upon the Count: he is being compared unfavorably to a swineherd. Hidden in Werther's choice of reading material is an implied sequence of emotional responses: the Count has insulted him, leading to resentment, which leads Werther to take covert revenge. The passage that Werther chose continues with a tale of violent revenge: one by one, Ulysses kills in cold blood the aristocrats who insulted him. It has already been suggested that resentment may be a compound of shame and rage. These emotions can be seen in less disguised form in the passage describing the aftermath of the incident:

[March 15, cont.]

23	In the evening I returned to the inn for dinner, there were only a few people left in the dining room; they had turned back the table
24	cloth and were playing dice in a corner of the table. Then Adelin, that honest fellow, came in, put down his hat, looked at me, came over and said quietly: "You've had an unpleasant experience?"
25, 26	"I?" I said. "The Count asked you to leave the company."
27	"The devil take them!" I said. "I was glad to get out into the
28	fresh air." "Good," he said, "that you take the matter lightly; but
29	I'm annoyed, the story has already made the rounds." It was only
30	then that the matter began to nag at me. Anyone who came to the table and looked at me made me suspect: he's looking at you be-
31, 32	cause of that. That poisoned my blood. And today, wherever I appear, people pity me, I hear that my enemies are triumphant and say: you see where the arrogant end, those who feel superior because of their bit of intellect and think it entitles them to disregard
33	all convention—and all the rest of this rotten gossip. You feel like plunging a knife into your heart; for say what you wish about independence, I'd like to see the man who can bear to have rogues talk about him when they have him at a disadvantage; if their prattle is empty, well, then you can easily disregard them.

The sequence of emotional responses continues in the next letter:

[March 16]

34, 35	Everything conspires against me. Today I met Fräulein von
36	B—— on the avenue. I could not resist talking to her and, as

soon as we were a little distance from her companions, showing her
37   that I was hurt by her recent behavior. | —"Oh Werther," she said
      in a passionate tone, "can you interpret my confusion in this way
38   when you know my heart? | What I suffered for your sake, from
39   the moment I stepped into the drawing room! | I saw it all in ad-
40   vance, a hundred times it was on the tip of my tongue to tell you. |
      I knew that that von S—— and T—— and their husbands would
41   sooner leave than remain in your company. | I knew that the Count
42   must not break with them—and now all this row!" | —"What row,
      dear lady?" I said, concealing my alarm; for everything Adelin had
      told me the day before yesterday rushed through my veins at this
43   moment like boiling water. | —"What grief it has already caused
44   me," the sweet creature said with tears in her eyes. | —I was no
      longer in control of my emotions, was on the point of throwing
45, 46 myself at her feet. | —"Explain yourself," I cried. | —The tears
47, 48 ran down her cheeks. | I was beside myself. | She dried them,
49   without trying to conceal them. | —"You know my aunt," she be-
50   gan; "she was there and saw it—oh, with what eyes! | Werther,
      what I endured last night, and this morning I was given a sermon
      about my association with you, and I had to hear you disparaged
51   and degraded, and I could and dared only half defend you." |
52   Every word she uttered pierced my heart like a sword. | She did
      not feel what an act of mercy it would have been to keep all this
      from me, and she even added what further gossip would be spread
53   and the sort of people who would feel triumphant about it. | How
      they would now gloat and delight in the punishment of my ar-
      rogance and my contempt for others, for which I have long been
54   reproached. | To hear all this from her, Wilhelm, in a tone of
      genuine compassion—I was devastated, and I am still in an inner
55   rage. | I wish someone would dare to reproach me, so that I could
      run my sword through his body; at the sight of blood I would feel
56   better. | Oh, I've seized a knife a hundred times, to ease this op-
57   pressed heart of mine. | I have heard of a noble race of horses
      which, when they are terribly overheated and excited, instinctively
58   bite into a vein to breathe more freely. | So it is often with me, I'd
      like to open a vein to gain eternal freedom.

The die is cast; in the next letter (March 24) Werther reports that he has asked
for his release from the court. He is adrift. He seeks no further employment.
On December 20 of the same year he kills himself. In order to suggest a relationship between the incident at the embassy and Werther's suicide, we must
consider first the passage just quoted, then the two passages together in some
detail.

To understand the significance of Werther's responses to this incident,
we should realize that it represents a flagrant act of discrimination against
Werther, solely on the basis of his social class. For reasons that will be sug-

gested below, it is possible that the modern reader may not fully appreciate this point. Suppose that this scene had taken place in the American South, and that Werther had to leave the reception not because of his class but because of his race. We would have no difficulty in appreciating that the treatment he received was insulting and unfair. Perhaps we still idealize aristocracy to some extent. Aristocrats may retain their glamour or sacredness in modern societies even though racial and religious elites have lost theirs. The issue of idealization of ruling classes, and the related issue of the shaming of the ruled class, will be discussed below. With respect to the incident to be analyzed, it is possible that like Werther, we too are somewhat mystified by it.

Werther ends the passage describing the incident on a very positive note. He seems not to be upset by the evening. Yet in the passage that follows, two events occur which cast the evening in an entirely different light. First, Adelin, an acquaintance, then Fräulein von B——, whom he considers his friend, inform him of their knowledge of the event and, what is worse from Werther's point of view, that "everybody" knows about it. His mood changes from satisfaction to torment and, finally, at the end of passage, to thoughts first of murder, then of suicide. How can we understand this sequence?

My interpretation of this chain of events is that Werther was humiliated when he was informed of his trespass by the Count, but that the shame involved was never acknowledged, not by the Count, not by Adelin or Fräulein von B——, and certainly not by Werther. Like the others, he was "gracious," which is to say that he cooperated with them in disguising the emotional meaning of the episode. In my interpretation, it was not the episode itself that caused Werther's limitless torment, but his *denial* of his emotional response to it. He and the three others cooperate in disguising the emotional content of the incident as if it had no more significance than the Count's employing Werther on an errand. His cooperation with the disguise is a form of what today would be called "identification with the oppressor." Werther's false consciousness grew out of the process which disguised his shame, a process in which he and the others cooperated.

The first false note is struck by the Count. He does not tell Werther than he (Werther) has broken the rules and must be punished. Nor does he protect Werther from humiliation by a stratagem (e.g., by legitimizing his presence by some pretense). The Count disguises his aggression against Werther by blaming it on his guests and informing Werther of the delict slowly enough that Werther is able to sentence himself to leaving and to apologize for his trespass. The Count's aggression is further disguised by the gesture of pressing Werther's hands as he is leaving, meant to assure Werther that the Count is acting against his will. The reality is that the Count is caught between his allegiance to the other aristocrats and his friendship with Werther. In this crisis, he chooses to side with the aristocrats, not with Werther.

Werther's cooperation with the Count in denying the emotional meaning of the incident is complete at the time that it occurs, and except for the carefully disguised significance of the passage from Homer, it is still complete afterward, when Werther is alone. Werther judges his behavior from the perspective of the aristocrats. He has heedlessly broken the rules. He does not permit the Count to request that he leave: Werther relieves him of the embarrassment of expressing the aggression of the aristocratic class; he takes the task on himself. He accedes to the judgment that has been passed on him, apologizes for his trespass, and leaves without creating a scene. After leaving the reception, he does not acknowledge to himself that he has been insulted, except surreptitiously in his choice of reading matter.

The particular way in which Werther fails to acknowledge his own emotions involves wholesale denial on his part. If left to himself, Werther may never have acknowledged any further emotional response to the incident. However, in the novel, Werther is not left to himself. Goethe traces out the sequence of emotional responses in fine-grained detail as they occur in stages in two subsequent encounters. The first takes place later the same day with Adelin, an acquaintance. When Adelin refers to the incident, Werther doesn't know what he is talking about: "You've had an unpleasant experience?" "I?" This bit of dialogue is an emotional gracenote in Goethe's description of the incident. Werther's denial of the emotional meaning of the event is so complete that he seems to have forgotten that it occurred. The incident has been *repressed*. Adelin persists: "The Count asked you to leave the company." "The devil take them! I was glad to get out into the fresh air."

When forced to recall the incident, Werther's first response is momentary anger (resentment) expressed by a curse; his second response is to deny that anything untoward occurred: he says he was in fact glad to leave. This sequence, understated anger, then denial of negative emotion, is reminiscent of his earlier response after leaving the reception: first resentment (as expressed by his reading the swineherd passage), then denial (the experience was "satisfying").

In showing his friendship to Werther ("Good that you take the matter lightly"), Adelin unintentionally forces Werther to confront an aspect of the reality of the incident, "the story has already made the rounds." Werther's torment, his confrontation with his emotions, has begun. Only now has the matter begun to nag at him, that is, come into consciousness. He now enters the prototypic shame context, viewing himself, in his imagination, through the eyes of scornful others: "Anyone who . . . looked at me made me suspect: he's looking at you because of that" (sentence 31). Next a very strong statement of painful emotion: "That poisoned my blood."

The shame context is still with him on the next day: "And today, wherever I appear, people pity me, I hear that my enemies are triumphant and say, . . ." (33). His friends are telling him in detail what everyone is saying about him. (Perhaps they are not the best of friends.) In any case, he has reached the point of obsessively imagining what everyone is saying about him, which further agitates him.

In the next sentence (34), the first indication of anger turned against himself occurs: "You feel like plunging a knife into your heart . . . ," and in the same passage, further acknowledgment from Werther that he acquiesces in the scornful judgment of his actions and his deserts: "I'd like to see the man who can bear to have rogues talk about him when they have him at a disadvantage."

The next letter, of March 16, shows the third stage of Werther's responses to the incident, his conversation with Fräulein von B—— on the following day. He thinks himself secure in her friendship, so that he complains about her part in the incident (37). Her story (38–43) confirms Adelin's and further agitates him. At first he hides his alarm, even though his feelings are so strong they are like "boiling water rushing through his veins" (43). Her own strong emotional response distresses him to the point that he can no longer conceal his feelings: "No longer in control . . . I was beside myself" (45, 49).

The passage ends with two final developments. Lines 53–56 show the further intensification of Werther's consciousness of himself as seen through the eyes of the scornful others, envisioning not only the relentless spread of gossip about the incident among his detractors but also their reaction to it, feelings of triumph, gloating, and delight. According to Lewis's theory, this kind of self-consciousness can be taken as a marker of intense but unacknowledged shame.

Werther's expression of agonizing emotional pain and loss of control over his emotions at this point suggest that the shame is of the overt, undifferentiated type. He refers to the pain only metaphorically, piercing his heart like a sword, being devastated, rather than use words which concretely express shame (embarrassment, humiliation, mortification, etc.). The rage phase of the shame-rage feeling trap is acknowledged, however, at least verbally, in line 56, "I am in an inner rage."

The second development in this final passage is imagery expressive of the intense emotion he is feeling—*humiliated fury.* In line 55 he considers the possibility of revenge through murder, running his sword through anyone who dares reproach him openly. But in the last two lines the imagery of violence is turned on himself. He says that he had already considered killing himself a hundred times, equating death with freedom.

It is important to note that in this last passage, in which he considers violent measures of redress, he shows no recognition of the actual source of his humiliation, the Count and the aristocratic class the Count belongs to and represents. The closest Werther comes to this recognition is the thought that he might kill one of his detractors: not the Count, who was so courteous and kind, but any anonymous aristocrat who might make the blunder of an open reproach. Since he views himself only from the point of view of his oppressors, he must seek a pretext for violence which falls within their system of etiquette. It is ironic that his position forces him to want to punish anyone who acknowledges the reality that he is denying. Most of the imagery of violence he turns against himself in suicidal thoughts and gestures. At the brink of suicidal despair, Werther is in a state of false consciousness.

Werther's consciousness is false in the sense that he has no understanding of the personal, social, political, and economic forces which are oppressing him. From my analysis of his emotional reactions to this incident, it would seem that his understanding was obscured by overwhelming emotions of shame and rage. His *rage*, though acknowledged inwardly, is not expressed. His *shame* is neither acknowledged nor expressed. He is caught in a feeling trap of rage bound by shame. When both components of the shame-rage spiral are at least partially experienced in consciousness, the affect feels like resentment, guilt, or jealousy, depending on whether the rage is directed at others, self, or a rival. Werther's shame is so intense that he cannot identify to himself the real cause of his rage. With the shame completely denied and no target for his rage, he cannot define what he is feeling. Since both emotions are undischarged, they haunt him to the point that he feels that he can be free only through death.

Note how large a part of the passage is concerned with just two issues: Werther's denial of his emotions until forced to confront them, and his obsessive imagery of himself as seen through the eyes of scornful others, a context for intense shame. There are five sentences indicative of denial, beginning with the one concerning the passage from Homer, and eight concerning Werther's imagining himself as seen through the eyes of his detractors. These thirteen sentences make up a large part of the total passage, suggesting that shame, first denied, then almost continuously felt, is a major aspect of this incident.

If Werther had had pride in himself and his class, the incident might have taken a different direction. The humiliated fury which he ultimately turned on himself might have been directed toward those who rejected him instead. Fury directed outward is more likely to lead to at least some understanding of class oppression than if it is directed back at oneself. Instead of volunteering to leave the reception, as he did, Werther might have forced the issue by making a scene. Scorn for the Count and his friends might have cost him his connection with the court, but it might have been less likely to cost him his life. Werther seems to be the first of the modern characters in fiction, like those in Koestler and Kafka, who respond to oppression by being ashamed of themselves.

It is hazardous to generalize from a single incident, but the interpretation I have made tempts further speculation. If my analysis is correct, class domination has a basis in the emotions of the subordinate classes as well as in the control of force by the elite class. Passive acceptance of injustice may rest on two complementary movements in the dominated class: shame over its members' characteristics and *idealization* of the characteristics of the elite class. In England it is said that "everybody loves a lord." That is, an aura of ability and glamour is attributed to the aristocratic class, however ineffectual and banal they may be in reality. Similarly, blacks often overvalue white intelligence and ability, just as women may overestimate the intelligence and ability of men. In Durkheim's (1915) terminology, the social differentiation of the sacred from the profane could arise from the dynamics of shame and idealization.

If the members of the dominated class are ashamed of their own putative characteristics, and this shame is not acknowledged and dispelled, it might result in a permanent undervaluation of self and an overvaluation of the ruling class. In Italy in the 1960s, when labor organizers sought to alert workers to the effects of educational "streaming" on their children, the workers often rejected the organizer's analysis, saying, in effect, that the reason a child was being streamed into a manual career was not discrimination but that "my boy is stupid, just like me." Similarly, when a woman refuses to be treated by a woman doctor, it may be that her decision is caused by unacknowledged feelings of shame about her gender. My analysis suggests that the need for class pride, as in the movement for "black pride" in the sixties, rests on massive but unacknowledged class shame.

These comments on the role of shame in false consciousness suggest that glamour plays a powerful but disguised role in the structure of class domination. The idealization of the ruling elite as glamorous cuts two ways at once: it legitimates their political power and, in a subterranean way, reaffirms the shame of the underclass since its members see themselves as inferior because lacking in glamour.

The rituals and trappings of rulership provide an illustration of the role of glamour in maintaining class domination. In a society run by a hereditary aristocracy, the pomp of coronations and changing the guard, the crowns and crown jewels, the scepters, maces, and ermines dramatically differentiate the rulers from the ruled, as if they were members of a different species. In a republic the manifestations of the glamour of power and possession are equally pervasive but less obvious. In the absence of traditional symbols of sacredness, the mass media seem to create sacred myths on the basis of personal style. Ronald Reagan's personality and his wife's clothing received an inordinate amount of attention from the mass media, attention which might have been better directed toward his covert political and military policies. The public demand for idealization is not only a matter of mass-media chicanery; both the media and the mass public seem to want idealization of the status quo.

The idealization-shaming process appears to flourish well below the threshold of consciousness in the everyday activities of members of the dominated class. In a monarchy, any penchant that members of the ruled class have for fairy tales in which the kings and queens, princes and princesses, are heroes and heroines rather than villains or bumbling incompetents, indirectly contributes to the idealization of the ruling class and therefore to maintenance of the status quo. In a republic a similar role would be played by the legends which grow up around presidents, generals, and other leaders. For example,

John Kennedy has a large constituency who remember him as a romantic figure, a man with good looks, courage, and a beautiful wife rather than for his philandering in political and private life.

Class humor probably plays an important role in the shaming of the ruled class. Most humor based on class characteristics shames an underclass: for example, the French minority and the "Newfies" (Newfoundlanders) in Canada, the blacks and Poles in the United States. Most of the jokes concerning these four classes ridicule their alleged stupidity. Jokes about Jews and women usually also are shaming, but the characteristics that are ridiculed go beyond the single issue of intelligence. For example, jokes about Jews may ridicule their alleged avarice or the undesirability of their physical features. Male jokes about women often concern alleged female stupidity but may also ridicule other class characteristics, such as sexual features (like the vagina), which differentiate women from men. These jokes do not idealize the ruled class so that it is perceived to be sacred or magical; they perform the opposite function: the ruled class is profaned by shaming or ridicule.

This is not to say that all class humor is shaming. Ridicule of the characteristics of one's own class may serve the opposite function of dispelling shame through cathartic laughter. Good-natured laughter at one's own foibles occurs when shame, and shame alone, is aroused at an aesthetic distance (Scheff and Bushnell 1984; Retzinger 1985, 1987). Humor which shames a class other than one's own usually is based on shame and anger directed away from one's self. As already indicated, resentment may be a shame-rage compound. Shaming class humor expresses resentment without discharging it.

I end this section by discussing two further implications of the analysis. The idea that idealization rests on an invisible base of shame is a way of uniting two seemingly disparate elements in the story of Werther, his hopeless love for Lotte, on the one hand, and the way he identifies with his oppressors, the Count and the aristocratic class he represents, on the other. (As will be suggested in chapter 10, the deterioration of his last two important social relationships also connects suicide with threatened social bonds.) Infatuation and hero worship may both be manifestations of unacknowledged shame, idealization in one's personal life and in one's political life. This idea unites what is usually assiduously kept apart, personal troubles and public issues, to use C. Wright Mills's (1963) haunting phrase.

My discussion of the idealization-shaming process suggests a new approach to the problem of class domination in terms of its social and emotional roots. We argue that the social differentiation of classes into the sacred ruling class and the profane ruled classes rests not only upon the legitimate control of force but also upon the collective dynamics of shame. Indeed, the concept of legitimacy itself may be seen to have roots in collective emotions.

In antiquity the differentiation of classes into the sacred and the profane was highly visible in the principle of the divine right of kings. Sacredness was present in the single person of the ruler and was diffused from this source downward through the ranks of the hierarchy. This arrangement was completely explicit—the subject of law, theology, legend, and myth. Its apogee was heralded by Shakespeare's Richard II: "Not all the water in the rough rude sea can wash the balm from an anointed king!" Its hold on the imagination could be seen in the paradox that it was reaffirmed even by the death of kings: "The king is dead; long live the king!"

Hitherto it has been thought that the decline of the sacralization of the ruling class began with the civil war in England and was speeded precipitously on its way by the French Revolution. My analysis suggests, however, that this was not the case. The sacredness of the ruling class is hydraheaded, easily surviving the demise of specific social institutions because of the invisible, protean base on which it rests, the idealization-shaming process that has been described here.

Conclusion

My analysis of an incident from *Werther* has suggested that his false consciousness had an emotional basis: in Goethe's description, suicidal despair seems to arise from an endless spiral of unacknowledged shame and rage. My analysis was intended not to demonstrate this proposition but only to outline its contours. Perhaps application of this line of inquiry to further incidents would lead to more precise statements that could be systematically tested. In the meanwhile, my discussion points to the possibility that class domination rests in part on the emotional process I refer to as idealization-shaming. My discussion of how this process might function in the symbolic treatment of the ruling class in the mass media and in secular myth, and in regard to the dominated group in class humor, might also give rise to testable propositions.

The next chapter examines the gap in modern society between expert and commonsense knowledge. I show how abduction and part/whole thinking can be used to unify the two seemingly antagonistic stances.

Addendum to second printing: For further analysis of *Werther*, with emphasis on the revenge motive in both the character Werther and the author (Goethe) in writing the novel, see Scheff and Retzinger (1991, chapter 6).

Part 4

Applications

8
Expert and Commonsense Knowledge: A Proposal for Integration

. . . there is One Man,—present to all particular men only partially, or through one faculty; and that you must take the whole society to find the whole man. Man is not a farmer, or a professor, or an engineer, but he is all. Man is priest, and scholar, and statesman, and producer, and soldier. In the divided or social state, these functions are parcelled out to individuals, each of whom aims to do his stint of the joint work, whilst each other performs his. The fable implies, that the individual, to possess himself, must sometimes return from his own labor to embrace all the other laborers. But unfortunately, this original unit, this fountain of power, has been so distributed to multitudes, has been so minutely subdivided and peddled out, that it is spilled into drops, and cannot be gathered. The state of society is one in which the members have suffered amputation from the trunk, and strut about so many walking monsters,—a good finger, a neck, a stomach, an elbow, but never a man.

Man is thus metamorphosed into a thing, into many things. The planter, who is Man sent out into the field to gather food, is seldom cheered by any idea of the true dignity of his ministry. He sees his bushel and his cart, and nothing beyond, and sinks into the farmer, instead of Man on the farm. The tradesman scarcely ever gives an ideal worth to his work, but is ridden by the routine of his craft, and the soul is subject to dollars. The priest becomes a form; the attorney, a statutebook; the mechanic, a machine; the sailor, a rope of a ship.

In this distribution of functions, the scholar is the delegated intellect. In the right state, he is, *Man Thinking.* In the degenerate state, when the victim of society, he tends to become a *mere thinker,* or, still worse, the parrot of other men's thinking.

In this view of him, as Man Thinking, the theory of his office is contained. Him nature solicits with all her placid, all her monitory pictures; him the past instructs; him the future invites. Is not, indeed, every man a student, and do not all things exist for the student's behoof? And, finally, is not the true scholar the only true master?

—Emerson, "The American Scholar"
[Emphasis added, but I have left the male language uncorrected]

In this chapter I first characterize systems of commonsense knowledge, distinguishing their qualities from those of expert knowledge.[1] Suggesting that the advance of specialization seems to encourage the worst features of both

---

1. I am indebted to Norbert Wiley's discussion of reflexiveness in his "History of the Self" and "A Note on Goedel's Proof," both unpublished as of this writing.

worlds, I propose a mode of thought and of social organization to slow this trend. The mode of thought is abduction, which allows one to review rapidly and continuously the relationship between parts and wholes. The change in social organization involves the establishment of a new kind of expert, the specialist-generalist, who is both a jack-of-all-trades and a master of one (or more). The intent of my proposal is to reduce separation between theory and method, basic and applied research, art and science.

I start with Geertz's (1983) analysis of common sense. Since his essay points toward two crucial differences between commonsense and expert systems, I refer to it extensively. The main impediment to describing systems of common sense, he notes, is their virtual invisibility. The problem is becoming aware that they exist and that they may be described and commented upon: "There is something . . . of the purloined-letter effect in common sense, it lies so artlessly before our eyes it is almost impossible to see" (92). Like any classic essay, Geertz's enlarges our vision. "Of course!" we say, "Why didn't I think of that?"

His essay begins with one of Wittgenstein's comments about the difference between invented and natural languages:

> [Chemistry, calculus, and similar invented languages] are suburbs
> of our language. And how many houses or streets does it take be-
> fore a town begins to be a town? Our language can be seen as an
> old city: a maze of little streets and squares, of old and new houses,
> and of houses with additions from various periods; and this sur-
> rounded by a multitude of modern sections with straight regular
> streets and uniform houses.

The old city and the modern suburbs, an evocative image. Geertz provides another—natural language as "ancient tangle": ". . . the ancient tangle of received practices, accepted beliefs, habitual judgments, and untaught emotions. . . ." Unlike the modern suburb, the old city is not systematized, even though, as much as calculus, it is a functioning system. That is to say that unlike calculus, common sense is unself-conscious: "Religion rests its case on revelation, science on method, ideology on moral passion; but common sense rests its case on the assertion that it is not a case at all, just life in a nutshell. The world is its authority" (75). Common sense, Geertz says, is the system made up of whatever the members of a group take to be *self-evident*, of what is taken for granted, of what goes without saying and, in fact, had better not be said or talked about. To talk about it is to undercut it, to challenge its status as completely self-evident. In a functioning social group, common sense is seen as untouchable and complete. In his words (84):

> As a frame for thought, and a species of it, common sense is as
> totalizing as any other: no religion is more dogmatic, no science
> more ambitious, no philosophy more general. Its tonalities are
> different, and so are the arguments to which it appeals, but like

them—and like art and like ideology—it pretends to reach past
illusion to truth, to, as we say, things as they are.

Geertz's essay enlarges upon and extends Schutz's idea of "the attitude of
everyday life" considerably because he considers not just the commonsense
attitude but also its components, "the ancient tangle" of practices, beliefs,
judgments, and emotions, as together making up a working system.

Geertz attempts to describe the attitudes toward reality common to all cultures. Acknowledging the difficulty, he tries five "quasi-qualities"; in systems
of common sense, reality is seen as *natural, practical, thin, accessible,* and
immethodical. (For reasons that will be discussed below, I have changed
Geertz's order by putting immethodical last.) Of these qualities, Geertz thinks
that *naturalness* is the most fundamental (85):

> Common sense represents matters—that is, certain matters and not
> others—as being what they are in the simple nature of the case. An
> air of "of-courseness," a sense of "it figures" is cast over things—
> again, some selected, underscored things. They are depicted as in-
> herent in the situation, intrinsic aspects of reality, the way things go.

Geertz's descriptions of *practicalness* is droll (87):

> What we most often mean when we say an individual, an action, or
> a project displays a want of common sense is that they are imprac-
> tical. The individual is in for some rude awakenings, the action
> is conducing toward its own defeat, the project won't float. But,
> simply because it seems so more readily apparent, it is also more
> susceptible to misconstruction. For it is not "practicalness" in the
> narrowly pragmatical sense of the useful but in the broader, folk-
> philosophical sense of sagacity that is involved. To tell someone,
> "be sensible," is less to tell him to cling to the utilitarian than to
> tell him, as we say, to wise up: to be prudent, levelheaded, keep his
> eye on the ball, not buy any wooden nickels, stay away from slow
> horses and fast women, let the dead bury the dead.

There is also comedy underlying his description of the third quality, *thinness* (89):

> The third of the quasi-qualities common sense attributes to reality,
> "thinness," is, like modesty in cheese, rather hard to formulate in
> more explicit terms. "Simpleness," or even "literalness," might
> serve as well or better, for what is involved is the tendency for
> commonsense views of this matter or that to represent them as
> being precisely what they seem to be, neither more nor less, . . .
> "everything is what it is and not another thing"—expresses this
> quality perfectly. The world is what the wide-awake, uncomplicated
> person takes it to be. Sobriety, not subtlety, realism, not imagina-
> tion, are the keys to wisdom; the really important facts of life lie
> scattered openly along its surface, not cunningly secreted in its

depths. There is no need, indeed it is a fatal mistake, to deny, as poets, intellectuals, priests, and other professional complicators of the world so often do, the obviousness of the obvious.

It is not unusual to see others' systems of common sense as comical. Geertz's description, however, seems to suggest the humor in one's own. It is important to realize, however, that even though systems of common sense can easily be seen as absurd, they are, at the same time, vastly powerful, since they function as general problem solvers. Although unsystematic and nonreflexive, common sense functions in the intuitive mode, using the vast resources of natural language. For this reason, as pointed out in earlier chapters, common sense is incredibly swift, broad, and flexible in comparison with expert systems. I return to this issue in the discussion below.

The fourth and last of the qualities which seem to me to be similar is *accessibleness* (91):

> the assumption, in fact the insistence, that any person with faculties reasonably intact can grasp commonsense conclusions, and indeed, once they are unequivocally enough stated, will not only grasp but embrace them. . . . Common sense, to put it another way, represents the world as a familiar world, one everyone can, and should, recognize, and within which everyone stands, or should, on his own feet.

These first four qualities overlap considerably, with accessibleness especially similar to thinness (note the similarity of the last sentence above to the passage [89] defining thinness). I return to this issue after discussing the last quality, *immethodicalness,* which seems quite distinct from the first four.

In systems of commonsense knowledge, Geertz says, reality is represented as inconsistent and possessing an "intractable diversity" (90):

> Commonsense wisdom is shamelessly and unapologetically ad hoc. It comes in epigrams, proverbs, *obiter dicta,* jokes, anecdotes, *contes morals*—a clatter of gnomic utterances—not in formal doctrines, axiomized theories, or architectonic dogmas.

The ad hocness that Geertz attributes to commonsense reality returns him to his initial quote from Wittgenstein about the old city as against the systematized suburbs. It also relates to my discussion of ad hocing and total association in chapter 4, as I indicate below. First, however, it is necessary to return to the underlying similarity among the first four qualities.

The first four qualities of commonsense reality that Geertz names, naturalness, practicalness, thinness, and accessibleness, seem insufficiently distinct from one another. The four might be subsumed by a more abstract concept: cultural systems of common sense are *nonreflexive.*

The system of common sense operates outside awareness. An outsider can reflect and comment on it, but an insider cannot; it is not just that the insider *does* not consider its operation, but unless he or she is willing to start at square one, the insider *can*not.

The obviousness of another's system of common sense, and its invisibility to the insider, is illustrated by the story of the Brahmin and the Englishman:

> The world is held up on the back of a water buffalo. The English-
> man asks what holds up the water buffalo. A turtle. The English-
> man: What holds up the turtle? A water buffalo. The Englishman
> persists: But what holds up the water buffalo? The Brahmin replies:
> From there on, it's turtles all the way down.

The insider feels that to consider any single item of common sense would require starting over from scratch, considering everything in the universe. The commitments have come too early, they are too deep, they are too vast. Rather than examine one's own commitments, they are projected onto the outside world: it is not I that is committed; its just the way things are: "Like its naturalness, the practicalness of common sense is a quality it bestows upon things, not one that things bestow on it" (88). This is to say that a cultural system of common sense is a collective mechanism of defense, an intensely defended individual and collective projection of inner commitments onto the outside world.

This explanation of the nonreflexiveness of common sense in terms of collective psychodynamics parallels Freud's (1927) analysis of religion in traditional societies. He had the temerity to argue, in a society that was still sufficiently traditional that he might have been lynched, that religion functioned as a mechanism of defense. In modern societies, religion has lost much of its sacredness, but common sense has not. As Geertz (84) suggests, when insiders consider something real, they "damn well mean it," and no fooling around, as we say.

Common sense imposes an ideological, that is to say, inviolate order upon reality. The outsider's vision is utopian; it shatters what is felt to be the natural order of things, everything that is possible, natural, and decent. It is a tribute to Geertz's good sense and the charm of his prose that he can lead us to reflect upon our own system of common sense without insulting us. We are programmed to be unaware of the operation of our own system and to be indignant when it is brought to our attention. Although human beings, both individually and collectively, have the capacity for instant reflexive awareness about many things, one's own system of common sense is not one of them.

I consider the quality that Geertz calls "immethodicalness" last because it seems to point to an aspect of systems of common sense different from the first four qualities. This last quality points to the elusive quality of human thought which is usually referred to as intuitiveness: the ability to understand a complex issue without any obvious attempt or labor, almost instantaneously.

The intuitive capacity is distinct from, yet closely related to, natural language. Intuition, or mother wit as it is sometimes called, depends upon our mother tongue. I think that this is the import of another of Wittgenstein's quotes (Geertz, 92): "In the actual use of expressions we make detours, we go by side roads. We see the straight highway before us, but of course we cannot use it, because it is permanently closed." Geertz also quotes an African proverb which makes the same point: "Wisdom comes out of an ant heap" (91).

Geertz emphasizes the antagonism between systems of common sense and expert knowledge. Since common sense is seen as accessible to everyone, without need of special training, its tone, he says, is antiexpert, if not anti-intellectual. By the same token, the adherents to an expert system of knowledge usually see common sense as a mere tissue of superstitions, especially if it is the common sense of an out-group. In modern societies, experts usually see laypersons in their own society, that is, nonexperts, as an out-group whose common sense is tantamount to ignorance. The antagonism between the two systems is a crucial issue in modern societies: it reflects and maintains the separation and suspicion between experts and the public.

However, the two systems are not inherently contradictory. The operation of common sense seems unmethodical, ad hoc, antisystematic only in comparison with the rules used in expert systems, which are governed by the Cartesian "*esprit de géométrie.*" That is, procedures are analytic, linear, serial, and explicit. The system of common sense is synthesizing, nonlinear, parallel, and implicit, as indicated in chapter 4. In that chapter I suggested that commonsense reasoning can be described as what Peirce called abduction, the extremely rapid internal dialogue between observation and imagination. Furthermore, the mental operations used in common sense are broader than those used in expert systems since they include not only classification but all types of association, a process of total association which allows problem-solving processes to be extraordinarily rapid, broad, and flexible.

Like Geertz, Pascal (1656, 211) stressed the antagonism between the two systems:

> . . . mathematicians [who in Pascal's day represented all experts] try to treat these intuitive matters mathematically, and make themselves ridiculous, by trying to begin with definitions followed by principles, which is not the way to proceed in this kind of reasoning. It is not that the mind does not do this, but it does so tacitly, naturally, and artlessly.

He goes on to state that minds guided by finesse have the opposite weakness (211–12):

> Intuitive minds . . . being accustomed to judge at a glance, are taken aback when presented with (abstract) propositions . . . (of which the necessary preliminaries are definitions and principles so barren that they are not used to looking at them in such detail), and consequently feel repelled and disgusted.

Pascal's discussion of system and finesse, in the round, however, suggests that the two styles are not incompatible. He does not say, for example, that mathematicians are never intuitive, or that the intuitive are never mathematicians, only that it is *rare* (211). Since he goes on to mention "mathematicians who are merely mathematicians" and "intuitive minds that are merely intuitive" (212), he seems to imply that both the spirit of system and the spirit of finesse can function in one mind. Indeed, his own case provides an example: Pascal himself was both a great mathematician and one of the first experimental physicists, as well as philosopher, theologian, and poet.

Specialization and the Spirit of System

It is customary in modern thought to assume that finesse and system, art and science, are mutually exclusive, indeed to make a virtue of their separation. Since the development of modern science, knowledge has been increasingly dominated by the spirit of system, as reflected by the division of inquiry into ever smaller domains of specialized learning. The emphasis on system leads directly to specialization: in order to define all terms explicitly and uniquely, to avoid the ambiguity of natural language, one must narrow one's field of vision. Instead of trying to understand everything under the sun, one specializes in one small domain, either an empirical domain (such as kinship in East Africa) or a conceptual one specializing in a particular approach (a theory such as Marxism or a method such as the sample survey).

Thomas (1974), a noted scientist and essayist, seems to assume that specialization in science is an unqualified blessing. In an essay in which he compares the social organization of science to that of the nest-building insects (such as termites), he quotes Ziman (1969): "The invention of a mechanism for the publication of fragments of scientific work may well have been the key event in the history of modern science." He argues that through sharing fragmentary information, science can advance, even though individual scientists, like individual insects, do not understand the larger meaning of their own activities.

Specialization was a key event in science, as Ziman claims, in the sense that it broke the impasse represented by the medieval worldview. In the sixteenth and seventeenth centuries, scientists realized that in order to move beyond the received view of nature, they would have to proceed piecemeal with fragments of knowledge because the premises of general understanding were unsound. Tycho Brahe is a representative figure. His patient sightings of the position of Mars meant little to him since he believed, like everyone else, that the sun and the planets moved around the earth. But Kepler took his data and in what seems to have been an agonizing process, wrestled free from the geocentric premise. After years of toil, he realized that the complex mathematical system of epicenters was a product of the wrong premise: the orbit of Mars is a simple ellipse if one postulates that it moves around not the earth but the sun.

Just as modern specialized knowledge deals mostly with parts, premodern knowledge dealt almost entirely with wholes. Traditional societies insisted on a single encompassing worldview, as did philosophy. The unity of knowledge of these views was arbitrary, based entirely on authority and precedent; it excluded innovative knowledge as disruptive. Since the established views were absolute, there was no room for modification and renewal.

In such a context, specialization was a corrective. Liberation from the status quo, the total systems of belief in traditional communities, required the work of an army of specialists. Religion and the Schoolmen taught that fragmentary details must be ignored when they clashed with doctrine. To counter this practice, the new researchers did the opposite. Art and science, William Blake proclaimed, must deal with "minute particulars." Positivism, the reliance on specialized methods and evidence rather than whole systems of belief, breathed new life into knowledge.

It may be fallacious to conclude, however, that if specialization was necessary at the birth of modern science, then unlimited specialization is necessarily beneficial. Thomas goes on to quote Ziman's lyric celebration of specialized science:

> A regular journal carries from one research worker to another the
> various . . . observations which are of common interest. . . . A
> typical scientific paper has never pretended to be more than another
> little piece in a larger jigsaw—not significant in itself but as an
> element in a grander scheme. This technique, of soliciting many
> modest contributions to the store of human knowledge, has been
> the secret of Western science since the seventeenth century, for it
> achieves a corporate, collective power that is far greater than one
> individual can exert.

Lewis comments: "With some alteration of terms, some toning down, the passage could describe the building of a termite nest" (16). The bizarre thing about Lewis's essay is that nowhere does he seem to realize that the similarity between specialized science and the insect world may bode ill for science, since insect social organization is essentially static. Hyperspecialization in science, the Balkanization of knowledge into disciplines, subdisciplines, theoretical and methodological camps, could produce stasis.

The spirit of system leads not only to specialization but also to an emphasis on explicit, linear analysis, step by step. Systematic work involves formalization, making explicit one's procedures. Finesse is still necessary but leads a shadow life, eclipsed by formalisms. Perhaps this drama is what T. S. Eliot had in mind when he spoke of the eternal struggle between art and education.

System has led to many triumphs in the history of science, but its role has been exaggerated. Many events in the history of physics illustrate this point. Most scientists now believe that Kepler's discovery of the orbit of Mars was accomplished through passive induction, the use of systematic methods in empirical observation. But Peirce has pointed out that the crucial step that Kepler took was not systematic: his intuitive realization that the problem was not with his and Brahe's observations but with the premises, the geocentric model. The mathematical astronomers of his day were lost in bizarrely complex models of centers and epicenters, mathematical formalizations which served to distract researchers from the imaginative leap necessary to leave the geocentric model. Discovery depends as much on imagination as on observation.

Einstein's formulation of the theory of relativity is another example of the way in which mathematical formalization not only does not help, but may impede the advance of knowledge. As mentioned earlier, David Hilbert, one of the greatest mathematicians, raised the issue of why Einstein, rather than others (like himself or Poincaré) immeasurably better qualified, made the discovery: "Because he had learned nothing about all the philosophy and mathematics of time and space" (quoted in Feuer 1982, 62).

Hilbert's point is so important that it requires elaboration. Einstein's first statement of the theory of relativity was proposed as a joke; it came out of his direct *intuition* of the natural world. The theory, in its original conception, was not mathematical. In analogy to Kepler's leap from a geocentric universe, Einstein intuitively understood that the problem was not with the new observations but with the premises of classical physics. Hilbert and the other better-qualified mathematicians, however, were busy building complex mathematical formulations designed to save classical physics, a system of centers and epicenters, to pursue the analogy. Inadvertently they had become wedded to the status quo in physics. Einstein's weak mathematical preparation freed him of this commitment. For this reason, he was able to use his direct intuitive understanding to solve the problem.

Boltzmann's solution of the problem of heat and electric transport in metals provides another variant of the use of intuitive understanding. Ultimately he worked out an extremely complex equation which yielded not only answers to the initial questions he raised, predicting the conductivity of metals from their atomic structure, but also solutions to problems of which he was unaware, for example, second-order effects such as piezoelectricity.

As in Einstein's case, however, the solution was not initially based on mathematical formalization but on an imaginative leap. He proposed that the valence electrons in metals could be treated as if they were completely free of the molecules, so that in effect they would make up a gas. Although an extremely implausible idea, an image of chaos, it led to the solution. No one had thought of this idea because valence electrons form the chemical bonds that hold metals together. Intuition lies at the core of scientific discovery.

A similar theme can be found in Feynman's complaints about mindless formalization in contemporary physics. He liked to find errors in the complex formalizations of his colleagues, especially when he was entirely ignorant of the mathematics involved. His secret: "[Rather than following the mathematical steps] I have the specific physical example of what he is trying to analyze in mind and I know from *instinct* and experience the properties of the thing" (Feynman 1985, 224; emphasis added). By instinct he means intuition, the free play of his direct understanding of the physical world. Although not as blunt as Pascal, he derides the results of pure system without finesse.

These comments on physics suggest a general point. Expert systems of knowledge initially have the capacity for reflexiveness, the attitude and procedure necessary for self-reference. In order to invent the new system, the originator(s) had to call upon the resources of both worlds: the intuitive understanding that led to the discovery, and the formalizations necessary to understand its implications and to communicate it to other workers. However, as the workers begin to function as a social group, the new system becomes their particular brand of common sense. As their system is transformed into commonsense knowledge, it gains speed, breadth, and flexibility in comparison with the original explicit statement. But at the same time, it looses its reflexiveness, its ability to comment on itself. It becomes as absolute for its members as any other system of common sense.

The transformation of systematic knowledge into common sense often produces a system which is static since it moves toward the disadvantages of both worlds. As a commonsense system, it loses the capacity for self-reference without completely gaining the fluidity of the "ancient tangle," the common sense associated with natural language. The crisis in physics at the beginning of this century was a product of the clash between new observations, on the one hand, and rigid adherence to Newtonian mechanics, on the other. Physicists had come to believe that elegant differential equations were a direct expression of the laws of nature rather than provisional formulations. These equations solved the problem of the movement of the planets but were contradictory when it came to the propagation of light from the stars and to the actions of electrons within an atom.

The term "jargon" is often used as a mere epithet, but it can be given a specific meaning. As suggested in chapter 4 and above, when expressed in natural language, common sense functions as a general problem solver. Natural language is extraordinarily powerful because it connects its user instantly with the lore, techniques, and feelings of the entire history of a society, with a functioning culture. Each use of a correct sentence is like riding the locomotive of one's society. The invented language of an expert group lacks this resonance. Even after it has become the language of common sense for the group, it is *arriviste;* it is useful only for special problems, not for general problem solving. Jargon lacks organic connection to the reigning culture.

The tendency toward stasis in expert knowledge may have been the basis for Weber's (1946) pessimism about the "iron cage," the suffocating hegemony of *formal* rationality in modern societies. His analysis of traditional and bureaucratic forms of organization concerns the end products of interpretive procedures rather than processes. He argued that bureaucratic thought and procedure were inevitable in advanced civilizations. Traditional societies depended upon substantive rationality: decisions were arrived at ad hoc, without resort to explicit, systematic procedures. The results were understandable, but capricious, since they depended entirely on the judgment of the decision maker(s): the ruler, scholar, or council.

Formal rationality arose as antidote to the whims of kings, Schoolmen, and priests: its goal was universal knowledge. This type of rationality is the outcome of the spirit of system. Since Weber did not consider the underlying process, he thought that the two forms of rationality were mutually exclusive. His scheme was tied to powerful images: "Kadi justice," substantive rationality, depending entirely on the personality of the particular sheik or scholar. The authoritative figure might be enlightened, a philosopher-king like Solomon, but he could also be a benighted tyrant (a contemporary figure like Kadafi, the dictator of Libya, comes to mind). Since Weber thought that one has to choose between the unpredictability of the one and the mediocrity of the other, bureaucratized thought and procedure would inevitably prevail.

In terms of my discussion of systems of knowledge, however, which concerns process rather than structure, formal and substantive rationalities are not contradictory. It is not difficult to visualize the meeting of the two worlds in a single gifted individual, as already suggested by the example of Blaise Pascal, the poet-mathematician. Another example will be discussed shortly, Goethe, whose life also combined system and finesse, science and poetry.

There is a danger, however, in offering individual examples; the reader may discount them as the result of transcendent genius, which is rare. It is important to understand, as already indicated, that the usual structural view of knowledge needs to be supplemented by analysis of the underlying process. It is also important to move beyond individual process and structure to social process and structure. The broader view will suggest that static systems of knowledge are not inevitable. In the remainder of this chapter, I outline proposals that might combine the best features of common sense and expert knowledge.

Goethe as Scientist

As introduction to this section, I review an incident from the history of science, Goethe's discovery of the human intermaxillary bone. I argue that Goethe's method of thought, part/whole thinking, and his social and intellectual position as a generalist enabled him to make discoveries which neither expert nor layperson could have envisaged.

Although Goethe's scientific activities and achievements have been obscured by his fame as a poet, and possibly for other reasons discussed below, he considered himself, and was considered by many of the eminent scientists of the time, as much a scientist as a poet. He also thought that his art and science were closely interrelated, an issue to which I will return.

There is considerable controversy in the evaluation of Goethe's scientific contributions, with opinion polarized, for the most part, between that of people such as Rudolph Steiner (1926), who argued that Goethe was one of the greatest scientists who ever lived, and the more common opinion, especially among contemporary scientists, which discounts his scientific work. More balanced views can be found in Magnus (1949), Vietor (1950), and Amrine, Zucker, and Wheeler (1987).

Most historians of science agree that Goethe made original scientific contributions, both theoretical and empirical, in many fields but especially in botany, optics, osteology, mineralogy, geology, and meteorology. He is usually considered the founder of both the comparative morphology of plants and comparative anatomy in zoology. Many of his observations are still current, for example, his work on afterimages in color vision. His study of plants is of extraordinary interest because of the combination of bold ideas and detailed observations. For brevity, I will limit my discussion to one of his discoveries, in osteology, since it most clearly illustrates my point.

In 1784, at the age of 35, Goethe finished his first scientific paper, an extremely detailed study of the intermaxillary (the section of the upper jaw which carries the incisors) in humans and other vertebrates. His study illustrates the approach that was to characterize his scientific work: viewing a problem in a way that combines the largest outlook with the diligent pursuit of the smallest detail. He started on the track of the intermaxillary in response to what was considered the key finding of the then-current work in osteology, that this bone was found in all vertebrates but with one great exception, human beings.

This "finding" offended one of Goethe's basic beliefs, his sense of the unity of nature. Since this was almost three-quarters of a century before Darwin, Goethe's idea was shockingly heretical. The finding was in accordance with contemporary belief that humans have a special status in nature. Instead of writing a speculative essay, however, Goethe began an extensive empirical investigation.[2] Examining every skull that was available to him, he made extremely precise and detailed drawings. His work showed that although the human intermaxillary was very small, in many cases vestigial, it had exactly the same form as the much larger ones in the walrus and elephant.

At first his report was uniformly rebuffed, much to Goethe's chagrin. The work of the osteologists was influenced by the cultural frame, which supposed a special status for humans separate from the rest of nature. Since the intermaxillary was usually vestigial, they were unable to see it. The generative idea for Goethe's labor was the opposite; since he presumed that the bone must be present, it enabled him to find it and to persist even though in some cases the outlines were barely visible. In some cases, however, the bone was obvious. By 1791, most of the osteologists had accepted Goethe's finding. Many years later, the last holdout, an eminent scientist, capitulated when one of his friends, a surgeon, showed him drawings of a patient whose intermaxillary was so prominent that it required an operation.[3]

This case is instructive for a number of reasons. Once again it shows the need for symbiosis between theory and research. The intermaxillary in hu-

2. For an example of a sweeping, Goethean idea in contemporary physics which was not developed further than the essay, see Bohm (1980), already mentioned in chapter 2.

3. Goethe's discovery is not universally acclaimed. Wells (1967) seems to suggest that it has been overrated since modern osteologists have established that the intermaxillary is usually present only during the fetal stage.

mans was invisible to osteologists because of a hidden premise, the special status of humans, outside nature. Goethe's intense theoretical conviction of the opposite enabled him to find what the others had missed.

In terms of the earlier discussion, this case illustrates the possibility of combining finesse and system, substantive and formal rationality. Goethe was not content with complaining about the special status attributed to humans in an essay or polemic: he conducted an exacting empirical study, just as any scientist would. He did not see himself as limited to the special role of poet or philosopher, nor did he mind impinging on the special role of the osteologists. His freedom and resourcefulness were not just a matter of his style of thought, although that was a help. It also involved his social position.

Goethe never held a social role which officially involved him in the production of expert knowledge. Instead he was detached from it—his profession was that of a government official. Initially he was a private secretary to the ruler of a small German state but progressed to become the first minister, that is, the manager of that state. He held this post for ten long, active years. Since he experienced his professional duties as undemanding, and since his artistic and scientific endeavors were informal, he was free to spend his time according to his own bent and to choose his associates as he saw fit. For most of his life, he was in close contact with various scholars, scientists, and artists. His attempt to be inclusive of all viewpoints will figure in my argument below.

In my earlier discussion, I offered one possible reason for the contemporary neglect of Goethe's scientific work: his eminence as a poet seems to overshadow his role as a scientist. There are two further reasons, however, both of which may have some bearing on current concerns in the quest for knowledge. The first concerns Goethe's particular scientific methodology; the second, what might be called conflict between his role as a poet and his role as a scientist. Detailed discussion of either of these issues would require a chapter in itself. For this reason I will describe them only very briefly.

Goethe developed a scientific methodology which is out of fashion in contemporary science. His philosophy of method was to study nature *in vivo,* and in the round, in a way which was not destructive—not destructive physically, certainly, nor even, one might say in current terms, intellectually and emotionally. He thought of nature, and humans in nature, as a harmonious whole which could best be understood as a whole using methods which did justice to its harmony. For this reason, he opposed extended analysis, including mathematical analysis, and the use of instruments or methods which ignored or disturbed the harmony of nature. His approach to science was "bare-handed," because he thought that in the long run, overemphasis on analysis and instrumentation would lead to results which were invalid or destructive, or both. These ideas are given poetic expression in his masterpiece, *Faust:* there is some fruit from the tree of knowledge which should not be eaten.

Goethe's philosophy of science was neither fully developed nor explicit. It must be gleaned from his poetry and his scientific and scholarly reports. At times it seems particularly unclear. The extreme case is his theory of light. He seems inconsistent (he objected to prisms but not to telescopes) and, at times, even foolish, as in his scurrilous attacks on Newton's rival theory. However, since in all but this one area, his approach bore extraordinary fruit, we might allow him this one mistake. (I should say that although the majority of scientific and historical commentary is in agreement that his theory of light is without merit, there is by no means unanimity among scientists and historians. Some argue that his theory complements, rather than contradicts, Newton's approach.)

The controversy over Goethe's *Farbenlehre* leads to the final reason for current neglect of his scientific achievements: role conflict. It is clear that one of the reasons that his scientific colleagues initially rejected his findings was emotional: they were affronted by a "mere poet" who deigned to tell them their business. Perhaps since they themselves were specialists, they seem to have felt humiliated that a layperson, a nonspecialist, would tell them that they were mistaken.

When we read between the lines, many more scientists than historians involved in the debate over Goethe's science seem to react much as their colleagues did during Goethe's time. Most of the present-day scientists who are aware of Goethe as a scientist seem to know only his color theory, which they peremptorily dismiss. Even Heisenberg (1974), both a great physicist and something of a savant, seems to acknowledge only a very small part of Goethe's scientific work, his color theory, and his role as a philosopher of scientific method. (Heisenberg is particularly appreciative, in the era after Hiroshima, of Goethe's warning of the dangers of a purely analytic science.) Perhaps the more narrowly specialized the scientist is, the more threatened by the scientific work of a nonspecialist.

It may be possible to learn from Goethe's case how we might decrease the separation between expert and commonsense knowledge in the modern world. Part/whole thinking and the social role of generalist complement each other. In the modern world publication and advancement occur almost entirely within specialized fields. The modern expert is a specialist and usually feels compelled to work on highly specialized topics. In the academy, there is no department of general art and science, few periodicals of general knowledge, and no professional organization which embraces all art and science. The alienation between art and science is symbolized by the existence of two giant organizations, one for the humanities (MLA), one for science (AAAS)—and none for the arts.

Goethe was a generalist who also felt free to specialize in topics as they became interesting to him. He seems to have been a master in part/whole thinking, of seeing a whole, a large enveloping framework, and the parts, the details which both attest to and develop from the large framework. In our own day we have divided this process into two separate functions, the specialist in wholes (the theorists and critics) and the specialist in parts (the empirical researchers and artists). The divorce between theory and practice is both cause and result of this division of function.

In view of my earlier discussion of contextual meaning in chapter 3, and of general problem solving in chapter 4, it seems likely that the human mind is at its best when the two functions, a focus on wholes and a focus on parts, combine within a single mind. It seems particularly crucial that any particular problem be viewed both from the point of view of expert knowledge and from the point of view of common sense. The expert view brings to bear systematic analysis, common sense—the natural language problem solver. The worker who uses part/whole thinking, who shuttles back and forth between expert and commonsense systems, I call a specialist-generalist (s-g). The s-g practices *bricolage* (Lévi-Strauss 1966), being a jack-of-all-trades, as well as being an expert in a particular field.

The s-g is in a position to use universalistic procedures, formal rationality, and intuitive, contextual processes that result in substantive rationality. This combination is likely to lead to quicker and more effective problem solving than the separation that characterizes current practice. To be sure, the system of specialized functions as described by Ziman will still be needed to supplement and test the work of the s-g's. Perhaps workers should usually begin as specialists as in current practice. With appropriate social organization and incentives, most specialists could learn to function as s-g's.

The development of s-g's might help to close the gap between expert knowledge and common understanding. The example of Emerson, the first of the American pragmatists, illustrates some aspects of my proposal. In his essays, Emerson embodied most of the ideas later advanced by James, G. H. Mead, and Dewey. But unlike these later specialists, Emerson was a generalist as well as a philosopher and poet. For this reason, his proposals are stated in ordinary language; they are virtually free of jargon. Emerson's social position was not that of a specialist: he gave public lectures for his livelihood. Although he dealt with many of the same problems which engaged the later pragmatists, he did so in a language which is forceful and clear, in contrast to that of his successors, whose message was usually so involuted as to be almost inaccessible. Perhaps if experts spoke to the public as well as to each other, there might be less confusion within art and science, as well as less alienation from society.

The discussion of expert and commonsense knowledge clarifies a point made by Mannheim (1936) in his discussion of the role of intellectuals in society. He attempted to specify how intellectuals might decrease the otherwise all-pervasive distortion of knowledge caused by ideological commitments. The problem of ideological distortion is currently the focus of "critical theory," a specialized critique of ideology, which ironically has become something of an ideology itself. Mannheim's position is like the one taken here: the free-floating intellectual, exposed to all ideological commitments, might be able to shake free of them. This is a variant of the argument in favor of marginality: the person who participates equally in more than one cultural world is troubled by conflicting demands but also is apt to be creative. Mannheim took this familiar argument further by characterizing the intellectual as someone who participates, in principle, in *all* cultural worlds, thereby decreasing ideological distortion. As indicated, Goethe provides an example. The epigraph by Emerson at the beginning of this chapter makes the same point.

My discussion of common sense as a general problem solver adds force to Mannheim's idea. An intellectual who participates in all ideologies would, perforce, employ the ideology of the reigning system of common sense: he or she would be a specialist-generalist. It is important to note that participating in more than one system of *expert* knowledge, by this definition, does not make one a free-floating intellectual, an s-g. A psychoanalytically oriented, feminist Marxist is still a specialist, since the system of common sense is not given a special position. For one to be a generalist, common sense must be used as a touchstone. An s-g is positioned between the worlds of special expertise, on the one hand, and the world of common understanding, on the other—neither specialist nor layperson. A group of s-g's would form a new class of intellectuals who might serve as intermediaries, translators, between the conflicting worlds, as well as experts in their own right.

Conclusion

I end this discussion by outlining proposals implied above. In order to encourage the specialist-generalist orientation, we need changes in the academy, particularly in the graduate programs, which produce the class of experts, and in the organization of the university and its system of incentives. I begin with the procedures that are used in teaching graduate students.

Although there are exceptions, most teaching overemphasizes either parts or wholes, rather than provides balance. Perhaps the strongest modern tendency is to focus on the parts, the details, with insufficient reference to wholes. C. Wright Mills (1959) called this mode "abstracted empiricism." Although it can be found in any field, it is more highly concentrated in the natural and human sciences than in arts and letters. Teaching of this kind encourages passivity in the students: they are lost in the minutiae, unable to use their native intelligence to organize the torrent of detail. Many students simply submit to the organization proffered by instruction, suppressing their own analytic and synthesizing abilities. This mode is dominated by the spirit of system at the expense of the spirit of finesse.

At the other extreme is teaching which overemphasizes wholes, with insufficient attention to the necessary parts, the details which follow from and give meaning to the large framework. In this mode the spirit of finesse reigns at the expense of system. This style includes, but is broader than, what C. Wright Mills thought of as "grand theory," since it occurs in the arts and letters as well as in the classic styles of philosophy and the human sciences.

This style also leads to passive learning. The student may be stimulated by the sweep of the large ideas but has no way to test or apply them; instruction has not sufficiently illustrated the relationship of the whole to the parts. The student either accepts the ideas on faith or rejects them in toto, rather than engage in a critical dialogue. Since both this mode and the overemphasis on parts encourage passive learning, these modes perpetuate themselves: passive students become passive experts, who teach as they were taught and conduct research as their mentors did.

Passive learning in graduate programs can be discouraged by emphasizing problem solving rather than courses, requirements, and examinations. Perhaps apprenticeship remains the best model for dealing with the real problems of research and teaching. In this model it is possible to balance system and finesse; it does not exclude formal rationality, but it includes plentiful instances of specific problems to solve, encouraging *bricolage* as well as specialized expertise. Close contact between the student and his or her adviser is crucial so that the student can both observe the way that the adviser solves problems and have his or her own problem-solving techniques supervised.

Classes and lectures are necessary parts of graduate instruction since they are efficient in supplying broad overviews, on the one hand, and specific problem-solving methods, on the other. They would probably work best, however, if they were used by each student as needed in the course of his or her own work rather than be presented in lockstep as formal requirements.

Lectures can be an occasion for using and teaching part/whole thinking rather than encouraging passive learning and memorization. If the lecture begins with an abstract summary of the parts and the whole, and their interrelationship, the student is given an opportunity to be a participant in the development of the lecture, rather than a passive observer. That is, the summary allows students to use their mother wit to assess and collaborate with the lecture. Under these conditions, the classroom takes on drama, the audience is constantly anticipating, and testing its anticipation, of the steps in the argument.

The summary statement at the beginning of class serves as a signal of the goal of cooperative activity. Having an explicit goal known to both teacher and class makes it possible for them to arrive at the same conclusion at the end of the lecture. However, if collaboration is to occur, it is necessary not only to end together but also to begin together. If students are to follow the argument, they need it to be connected to their general understanding before proceeding.

Many teachers understand this step intuitively; they begin with a statement of the goal of the lecture and with attention to the content and level of understanding in the audience. Although the teacher may be able to assess class understanding intuitively, often it is necessary to check by asking questions or making statements at the beginning of class which invite student response. This step allows for the explicit announcement of the beginning point of the lecture and also encourages a collaborative stance rather than passive observation.

Active rather than passive learning in graduate instruction, although a necessary step, would probably not be sufficient to change the current system of expert knowledge. Even if graduate programs produced large numbers of specialist-generalists, the existing organization of the academy and its system of incentives would probably transform most of them into specialists. Discussion of all the changes required would be lengthy; I confine my remarks to what I consider three crucial avenues.

Perhaps the first step would be the establishment of academic units which would facilitate the development of general, as well as specialized, knowledge. Given the structure of universities, the initial unit might be a research institute, to be followed, allowing for the slowness of organizational change, by what is usually called a program, then a department, and finally, in the fullness of time, a college. The college-level unit is a necessary goal since it would draw not only on letters and science but also on the professional schools such as education, engineering, law, and medicine. To make inroads on the divorce between theory and practice, we would need the participation of these latter faculties.

A second organizational step would concern not the university system itself, but the professional organizations which exist outside that structure. In the present structure of expert knowledge, the organized disciplines are extremely powerful forces. Because of this power, the university is more like a confederacy than a federal organization: the lines of reward and communication flow as much through the professional organizations as through the university system. To symbolize a dramatic move toward general knowledge, perhaps a new organization subsuming all disciplines in art and science would be needed. Such an organization (the International Association for the Advancement of Art and Science [IAAAS]?) would not replace the existing disciplinary associations but would encourage the development of s-g's by providing them with a forum for their concerns.

A final proposal concerns changing the incentive structure in the university system to reward general knowledge. Ostensibly, publication aimed at general understanding is now rewarded. According to academic manuals, such publication (e.g., an introductory textbook) may demonstrate teaching competence and should therefore be part of the case for overall competence. There are substantial drawbacks, however. It is no secret that there is very little reward in the academy for teaching competence or for anything other than research competence. The reward structure recognizes virtually nothing but publication of specialized research.

Except under unusual circumstances, textbooks and what is called "popularization" are not only not rewarded, but punished. This kind of writing is seen as competing with "serious," that is, specialized, research and therefore usually deemed inappropriate for the scholar or the scientist, or even calls into question the merit of the popularizer's specialized work.

It might help to *require* some kind of popular writing at regular intervals, in which each worker is called upon to write for the public at large about his or her work. This step would encourage all experts in the academy at least to consider moving toward the s-g role. It might also help with the current difficulty in adequately representing academic work to the public. There are very few periodicals which present the right blend of specialized and general knowledge. In science, *Scientific American* is too specialized, and a magazine like *Discovery* too simplified, to convey expert knowledge to public. In the arts and humanities the situation is still less adequate, since there seem to be no general audience periodicals equivalent to the two in science. Perhaps there are too few s-g's; the talent is not available at the moment to bridge the gap.

At present, all these proposals seem utopian in the face of the everyday reality of the academy, with its ever-increasing specialization. Even so, if they provoke discussion, they may help to bring further system and finesse to bear on the problems which face our quest for knowledge. The next chapter outlines a second application of my approach—the problem of the sources of genius.

9

Language Acquisition versus Formal Education: A Theory of Genius

The explanation of genius that is most common is that it is a product of inherited genes. Galton (1869) sought to demonstrate this point by studying the family lines of artists, scientists, and statesmen. Cox (1926) conducted a similar but more extensive study. Both show a strong relationship between genius in a certain field, for example, music, and a family background of talent in that field. Bach and Puccini, for example, were both descended from five generations of musicians. Although these two examples are extreme, the relationship is general; most of the great musicians came from families in which there was already musical talent.

This chapter is aimed not at dismissing the genetic argument but offers an alternative model of explanation which could either complement or replace it, depending on the findings of future research. As has been pointed out many times, family inheritance has both a biological and a social character. In the study of genius it is difficult to disentangle the two since we deal with a small number of cases. Since I propose only a necessary cause, not a sufficient one, there is no need to evaluate the validity of the genetic argument.

The theory proposed concerns two processes of development—one of *talent,* the other of *self-esteem.* I argue that both processes are necessary. The development of talent will be discussed first.

Modern linguistics has (unintentionally) contributed to the issue by the discovery that all humans have genius in language. Since this contention is not obvious, I first review the contribution that linguists have made: the competent use of language is an achievement of such staggering complexity that it seems a miracle.

There is a large literature on the complexity of even the simplest utterances. The attempt to program computers for automatic translation is one of the bases of the new appreciation of the immense intelligence required to use language. There is no way to program a computer to solve a relatively simple problem of competent language use: choosing from among fixed, multiple meanings of a word. This can be demonstrated by returning to the simple statement discussed in chapter 6, "The box is in the pen." Is pen to be construed as a writing instrument or an enclosure? To answer this question, the program would have to have access to an encyclopedia, not merely a dictionary, and would have to have the resources to know how to comb the encyclopedic reference for its relevance to the context in the sentence.

Compared with creating a metaphoric expression or even merely understanding one, words with two or more meanings are very simple problems indeed. There is the story of the computer program which translated the expression "The spirit is willing, but the flesh is weak" into Russian as "The whiskey is good, but the meat is bad," and "Out of sight, out of mind" as "First blind, then insane." These illustrations are apocryphal, but they make the point: using language correctly is a creative process beyond the power of even the most sophisticated computer program, or of living creatures other than humans, for that matter.

It will be helpful here to define what I mean by creative intelligence, the basis of genius. For my purposes, it is the ability to find a new solution to a new problem. In the living world outside humans, creatures that have even a modicum of this ability are very rare. The psychologist Köhler showed that a few of the most intelligent in the most intelligent of the primates, the chimpanzees, had a limited amount of creative intelligence. A representative problem was to reach fruit on a shed that was to too high to climb. The ingredients of the solution, jointed sticks and packing crates, were scattered around the yard. Only a few chimpanzees solved the problem: stacking the crates near the shed, carrying the jointed sticks to the top, joining them, using the pole created to get the fruit. This simple problem would confound almost all the nonhuman living world.

At the other end of the scale of complexity was the problem facing physicists at the turn of the century, already mentioned in chapter 8, when it was becoming apparent that classical physics was inadequate for dealing with the accumulating evidence on the nature of the physical universe. Hilbert (cited in Feuer 1982) raised the question of why it was that Einstein solved the problem rather than any one of a group of men, all of whom seemed to be so much better prepared than he: Lorentz, Hilbert himself, Poincaré, Mach, and Minkowski. His question can be used to illustrate my conception of creative intelligence. The others were all more erudite than Einstein, but their very erudition led them to keep applying the old solutions that were no longer appropriate. Only Einstein saw that it was the very successes of classical physics that were standing in the way of a solution. What was needed was not merely modifying the old solutions but discarding them entirely and starting over with new ones.

The physicist Boltzmann (1899) described the problem in general terms. He noted that when a new method yields "beautiful results," many become unconsciously wedded to it; they come "to believe that the development of science to the end of all time would consist in the systematic and unremitting application of it."

The method of "unremitting" repetition of a method that at first proved successful is the pattern of all life outside the human world. In all other living species, patterns of behavior are fixed during the lifetimes of individuals by genetic inheritance. As Darwin indicated, new solutions to new problems occur but only over immense spans of time, through natural selection. A particular bird, finding that its call is not attracting a mate, cannot observe the calls of its successful competitors in order to devise a new, more effective call. It is for this reason that all species of living creatures, except for humans, are ultimately doomed to extinction. Sooner or later, a change in the environment will occur more rapidly than the fixed repertory of responses can adjust. The Ice Age, for example, extinguished numberless species. But some brilliant human or humans created a new solution to this new problem—using caves for shelter.

Even among humans, many kinds of creative activity are rare: only a few solve an artistic or scientific problem in their lifetimes; that is, they do not create a new solution to a new problem. However, as already suggested, in one field, language, virtually every human by the age of five is a creative genius. Most five-year-olds can understand and even create a correct sentence that they have never heard before. Not infrequently, at a somewhat later age, a child can create a correct sentence that no one has ever heard before. In one field, language, almost everyone is creative, spontaneously creating new solutions to new problems as they arise in everyday life.

How do linguists account for the immense human creativity they have discovered? Chomsky (1957, 1965, 1969) offers what turns out to be a conventional genetic explanation. He suggests that linguistic competence is based on "deep structures," genetically programmed sequences, which would have been called instincts if that term had not been discredited. In his view, all humans are linguistically creative because that creativity has been genetically inherited.

I wish to broaden the linguists' question so that the issue includes all creative genius, not just language use. The question becomes: Why is it that almost everyone is a genius at language, but only a few rare individuals are geniuses in all other spheres of activity? As already suggested, Chomsky's answer to this question is genetic; he would assume that language creativity is genetically inherited by everyone and that genius in other areas belongs to only a few individuals with the right genetic inheritance, as Galton and Cox both tried to show.

My alternative explanation does not exclude genetics but opens several new areas of investigation. First, assume that the capacity for creative genius in all spheres of activity, not just in language, is genetically inherited by all human beings. Apparently the human brain is more complex and powerful than the largest and most sophisticated computer. Von Neumann estimated that it is capable of processing 140 million bits of information per second. The philosopher Emerson (whose conception of human nature will figure prominently in this essay) did not know this, of course, but he seemed to sense it: "We lie in the lap of immense intelligence" (1837).

If humans have the capacity for genius in all areas, not just in language, why does genius appear in everyone in language but almost never in other areas? Suppose we assume that the disparity is caused by differences not in genetics but in systems of instruction. That is, it is possible that the system of instruction which leads children to learn language is enormously effective, while the systems of instruction which lead children to learn other activities, such as musical composition or mathematics, are relatively ineffective. These two suppositions raise what seems to me to be a new question. How is the system of instruction of children in language different from other systems of instruction?

A careful answer to this question might require considerable investigation. In this paper I will attempt only a provisional answer in order to formulate a rudimentary theory of the origins of genius. I will describe only some of the most obvious characteristics which differentiate language instruction from all other types of instruction.[1]

1. Exposure to language begins at the moment of birth and goes on almost constantly throughout infancy and childhood, and indeed for the whole of the individual's life. In terms of sheer quantity, for most individuals, exposure to language is probably vastly greater than any other type of instruction.

2. Language instruction is supremely interactive. Only very early in infancy is the child merely passively exposed to language. Long before any speech is acquired, parents and others speak directly to the infant, usually seeking a response, any response, to their utterances. The immediate rewarding of the infant's responses, often with boundless enthusiasm, is the beginning of a process of interaction between the infant and competent speakers which instructs the child in correct usage.

3. Virtually all an infant's prelanguage and language tutoring is with tutors who are, as has already been pointed out above, extraordinarily competent in the subject they are imparting. This characteristic of language instruction surely differentiates it from instruction in other subjects. With subjects other than language, the instructors are often only routinely competent, if that. As will be illustrated below for the case of musical creativity, most of the children who go on to become creative geniuses had been instructed by a teacher, usually a parent or other close relative, of much more than routine competence.

4. Language instruction is built upon the infant's own spontaneous gestures and utterances. Virtually all other systems of instruction require the learner to conform to the conventions of the subject to be learned. With a baby, however, one instructs by responding to its cooing, crying, or babbling with language,

---

1. Howard Becker called to my attention a comparison of schooling and language acquisition which parallels mine, in Paul Goodman, "Education of the Young" (1969).

thereby gradually but relentlessly shaping native impulses. This characteristic may profoundly influence the results of instruction. It also serves to tie together the two parts of the present argument. Since language instruction appears to be so integral with the infant's spontaneous impulses and gestures, it would probably serve to affirm the infant's sense of self, resulting in small but cumulating additions to the level of self-esteem. By contrast, most other systems of instruction, which require the learner to adapt to an alien system of conventions, may cause small but cumulating deficits of self-esteem.

It is conceivable that a system of instruction for music or mathematics or other subjects could be constructed, as language is, out of the learner's spontaneous activities. In music, for example, the instructor could begin by responding to the infant's pitch and rhythms as if they were musical notes and shaping them as one does with language. Similarly a system of mathematical instruction could be built upon the learner's spontaneous counting activities.

The intention to build upon the learner's spontaneous actions appears to lie at the core of the Montessori method of teaching. Children are allowed to play with instructional toys which usually give rise to spontaneous mathematical, musical, and other types of activity. The teacher is trained to base his or her teaching on these spontaneous activities. Although this is an excellent idea, it is not able to capture many of the characteristics of language instruction in the family setting. It takes place only at certain hours of the day and only when the child has reached school age. The instructor may be at least routinely competent in the Montessori method but only routinely competent, if that, in the special area of music, mathematics, and so on. Finally, the teacher is a stranger, at least at the beginning of instruction, rather than being someone, like a parent or other relative, to whom the learner is already strongly attached.

The ideal teacher for a budding genius would be a close relative who is gifted in the area of instruction, always available because living in the same abode, who uses the learner's spontaneous acts as the basis for instruction. Also ideal would be the presence in the home of one or more back-up teachers, so that at least one teacher would be always available.

If we look at the families of the greatest composers, these conditions were usually met. Of course there is no way of knowing in detail their methods of instruction. Most of the greatest composers had at least one close relative who was a gifted musician: Bach, Beethoven, Bizet, Brahms, Chopin, Dvorak, Gounod, Grieg, Ives, Liszt, Mendelssohn, Mozart, Puccini, Rossini, Scarlatti, Schubert, Stravinsky, and Vivaldi. It would appear from their biographies that these composers had access to instruction from at least one gifted musician during infancy and early childhood. However, there are three composers who appear to be exceptions: Tchaikovsky, Verdi, and Wagner. I could find no obvious indication that there was a gifted musician available to them from the time of their births. Judging from these three exceptions, it would appear that although access to a gifted teacher from birth is strongly correlated with the appearance of genius, it is not a necessary condition. I will return to this issue after the discussion of self-esteem, below.

One last comment on musical instruction must be made with respect to Mozart, one of the most prodigiously gifted of the great composers. Like most of them, in his earliest years he had access to more than one competent musician. His father, Leopold, was a performer, composer, and teacher of music; and his older sister, Nannerl, a gifted performer. Of great interest for my argument, there is evidence that his father may have been extraordinarily gifted as a teacher of music. His manual of instruction for the violin, now almost two-hundred-years old, is still the standard text for that instrument. The vitality of his written teaching at least suggests that he may have also been a supremely competent teacher for his son.

The fifth characteristic which may differentiate instruction in language from instruction in other fields is the nature of the response to the learner's progress or lack of progress. In language acquisition in infancy, at least, the instructors seem to concentrate on rewarding correct speech rather than punishing error. Many parents seem to regard each new word as a miracle, often completely disregarding errors. One does not expect infants to know how to speak. We feel no contempt for their errors. (This is in contrast to our native reaction to the difficulties foreign adults have with our language.) At least in the earliest years of instruction, the young learner is not ridiculed for making errors. Perhaps this is one of the reasons for the remarkable effectiveness of learning in language and the ineffectiveness of most other kinds of instruction: early language use may be almost completely free of shame.

In this section I have suggested that the methods that lead to language acquisition are vastly richer than other kinds of instruction. They begin at birth and are virtually continuous during the child's waking hours. They are carried on by a close relative who is extraordinarily gifted in the use of language. One or more back-up teachers are also usually available to ensure continuous training even in the absence of the primary teacher. Language instruction in infancy and early childhood is also intensely interactive, with the learner's getting virtually instant feedback on her or his fluency. I have also suggested that language instruction in the family is built upon the shaping of the learner's native impulses rather than the acquiring of new ones. This method may lead to high levels of self-esteem. A fifth characteristic may also build self-esteem: the overwhelming prevalence of positive, rather than negative, feedback in the early years of language acquisition. There seems to be a moratorium on criticism in the initial response of adults to children's early efforts at language.

The Real and the False Self

I introduce the topic of self-esteem and its relation to genius by referring again to Emerson's thought. He believed that self-reliance was the basic virtue because, he argued, at the core of every human is a self of unbelievable brilliance (1837, 18):

What is the aboriginal Self, on which a universal reliance may
be grounded? What is the nature and power of that science-baffling

star, without parallax, without calculable elements, which shoots a
ray of beauty even into trivial and impure actions, if the least mark
of independence appear? The inquiry leads us to that source, at
once the essence of genius, of virtue, and of life, which we call
Spontaneity or Instinct. We denote this primary wisdom as Intuition, whilst all later teachings are tuitions. This aboriginal self is
the origin of intuition, and therefore of inspiration, of effortless
genius.

Emerson points out that one aspect of genius, the completely accurate perception of reality, is totally involuntary:

Every man discriminates between the voluntary acts of his mind
and his involuntary perceptions, and knows that to his involuntary
perceptions a perfect faith is due. He may err in the expression of
them, but he knows that these things are so, like day and night, not
to be disputed. My willful actions and acquisitions are but roving;
the idlest reverie, the faintest native emotion, command my curi-
osity and respect. Thoughtless people contradict as readily the
statement of perceptions as of opinions, or rather much more readily; for they do not distinguish between perception and notion. They
fancy that I choose to see this or that thing. But perception is not
whimsical, but fatal. If I see a trait, my children will see it after
me, and in the course of time all mankind—although it may chance
that no one has seen it before me. For my perception of it is as
much a fact as the sun.

If all humans have access to boundless intuition and perception, according
to Emerson, why is not everyone a genius? The answer he gives is that with
few exceptions, everyone is terrified by the specter of being deviants from the
collective vision of reality that is held in the community. We conform out of
shame.

A man must consider what a blindman's bluff is this game of
conformity. . . . most men have bound their eyes with one or another handkerchief, and attached themselves to some one of these
communities of opinion. This conformity makes them not false in a
few particulars, authors of a few lies, but false in all particulars.
Their every truth is not quite true. Their two is not the real two,
their four not the real four; so that every word they say chagrins us
and we know not where to begin to set them right.

Conformity to the popularly held version of what is real and what is possible blinds most individuals to their own inner visions. Only that person
whose self-esteem is so high that he can withstand social rejection will be able
to propose new solutions to new problems. Emerson's formulation of this
issue is so lengthy that I have separated and enumerated the main components
(emphasis added).

[1] To believe your own thought, to believe that what is true for you in your private heart is true for all men—that is genius. Speak your latent conviction, and it shall be the universal sense; for the inmost in due time becomes the outmost, and our *first thought* is rendered back to us by the trumpets of the Last Judgment.

[2] A man should learn to *detect and watch that gleam of light which flashes across his mind from within,* more than the lustre of the firmament of bards and sages.

[3] Yet he dismisses without notice his thought, because it is his. In every work of genius we recognize our own *rejected thoughts;* they come back to us with a certain alienated majesty.

[4] Great works of art have no more affecting lesson for us than this. They teach us to abide by our spontaneous impression with good-humored inflexibility then most when the whole cry of voices is on the other side. Else tomorrow a stranger will say with masterly good sense precisely what we have thought and felt all the time, and we shall be forced to take with *shame* our own opinion from another.

There are several important ideas in this passage, but they are not developed by Emerson, only mentioned casually in passing. Perhaps the most fundamental basis of his thought is found in (2): "A man should learn to detect and watch that gleam of light which flashes across his mind from within, more than the lustre of the firmament of bards and sages." The key word is "flashes." In the context of the sentence, he seems to be suggesting that the flashes are extremely fast, so fast, perhaps, that unless one trains one's self, it is almost impossible even to become aware of them, much less try them out.

This sentence may serve to clarify what is otherwise a confusing issue in the advice that Emerson gives us. He tells us to trust ourselves but, aside from this sentence, does not give us any further guidance about what self it is that we are to trust. In the passage quoted earlier he calls it the "aboriginal self" and identifies it with intuition and spontaneity. But we have many different types of spontaneous impulses and thoughts, some of which are notoriously unreliable. We need a more specific description of the type of spontaneous intuitive thought.

In the sentence about the gleam of light, Emerson may have provided an important clue to what he meant. He seems to have anticipated Freud's discovery of the unconscious, the "aboriginal self" as Emerson calls it. In order to teach his patients "to learn to detect and watch" the gleam of light, Freud developed the method of free association. He devised a practical workaday technique for giving his patient's access to their "aboriginal" selves. Once the patient discovered this access, therapy usually advanced more rapidly.

In systematically applying the method of free association, Freud made a discovery that went beyond Emerson. He found that most of his patients actively resisted acquaintance with their aboriginal selves (the repressed parts of their experiences):

> That which has ostensibly been forgotten is always lying ready
> "close at hand" and can be reached by associations that are easily
> accessible. It is merely a question of getting some obstacle out of
> the way. This obstacle seems once again to be the subject's will,
> and different people can learn with different degrees of ease to free
> themselves from their intentional thinking and to adopt an attitude
> of completely objective observation towards the psychical processes
> taking place in them. [Freud and Breuer 1895, 312]

The patient's resistance, Freud later found, was due to unresolved painful emotion that was often also a part of the aboriginal self. I will return to the issue of unresolved emotion below, in the section on shame and guilt. The last part of this passage, however, seems to corroborate and extend Emerson's description of the intuitive process.

Although not explicit, this early statement by Freud has an air of bland optimism which he was later to renounce. Note the words "easily" and "merely." The brevity and casualness of Emerson's references to the aboriginal self also seem to imply an unrealistic optimism in his thought. By the time Freud wrote *The Interpretation of Dreams* (1905), he realized that everyone has not merely one or two protective layers over his or her aboriginal self, but an intricate many-leveled structure of defenses, like a fortified city, whose development begins in earliest infancy. In his old age, Freud became as pessimistic about the possibility of self-discovery as he was optimistic in the beginning. Karen Horney, one of Freud's intellectual heirs, took a more balanced stance (1950). She proposed that neurosis occurs because of the suppression of the real self (read aboriginal self) beneath the false self. The real self can be reclaimed, but this process, she implied, is a lifelong quest.

If, as I have suggested, Emerson anticipated the discovery and use of the unconscious, how could everyone have missed his point? First of all, as already indicated, the key sentence is almost hidden in a paragraph in which there are many other ideas as well. Emerson did not call attention to it; it is buried in the middle of a lengthy paragraph, with three sentences coming before it and five after, some quite long, and all packed with matter. He seems to have taken this idea for granted, mentioning it almost as an afterthought.

Second, it would be very easy for most readers to understand the sentence not as a literal description of a particular kind of inner experience—as a very concrete, even flat-footed description of a phenomenon in nature, as I have—but, instead, as one more example of Emerson's floridly poetic, grandiloquent prose. Emerson's mixture of styles is confusing. Notice the similarity between the sentence which I have emphasized, concerning the gleam of light, and an earlier sentence in the passage where he names the aboriginal self: "What is the nature and power of that science-baffling star, without parallax, without calculable elements, which shoots a ray of beauty. . . ." Although at first glance this sentence seems similar to the other one, a close reading suggests that this latter sentence is as utterly devoid of factual description as the first sentence is loaded with it. The gleam-of-light sentence appears to have been written by the natural science side of Emerson's personality, a cross between Darwin and Freud; the star-without-parallax sentence by the bombastic orator, in the manner of William Jennings Bryan. It seems unfair of Emerson not to have bracketed this sentence in some way: "Stop! This next sentence is to be understood literally, rather than metaphorically." Perhaps, for reasons that are now obscure, he did not wish to be understood. If so, he certainly succeeded. He antagonized two of his greatest contemporaries, Hawthorne and Melville, and puzzled later commentators, like Knut Hamsun and John Updike (1984).

Emerson's idea and Freud's later work teach that intuitive thought is unsolicited and nonverbal, an "involuntary perception," to use Emerson's term; second, it appears and disappears so rapidly as to seem instantaneous; and finally, it is always the *first* thought, rather than the second, third, or later thought, that is unedited and uncensored and therefore uncompromised by bias. The unsolicited first thought appears always, "invariably" to use Freud's word, to be the most inclusive, complex, and original of our thoughts. (But this is not necessarily true; Emerson was careful to state that intuitive ideas always need to be tested in reality.)

Einstein, when he sought to explain the origins of his creative ideas, often hinted at these characteristics. He usually explained that ideas did not come to him in words but in "images." The greatest of the chess masters also explain their deliberation in a similar way, not in words or moves but in fluid images that come to them involuntarily. Like Einstein, they struggle in their descriptions because they are attempting to describe a nonverbal process in words.

Nietzsche, who acknowledged that he was strongly influenced by reading Emerson, also described the creative process: "Beneath thy thoughts and feelings there is a mighty Lord, an unknown sage; it is called the self; it dwells in your body." Nietzsche's "mighty lord" corresponds, it would seem, to Emerson's aboriginal self. Like Emerson, but much more explicitly, Nietzsche also attempted to describe the creative moment. The relevant passage is so long that for the sake of clarity, I have divided it into five sections. The first makes clear how involuntary the whole episode is:

> Can any one at the end of this nineteenth century possibly have any distinct notion of what poets of a more vigorous period meant by inspiration? If not, I should like to describe it. Provided one has the slightest remnant of superstition left, one can hardly reject completely the idea that one is the mere incarnation, or mouthpiece, or medium of some almighty power. The notion of revelation describes the condition quite simply; by which I mean that something profoundly convulsive and disturbing suddenly becomes visible and audible with indescribable definiteness and exactness. One hears—one does not seek; one takes—one does not ask who gives; a thought flashes out like lightning, inevitably without hesitation—I have never had any choice about it.

Note the echo of Emerson's flash of the gleam of light in the last clause: "a thought flashes out like lightning. . . ."

The next passage describes the painful emotion that is found in the aboriginal self:

> There is an ecstasy whose terrific tension is sometimes released by a flood of tears, during which one's progress varies from involuntary impetuosity to involuntary slowness. There is the feeling that one is utterly out of hand, with the most distinct consciousness of an infinitude of shuddering thrills that pass through one from head to foot;—there is a profound happiness in which the most painful and gloomy feelings are not discordant in effect; but are required as necessary colors in this overflow of light.

Emerson's description of the aboriginal self does not prepare us for Nietzsche's discovery: growing self-knowledge means confrontation with occluded emotions. This finding looks forward to the knowledge gained in the practice of psychodynamic psychotherapy, that patients resist acquaintance with their aboriginal selves because they anticipate that it will bring pain.

In a later passage, Nietzsche points to the extraordinary vividness of sensation; the perceptions are so vivid they have a hallucinatory quality. Words seem to become things, and the things themselves appear to present themselves, not just the images of the things:

> The spontaneity of the images and similes is most remarkable; one loses all perception of what is imagery and simile; everything offers itself as the most immediate, exact, and simple means of expression. If I may recall a phrase of Zarathustra's, it actually seems as if the things themselves came to one, and offered themselves as similes.

The passage ends on an unexpected note: "This is my experience of inspiration. I have no doubt that I should have to go back millenniums to find another who could say to me: 'It is mine also!'" Nietzsche seems to be saying that he might have to go as far back as Homer or Moses to find someone else besides himself who had a similar experience. This comment is surprising since we know that Nietzsche had read Emerson by this time and had even acknowledged that his reading of Emerson had influenced him profoundly. Perhaps, like almost everyone else, Nietzsche had not understood that Emerson had had similar experiences, or, much more likely, had understood it but only beneath the level of awareness.

If we return to Emerson's passage, a second idea is suggested in (1), "To believe your own thought, to believe that what is true for you in your private heart is true for all men—that is genius." This statement makes a connection between self-esteem and genius. It evokes the idea, in the strongest possible terms, that what differentiates the genius most strongly from other, ordinary persons is not talent—no mention is made of that—but self-esteem. Emerson seems to suggest that for the genius, his or her unique vision does not lead to a feeling of alienation from others, of being "different," that is, a freak, as is usually the case, but of feeling connected with others in that what is true for you is also true of all others. In the discussion of the relationship between self-esteem and shame below, I suggest how such an extraordinarily high level of self-esteem might come about.

One last thought in the original passage, (4), is in need of elaboration. I refer to the last part of this sentence, about the "whole cry of voices" being on the other side. The implication is that the person who expresses his or her unique vision will be persecuted for it. This sentence again implies a connection between genius and self-esteem. In this case it is implied that one will need a high level of self-esteem in order to withstand the cry of voices. The case of Galileo affords a familiar example. The tragic lives of the mathematician Georg Cantor and the physicist Boltzmann are less familiar. Relentless criticism of their work, which was far advanced over that of their contemporaries, drove Boltzmann to suicide and Cantor to the insane asylum. Emerson's paragraph appears to comprehend, in a single glance, the whole situation of the genius—his inner turmoil and his place in society.

What is not suggested in Emerson, but which may be necessary in order to understand the development of genius, is the idea that persecution does not await the full development of talent and its expression, as in the cases of Cantor and Boltzmann, but is present even early in childhood. The case of Galois, the mathematician whose ideas were formulated between his sixteenth and twentieth years, comes closer to this point. He was rejected uniformly by his teachers and examiners yet persisted, alone, in his mathematical work. Suppose that the unique vision of the genius makes her a target for oppression from earliest childhood. How could a person survive such relentless attack?

Self-Esteem: Coping with Shame and Guilt

One last reference to Emerson evokes another aspect of genius—single-minded dedication to one's work: "I shun father and mother and wife and brother, when my genius calls me." Once again the image which Emerson evokes refers to a high level of self-esteem, in this case, the absence of guilt. I suggest that self-esteem rests upon a very specific process, the management of shame and guilt, and that this process, in conjunction with the development of talent, gives rise to genius.

I have been using the term "self-esteem" as if its meaning were self-explanatory. Actually, there is no agreed-upon definition of this idea. The nearest thing to be found in the literature is the idea that level of self-esteem concerns the degree to which one has positive feelings about oneself. Although this idea is a good place to start, since it concerns feelings rather than thoughts or images, it is much too vague. It does not tell what kind of positive feeling: joy, love, pride, interest, thrill, and so on. In order to proceed further with the theory of genius, I discuss one particular feeling: shame. I define self-esteem as freedom from chronic shame.

Even a child who has no wish to express a unique vision, who wishes merely to be conventional in every possible way, must run a gauntlet of potentially shaming situations. The problem that the child faces is of almost inexpressible magnitude: in order to become an acceptable member of a community, she must learn a myriad of conventions and execute them in virtually perfect manner, as if each were second nature. There is a further characteristic of the job at hand. The child must learn to suppress her understanding that most of these conventions are completely arbitrary. The question "Why do we kiss on the lips rather than rub noses?" or a similar question is tolerated from a three-year-old, but in an older child it already is taken as intimating frivolousness or worse. These conventions "go without saying"; that is, they are sacred. Even to notice the arbitrariness of conventions, much less make an issue of them, invites ridicule and ostracism.

Rapid learning of a large mass of conventions makes errors inevitable. Mispronouncing a word is as much a part of learning as pronouncing it correctly, yet each error invites scorn or ridicule. (In a family I know, one of the members is still being teased about the time she thought that a friend of the parents named Dennis was a dentist.) A repeating error, such as lisping, stammering, or stuttering, creates a nightmare of ridicule. Language errors are particularly rife. There are millions of details of pronunciation, inflection, grammar, syntax, and nonverbal gesture that must be performed, letter perfect.

There is a further twist to language that must seem almost diabolical to the learner. On the one hand, the correct use of language requires creativity. As already indicated, one often needs to invent new linguistic solutions for new situations. A vexing problem faced by children, however, is that some of their inventions are accepted but others are ridiculed. The child who thought that the point of soccer was to hate the ball was mentioned earlier.

The Shame Construct

This digression on children's errors has been by way of introducing the topic of shame once again. A useful place to start is to compare shame with a much less complex and much more prestigious affect: guilt. In most cases, the feeling of guilt is evoked by a specific and quite delimited act or failure to act, for example, to forget one's spouse's birthday or to scream at one's helpless infant. The thread which seems to be common to the actions or inactions which produce guilt is that they all involve the possibility of injuring another. Whether one person steals another's purse or curses or berates him in public, the victim has been injured.

When a child misunderstands a word like "Dennis," however, or invents a motive for soccer players, no injury has occurred. Harmless errors of these kinds do not produce guilt in the perpetrator but a different emotion: shame.

The possibility that one could injure another assumes a potent, powerful, *capable* self. Making a gross error raises a question about the *adequacy* of the self, its basic worth: If you could make an error like that, are you really a person like me, or are you some kind of freak that need not be taken into consideration?

When one feels guilt, one's self feels *intact*. In feeling shame, one experiences what must be the most vertiginous of all feelings, the *disintegration of the self*, or its potential for disintegration. It is for this reason that guilt is infinitely more prestigious than shame. Guilty persons may even feel pride (the reverse of shame) that they are feeling guilt: it shows that they are basically moral persons; that is, they have intact, capable selves.

A vast ocean of errors is built into the child's existence. These errors, for the most part, are unavoidable, as is the normal shame that is the result of making errors. What may be avoidable, however, is to have innumerable experiences lead to *chronic* shame.

Shame is probably the most intensely painful of all feelings. Each person has spent what feels like an eternity of time and effort in constructing a competent, valuable self. The threat of losing that self may be more painful than the threat of losing one's life. In all cultures and historical eras, personal disgrace usually leads to extreme measures, even suicide.

There are two further premises about shame which need to be discussed before I return to self-esteem and genius. Many readers might agree that shame is a profoundly painful emotion but will assume that it seldom occurs and, when it does, one is fully aware of it. I am assuming, on the contrary, that shame is ubiquitous, not only in the lives of children but also in adult life, and virtually invisible. How can one be consumed with shame and still not be aware of it? To understand this issue, I will again review the concept of "unacknowledged shame" and the two forms this type of shame takes: "*bypassed* shame" and "*overt*, undifferentiated shame" (Lewis 1971).

According to Lewis, there are two opposite paths that one can take in order to avoid noticing the feeling of shame: one can bypass the feeling, swallow it, so to speak, so that one does not feel the pain at all (except for one extremely brief instant, when the shame is initially evoked). Although by following this path, one manages to decrease substantially the *intensity* of pain, at the same time the *duration* is increased. The shame is experienced as obsessive ideation or speech. During episodes of compulsive thinking or speaking, one experiences little feeling. On the contrary, one may be aware of an absence of feeling, of blankness or emptiness. Bypassed shame takes the form of too much ideation and too little feeling.

The other form, unacknowledged shame, the overt, undifferentiated type, leads to the opposite experience, too much feeling and too little ideation. One is so flustered by the threat of incompetence (paralysis, disintegration) that one is unable to observe and analyze what is happening. "I feel like a perfect idiot" is one rendering. "Embarrassment," "humiliation," and "mortification" are examples of words used to describe overt shame; "bashfulness," "shyness," "modesty," and "discomfiture" are less-intense but longer-lasting variants.

Many of the commonly used references to undifferentiated painful feelings appear to be shame experiences, or mixtures of shame with another emotion, such as anger: awkward, uncomfortable, foolish, silly, strange, and "in a stew" are examples. In adolescent terminology, one is "bummed," "freaked," or "weirded out." These words appear to be substitutes or euphemisms for shame, just as there are many euphemisms for sexual and "toilet" terms. Shame, like these other functions, appears to be subject to taboo (Scheff 1984).

The discussion so far has focused on shame as a *response*, a stereotyped biopsychological response which is virtually omnipresent in human communities. To describe shame further, it is necessary to shift to the *stimulus* that is common to all situations in which shame arises. This stimulus seems to be social in character: shame appears to be the stereotyped emotional response to a threat of loss of connection to another person or persons. This element is fairly obvious in most cases of overt, undifferentiated shame. One becomes painfully embarrassed and flustered when one "loses face" in public: caught in a lie, a gross error, or caught unawares by an obvious trick (we feel humiliated that we "swallowed it hook, line, and sinker" without a trace of redeeming suspicion).

In bypassed shame, the social source is less obvious since this experience often arises when one is alone. Here is a characteristic moment described by a male college student:

> I am on campus, walking to class. On the way, I am remembering
> an earlier conversation with a great deal of pleasure. I believe I
> made a good impression on this woman that I am interested in. But
> then I remember a remark I made about her ex-boyfriend. At the
> time I felt witty saying it, but suddenly I saw it from her point of
> view. I felt like a turd. I kept re-playing that scene, even when I
> was sitting in class, thinking what I might have said instead.

The obsessive replaying of the scene suggests that this experience involved bypassed shame. It occurred when the student shifted from his point of view to that of the woman. This shift exposes the social nature of the stimulus to bypassed shame. It occurred not in social interaction in the real world, as overt, undifferentiated shame usually does, but in imagined social interaction in the "internal theater," the interior dialogue that goes on in our minds.

The stricken feeling of shame indicated by the phrase "I just felt like an idiot" may occur in actual social interaction. Just as likely, it can occur in solitude, when one is reenacting a transaction from memory or inventing a meeting with another which has never taken place, and may never take place—imagining a conversation with "the man on the street" or with Shakespeare.

In interior dialogue, we are very often engaged with some other person, whose image we create for an inner enactment or reenactment: one's spouse, son, or daughter, boss or subordinate, or even one's self in some other guise, older or younger, in one or another of one's many hats or disguises. This internal theater often results in emotional responses. When we imagine the other as approving or accepting ourselves, we bask in the glow of self-generated pride. When we imagine the other as critical, contemptuous, or scornful, we roast in the hell of self-generated shame or guilt.

Emotion and Creativity

The last step in describing the relationship of genius and self-esteem concerns feeling traps (Lewis 1971). Normal emotions—fear, anger, grief, and shame—are usually quite short-lived, a few seconds perhaps. They ordinarily are crisis responses. Referring to anxiety, Freud suggested that it has a "signal function"; it is an interior warning that something is wrong. If normal emotions are short-lived, how is it possible that one may be constantly angry, frightened, and, especially for our purposes here, ashamed? Chronic shame states are significant because they are probably the basis of what is called low self-esteem: one is usually not proud of one's self but ashamed.

The concept of the feeling trap may explain what otherwise might seem to be a paradox: emotional states which are virtually life long. Feeling traps occur when one has an emotional reaction to one's emotional reaction, and another reaction to that reaction, and another and another, and so on, ad infinitum. Panic seems to be one outcome of a fear spiral: of being frightened that one is so afraid. In fear panics, people may stampede like animals, inadvertently killing each other, or, as in the case of voodoo death, die of anoxia. Being ashamed of being ashamed is another spiral that has runaway possibilities: "What an idiot I am (how shameful it is) that I should get so upset (ashamed) over something so trivial." One outcome of this spiral, stage fright, can reach such proportions that the victim is paralyzed in mind and body.

In interpersonal relations, the lethal feeling trap seems to be the shame-rage spiral, of being ashamed that you are angry ("How could I be so angry at someone who loves me? What a monster I am.") and angry at self or at the other that you are shamed: "You asshole. Don't stand around moping over your ego. Get your ass in gear." The anger may be directed at the other rather than one's self: "It's all your fault. You made me feel bad." This particular spiral may be experienced as humiliated fury (e.g., the "wronged woman")— anger bound by shame. This state may not be represented in consciousness, however. Frequently it is not experienced at all since it has been going on so long as a virtually automatic response. Another possibility is that it is experienced as the absence of any feeling at all, as blankness or emptiness.

Another of the isotopic representations of shame-rage is intermittent but lengthy bouts of resentment, jealousy, or guilt. These are all molecules of the same two atoms, but with the anger pointing in different directions. In resentment, the anger is pointed outward, at objects in the external world. Hitler's *Mein Kampf* has shame and rage bristling from every page (Scheff 1989c). In chronic jealousy, the anger may be pointed at the putative rival or at the love object or at both. In guilt, the anger seems to be pointed back at the self. One is enraged at the self for injuring another and, at the same time, ashamed both of one's actions and of being so enraged ("out of control").

Is there any possibility of escaping from a feeling trap, once caught up? The most common gambit used in daily life seems to be the attempt to talk one's self out of it, which seldom works. Telling one's self "You should be ashamed of being so upset at something so trivial" only sinks one deeper in the trap. In psychotherapy, a frequently used technique is to try to get the victim to express or discharge his anger. This seldom works either because it ignores the shame component of the trap. A common reaction is to become embarrassed (shamed) by the "artificiality" of showing anger when you are "not really mad," which is another variant of feeling that one's anger is not adequately justified, or feeling guilty about being loud or "selfish."

One method which almost always dispels shame is laughter, good-humored or affectionate laughter. This idea is very much in accord with popular belief that laughter relieves embarrassment. Lewis (1983) has shown that it is also supported by Freud's analysis of wit and laughter, although he does not make the idea explicit. Retzinger (1985, 1987) has shown that it is also implied by McDougall's analysis of laughter, although, like Freud, he does not make the sequence explicit.

If one laughs good-naturedly when shame is evoked, it will be quickly dispelled. If one does not laugh, one is often faced with unpleasant after effects. Usually the shamed person will blush or attempt to hide (cover face with hand, look away, try to leave the scene, or at least imagine he has left) or begin to talk or think obsessively. This is the setting for entry into a feeling trap. A common sequence is to become angry or hostile toward the other who is perceived as shaming one, then to feel guilty that one is angry, then to feel ashamed that one is so upset, and so on.

Good-natured laughter, if it occurs immediately when shame is evoked, avoids entry into the spiral. If it occurs when the spiral is in operation, it ends the cycle. Apparently when one laughs during a shame-rage spiral, the dispelling of the shame, which was binding the anger, allows the anger to discharge also. In her video studies of resentment, Retzinger (1985, 1987) has investigated the effects of laughter on anger. In the episodes where laughter occurred during the recalling of a resentment-laden memory, facial flushing and body heat, which are the markers of anger discharge (Scheff 1984), occurred simultaneously with the laughter. Retzinger showed that the frequency, intensity, and duration of verbal and facial anger expressions decreased dramatically after laughter.

The Laughing Genius

Having reviewed the concepts of unacknowledged shame and the shame-rage feeling trap, I return to genius and its relationship to self-esteem. I have argued that for genius to appear, the bearer must have extraordinarily high self-esteem, be able to catch his or her first thoughts in flight, and have the confidence to develop and express these thoughts. There are probably two paths which lead to this level of self-esteem. The first path concerns humane treatment: the budding genius may have undergone less humiliation than others and therefore spent less time in shame-rage spirals than the less gifted. Although it is conceivable that biographies and autobiographies would yield evidence relevant to this hypothesis, it would probably be very difficult to make a judgment unless the humiliation of the child or its opposite, acceptance, were particularly flagrant. One genius, Freud, does remark on this issue in his biographical comments. He attributed his success to being his mother's favorite. It is also clear from Proust's autobiographical comments and from his biographies that he was held in extraordinary esteem by both his mother and grandmother.

It seems likely, however, that the development of ways of managing shame would be far more important in the development of self-esteem than the extent to which one was treated with respect or contempt. Shame seems to be an unavoidable aspect of the human condition, even for those who are fortunate enough to have been treated well in most of their relationships. The gamut of errors through which children must pass in learning their culture, and the shame which results, has already been mentioned. A second universal source of shame is that love is always ambivalent. Intimate relationships are invariably a source of frustration, and therefore of anger, as well as fulfillment, and a source of shame as well as pride. That is, intimacy inevitably leads to a situation in which one is rejected or feels rejected, a basic source of shame.

If, as been argued here, shame is unavoidable, then self-esteem must rest on effective ways of dispelling shame. The most effective way of dispelling shame, I have suggested, is through laughter. If this is the case, the great geniuses should have been laughers. Unfortunately, it is very difficult to find information on this issue. We know from their biographies that Samuel Johnson and Byron were both inveterate laughers, given both to ordinary laughter and to prolonged fits of laughter. From his own accounts, Nietzsche appears also to have been a prodigious laugher. He also connected his laughter with his creativity, particularly with the writing of *Zarathustra* in only thirty days. I have heard from people who knew him that Einstein was also a laugher, although I can find no written record of it.

There is one written documentation of the connection between laughter and genius, however. It happens that Wagner's wife, Cosima, kept a diary with lengthy daily entries for the last fifteen years of her husband's life (Wagner 1976). As far as I know, this diary constitutes by far the best written record of the emotional life of a genius. A preliminary study of its contents substantiates the idea that Wagner's laughter was extraordinary in its frequency and intensity.

Laughter is not the only emotional response that Cosima noted. In the daily entries I found ninety references to Wagner's weeping. These events were not tantrums of self-pity, as one might suspect on the basis of Wagner's personality. His crying usually occurred, rather, when he was moved by the beauty of a passage in music or literature or touched with pity for another person's plight. The feeling, intuitive side of Wagner is much more appealing than other aspects of his personality, such as his florid anti-Semitism (abundantly evidenced in Cosima's diaries).

More frequent than his weeping, however, was Wagner's laughter. Although some of the laughing recorded in the diary is relatively brief, most of it is not: prolonged, hearty, and completely involving fits of laughter. There are more than *three hundred* entries. It is relevant to my argument that most of the entries occur in the first half of the diary, which is the time in which Wagner was still creating music. During the last seven years, there are far fewer entries for both laughter and crying. During this latter period, Wagner's creative work had virtually ended; he was organizing and editing his earlier work.

The possibility that the genius's unique vision leads to a life of persecution casts a new light on the often-discussed connection between genius and madness. In terms of the discussion here, it would seem that it is genius which leads to madness, rather than the other way around: the genius may be tormented until driven to madness or suicide. The case of the mathematician George Cantor, who invented set theory, is instructive. His mathematics was so innovative that it revolutionized the field, but not until long after his death. During his life, he was persecuted for his efforts. His opponents were led by the mathematician holding the most powerful position in Germany, Kronecker, a professor at the University of Berlin. They saw to it that his papers were not published in professional journals and that he received no job offers or even advancement at the small rural university, Halle, where he taught. The cases of Boltzmann and Galois, already mentioned, were also tragic. Boltzmann committed suicide; Galois died in a duel at the age of twenty. During his lifetime, he was rejected by all his examiners (he was never admitted to college) and by most of his teachers.

Although it is difficult to test the laughing-genius hypothesis with written biographies, it might be possible in interviews with living artists and scientists. I think that the laughing hypothesis probably is much more relevant to a certain type of creator, which I have termed the "easy" creator. These creators work very rapidly and with little revision. Goethe wrote *Werther* in 24 days; Nietzsche, as already mentioned, wrote *Zarathustra* in 30 days. I suspect that creativity is extraordinarily rapid with this type because there is freedom from self-censure and therefore access to the aboriginal self. Schubert and Mozart were certainly composers of this type, and also the mathematician John von Neumann (the person most responsible for the invention of the computer). By investigating the nature of the emotional lives of these creators, and particularly the amount and quality of their laughter, it might be possible to clarify some of the issues that have been discussed here.

Conclusion

This chapter has outlined a rudimentary theory of genius. Creative intelligence may arise out of two interrelated processes, the development of extraordinary talent and the growth of extremely high levels of self-esteem. Extraordinary talent, whether or not it also involves genetic inheritance of talent, also requires a system of highly effective instruction. The model for this system of instruction may be the kind of language instruction children receive for the first five or six years. The formulation of this model raises what may be an important question for investigation: In what ways is early language instruction different from all other types of instruction, and do these differences account for the creativity that occurs in the correct use of natural language?

The second process in the growth of creative intelligence may be the development of high levels of self-esteem. I argue that self-esteem is essentially freedom from chronic shame. This type of shame is usually unacknowledged. It is virtually invisible because it appears in multiform guises. The basic mechanism of chronic shame, it is argued, is the feeling trap, which may convert emotions, normally brief, into lifelong states. Finally it is suggested that chronic shame is most effectively dispelled by good-humored laughter. If this is the case, we should expect to find the genius, especially the easily creative genius, to be a laugher.

One final question: Is there any reason to believe that one or the other of these two processes, the one involving talent, the other, self-esteem, is in any way more important than the other in the appearance of genius? No doubt they are equally important in the lives of most geniuses. However, it seems possible, for theoretical reasons, that the development of self-esteem may be more important. It is possible that the early growth of high levels of self-esteem may allow the potential genius to find the effective instruction needed to develop extraordinary talent. This is one way of interpreting the three deviant cases—Tchaikovsky, Verdi, and Wagner—who do not appear to have had early access to a musically talented teacher. This possibility, like the others suggested here, awaits future research for clarification.

In the concluding chapter of this book, some of the basic themes will be reviewed, leading to a summary of my conclusions.

Part 5

Conclusion

10

The Microfoundations of Social Structure

> Those who have handled sciences have been either men of experiment or
> men of dogmas. The men of experiment are like the ant; they only collect
> and use; the reasoners resemble spiders, who make cobwebs out of their own
> substance. But the bee takes a middle course; it gathers its material from the
> flowers of the garden and of the field, but transforms and digests it by a
> power of its own. . . . Therefore from a closer and purer league between
> these two faculties, the experimental and the rational (such as has never yet
> been made), much may be hoped.
> —Francis Bacon, *Novum Organum*

The thread that connects the preceding chapters is the concept of the social
bond, and its accompanying emotions of pride and shame.[1] I have proposed
that the human behavior is determined in large part by activities relevant to the
bond, but at the same time the importance of the bond is carefully hidden or
denied. To become aware of the role of bond-related actions, it is necessary to
explore certain crucial themes: the ambiguity of human expressions, abduction, and the role of emotion in human conduct.

I have argued that traditional societies were underdifferentiated: the balance
between the individual and the group favors the group. In such societies, the
group is everything; the individual is *engulfed*. In modern societies, the balance is usually upset in the opposite way: the individual is everything, the
group nothing; the individual is *isolated*. In modern societies, there is a continuing attempt to erase the last vestiges of the importance of the social bond.
At the cognitive level, this attempt can be seen in the ideology of individualism and simplicity; at the level of emotions, in the collective denial of the
emotions that signal the state of the bond, pride and shame.

One tradition in the human sciences, centered on the work of Cooley,
Goffman, and Lewis, has been used here to point to the direction needed to
understand human conduct in modern societies. Goffman's specialty was describing the devious ways in which interaction ritual maintains what bonds
there are and at the same time hides its own trail. His emphasis on deference
and demeanor, respect and disrespect, character contests and embarrassment,
point to the motive that is usually hidden and disavowed.

Of particular importance for my approach is the motive that Goffman's implies for modern societies—impression management and "face." Although
Goffman did not develop this analysis at the societal level, it may have considerable relevance there, as well as in the interpersonal interaction he surveyed.

---

1. My analysis of bases of domination in this chapter is indebted to discussions with Suzanne M.
Retzinger.

It implies that collectivities in modern societies may become more interested in outer appearances than in the underlying reality. The Italians say *fare una bella figura* ("By all means, cut a good figure, no matter the cost"), which I call the *"bella figura"* syndrome.

As indicated in chapter 5, the French were so preoccupied with outer appearances of honor, glory, and revenge, before helping to instigate World War I, they seemed to have forgotten to prepare for the war. Their use of the bulk of their troops to occupy Alsace-Lorraine rather than resist the German thrust toward Paris is a particularly striking example of the *bella figura* mentality. Another example may be the extraordinary popularity of Reagan during his incumbency in the White House; he was a master of *bella figura*. If carried to extremes, as seems to be happening in our era, *bella figura* is suicidal: never mind survival; we just want to look good. It should be pointed out that the preoccupation with outer appearances implies a shame dynamic; one is seeing one's self in the eyes of others rather than attending to business. At least at the interpersonal level, Goffman implied that this motivation dominated modern societies.

Although Cooley's approach was much less detailed than Goffman's, it conveys, in its offhand, abstract way, the completeness of a vision uncluttered by distracting detail. Cooley saw clearly both components of the bond construct: the central importance of the bond, in his emphasis on the primary group and the looking-glass self, and, equally important, the crucial relevance of pride and shame, both of which he called by their right names.

Lewis, like Cooley, saw the significance of the social bond, particularly in her book on gender (Lewis 1976). She went much further than either Cooley or Goffman in specifying the exact details of shame as a signal of the state of the bond. As I have indicated, her work has served as the foundation for my approach—the analysis of social solidarity in actual discourse.

She went far beyond the other theorists of the social bond in demonstrating the usefulness of her theory in application to actual social transactions. She found that shame is virtually ubiquitous in psychotherapy sessions and that it is seldom noticed, much less acknowledged and discharged. This last finding emphasizes the prevalence of disguise, denial, deception, and self-deception in social encounter, particularly with respect to emotions.

Deception and self-deception with respect to feelings are issues seldom raised in current human sciences. Quantitative studies usually exclude feelings entirely. Qualitative studies seem to assume that self-deception is not a researchable issue: one's goal is to determine only the subject's point of view. With a few exceptions (e.g., Goleman 1985), self-deception has been little studied or discussed. The issue of self-deception is one of the themes of the earlier chapters.

A second theme has concerned abduction, the process which humans seem to use unself-consciously when attempting to understand and solve problems. Abduction solves the enigma of context, how it is possible to relate the specific to the general, the part to the whole. According to my thesis, most human action is deeply contextualized, not understandable without a thorough knowledge of context. It is for this reason that I have urged the study of discourse as a complement to studies of aggregate data. Detailed, micromomentary study of discourse, I argue, affords a method of bringing together the seeming opposites that fragment and confuse understanding, theory and research, inner and outer, thought and feeling.

The use of abduction allows one to investigate the degree of disclosure and knowledge of self and other in discourse. Assessment of self-knowledge and self-deception requires analysis of discourse in context. In this book I have used two kinds of contextual information to interpret meaning. One type was analysis of the thick description of the extended lives of the characters in novels and biographies: biographical details that allow the understanding of meaning in context. The second kind of context used was the analysis of the *microworld* of word and gestures available in mechanically recorded discourse. Both types provide the dense cloud of information that allows one to enter the lifeworld of the characters, what I have called an open domain. This cloud seems to be needed to describe the interplay between deception and self-deception, ambivalence and ambiguity, that characterizes the human condition.

In the first section of this chapter, I return to dialogues discussed earlier, this time with a focus on issues of deception and self-deception. I show the application of my approach to one problem: the microroots of domination. I argue that domination in modern societies is usually a joint action involving unwitting collaboration between the dominated and the dominant. Although at first sight this point of view may seem unsympathetic to the plight of the dominated, paradoxically, it can point the way to their empowerment. Through discourse analysis, fundamental issues involving levels of disclosure, self-awareness, and self-deception can be investigated.

Applying the method of abduction to discourse allows one to make explicit the relationship between parts and wholes. In the second section of this chapter, I use a literary analysis of poetic closure to illustrate some of the ramifications of this idea. Finally, I return to the central idea, the micro-macro link, suggesting a format for intensive-extensive research designs. As an example, I discuss a design for a study of suicide that might further develop Durkheim's approach.

Consensus and Acknowledgment of Conflict

In order to understand modern societies, one may need to conduct detailed studies of discourse because only such studies will show intricate mixtures of understanding and misunderstanding, self-knowledge and self-deception. To do such studies, one may also need to improve on current models of consensus.

The reigning paradigm of consensus in contemporary social science involves simple agreement, as exemplified in Parsons's theoretical work and in many empirical studies of "conflict and consensus." The agreement model, because it is so simplified, obscures the problem of solidarity, of the binding force that connects people in a well-ordered society. It equally obscures the problem of alienation in modern societies, of the forces that divide and disrupt. Agreement/disagreement is only one facet of complex, multilayered structures of consensus-dissensus. Seeming agreement on the surface, masking fundamental disagreement, is a potent source of insecure bonds, bonds not only in personal relationships but also more generally in whole societies.

It may not be possible to understand current American electoral politics without recourse to studies of discourse, since these could provide models of the complex link between deceptions practiced by governments, on the one hand, and self-deceptions practiced by voters, on the other. Social science is well equipped to show the deceptive practices of governments since they occur in the outer world. But existing social science cannot even detect, much less demonstrate, self-deception. It is even further distant from showing how deception and self-deception form a self-sustaining system of voting publics who want to be deceived, in symbiosis with governments all too happy to give them what they want. If we are to understand the crisis of consciousness in our civilization, we may need to begin with the study of discourse.

Some of the findings of the experiments on conformity in social psychology can be used to illustrate my point about self-deception further. Asch, Sherif, Milgram, Zimbardo, and literally hundreds of others have documented the link between conformity and self-deception: the majority of subjects act as accomplices in unreal or unjust scenes by deceiving themselves about the meaning of their actions. Yet none of the original experimenters nor any of the reviewers of the studies have made this point explicit. The concept of self-deception falls outside the net of current paradigms.

In an earlier work (Scheff 1967), I pointed to a further dimension of consensus, the extent of awareness of agreement or disagreement by the participants, their awareness of that awareness, and so on. Giddens (1987, 67) evokes this dimension in his discussion of "mutual knowledge." This one dimension quickly produces complex structures, some involving simultaneous understanding and misunderstanding.

In chapters 2–5, I introduced two further dimensions. First, distinguishing between cognitive and emotional consensus introduces a crucial issue. Emotional attunement may be a powerful binding force leading to solidarity, even in the absence of agreement at the cognitive level. Similarly, alienation from feelings may produce discord, even in the presence of cognitive agreement. These two propositions are implied in my approach to the social bond. Since they may turn out to be fundamental for understanding social structure, I will elaborate them further.

In his seminal work on family systems, Bowen (1978) has suggested an idea that may prove fruitful for analyzing the two types of consensus. He proposes that *level of differentiation* is the key to understanding family systems.

In a differentiated family, loyalty is not measured by agreement. For example, when a son tells his father that in good conscience, he has voted for a different candidate from the father's, the father might say, "Naturally I'm disappointed I wasn't able to convince you, but I am also gratified to see that you are your own person, that you are able to think for yourself." In an undifferentiated family, disagreement is taken to be a sign of disloyalty or betrayal. Bowen's analysis of level of differentiation implies that emotional consensus, the sharing of emotions, may signal a secure bond, even in the absence of agreement, and that lack of emotional consensus may signify an insecure bond, even where agreement prevails. Distinguishing between the two types of consensus further complicates the structure of consensus-dissensus.

Finally, the distinction between the immediate meanings in messages and their long-range implications, as in motives, intentions, and character, was introduced in chapter 3. Even if the participants in a dialogue were attuned both emotionally and cognitively, the nature of the social bond involves more than just momentary attunement. A secure bond probably involves a history of disclosure and knowledge of self and other. Under these circumstances, mutual trust arises. Intricate mixtures of trust and distrust characterize insecure bonds.

The idea of false consciousness provides an example of the possible usefulness of a complex model. This idea implies a many-layered structure of consciousness involving both deception and self-deception, understanding and misunderstanding, reality and illusion. As suggested in chapter 7, Marx's use of this concept was casual; he merely meant that coercion by the ruling class was not sufficient to explain domination. Because of false consciousness, ruled groups contribute to their own domination. Marx had no way of using this insight to analyze the details that make up historical events. Nor do current theory and method provide a framework: the conceptual and methodological equipment is not available. By calling upon studies of discourse, however, one may suggest such a framework. To make precise interpretations of events in the microworld, one needs to call upon the extended context, that is, not just the biographical details of the participants in the discourse but also the larger institutional framework in which the discourse and the relationship take place. As the concept of the hologram suggests, we understand the smallest cell in the system by understanding the system as a whole, and vice-versa.

Relationships and Social Structure

I now return to some of the discourse that was discussed in earlier chapters to highlight issues of self-knowledge and self-deception. In chapter 6, I emphasized the *initial exchange* between the patient (P) and the therapist (T). Here, because I focus on domination and self-knowledge, I refer to the entire interview. As indicated in the earlier discussion, the major conflict between P and T concerns her emotionality: both the form and content of her discourse concern emotions. She wants to talk about her emotions, and her manner is emotional. In contrast, T seldom talks about emotions or responds to hers, and his manner is unemotional and detached.

This difference continues throughout the interview. In the fifty-minute session, P refers to emotions seventy-seven times, more than once a minute. Many times she refers to her own emotions, but she also refers to those of others, for example, her husband's and her children's. She uses the terms "emotion," "feeling," and "I feel" frequently. She also uses vernacular terms which signify emotion: "wound up," "bothered," "miserable," "in a constant stew," and so on. In contrast, T rarely uses an emotion word, only nine times. In all but one of these times, he is not initiating the use of an emotion word but only responding to her use of one.

The difference between T and P in the use of emotion words can be conveyed by examining the eighty-six *exchanges* (an utterance by one person, followed by the utterance of the other) in which there is at least one emotion word. Virtually all of these exchanges, eighty-five out of eighty-six, are initiated by P. The usual response of T is to ignore the reference by asking her a factual question. One such exchange occurs in P8–T9. In her eighth utterance, P has complained about her husband's insistence that she take care of the children and not work at her job, saying, among other things, that "he makes it so miserable for me that I'm in a constant stew." Rather than responding to the strong feelings she has expressed, however, T merely asks her, "How many kids are there?"

P dutifully answers this factual question with a fact, as well as two more such questions (T10 and T13), but then she returns to her agenda in P14, P16, P17, and P20—strong feelings that are generated by her marriage. Each of these turns, which Pittenger et al. refer to as "emotional outbursts," is duly parried by T with a factual question. And each of these parries is duly answered, factually, by P.

In a sense, this interview involves a series of impasses because the interactants have two different agendas. These agendas are never stated but can be inferred from the words and gestures. P wants to talk about her intense feelings, most of which result from her marriage. Apparently, T does not want her to talk about her feelings but appears to want to find out the facts of her life. Underlying his tactics appears to one of the typical strategies in the practice of psychotherapy, attempting to lead the patient toward taking responsibility rather than blaming outside circumstances, in this case the husband.

What never happens in this session is a question which might lead to the underlying agendas. For example, P: * "I notice that you always ignore how upset I am, and ask me about some fact. What is going on?" Or T might have said: * "I am trying to understand the facts of your situation. You answer my question, but then go back to some feeling you are having. Why is that?" Each person relentlessly follows his or her own agenda as if not noticing that the other person is on an entirely different course. Since neither person comments on, or asks questions about, the conflict, no negotiation about a joint agenda is possible.

The participants in this interview are not in attunement. They bounce off each other in a way that must have been frustrating for both. Indeed, a close reading of the words and gestures suggests that both parties are embarrassed and angered by the encounter: P might well feel continually cut off, even insulted, by T's tactics. In turn, T is perhaps feeling frustrated, defied, and inadequate because of P's tactics. The interview ends on a painful note: P is tearful, indecisive, not finished, but T cuts her off; her time is up.

Why does neither person say: * "Wait a minute. What is going on here?" The seeming inability of participants in discourse to comment on the discourse itself has been the topic of considerable discussion in the literature on family systems. Bateson and his co-workers (1951) suggested that there are levels of communication which need to be bridged. Watzlawick, Beavin, and Jackson (1967) developed a very general treatment of these ideas. Communication about communication they called "meta-communication." To comment on one's own discourse requires stepping outside it, an interruption of an ongoing process. Ordinarily people seem unwilling or unable to take such a step.

Although the Bateson's analysis is relevant to this discussion, it has less force than Watzlawick et al.'s. In the application of abstract ideas to real dialogue, the exact terminology seems to be crucial. Watzlawick et al. make a distinction between "content" and "relationship" levels in dialogue. Ordinarily people converse about content, that is, topics, and refrain from commenting on the relationship as it is occurring during the discourse. Because the idea of topic is more concrete than the idea of content, I modify Watzlawick et al.'s terminology and show how it may be applied to concrete episodes.

The dialogue between Gwendolen and Grandcourt illustrates this idea. The verbal discourse involves certain topics such as archery, hunting, and so on and implies a covert topic, marriage. But there is no reference to the relationship between the two as it unfolds: for example, do Grandcourt's fixed stare and slowness of response imply inadequate deference toward Gwendolen? If not, what do they imply? To be sure, the author reveals that Gwendolen notes his manner and worries, to a limited extent, about its implications for their relationship. But neither she nor Grandcourt openly comments on it. Since his manner is not discussed, Gwendolen does not allow herself to understand its implications for their future relationship.

Similarly, in the interview discussed above, neither T nor P talks about their relationship as it is occurring, but they battle over topics: P wants to talk about her feelings; T wants her to talk about her factual circumstances. The same thing happens between Werther and the Count in the Embassy incident. Their exchange concerns a topic, his unwanted presence at a gathering of aristocrats, but not the implications of this exchange for their relationship.

These microepisodes suggest a crucial sociological point: social structure is manifested and maintained in social interaction, but this manifestation is usually hidden from the participants. *To the extent that participants discuss top-ics, and suppress discussion of their relationship, social structure becomes invisible to them.* In the conflict between the Count's "friendship" for Werther and his allegiance to his own class, the Count chooses his class. But his choice is denied; neither he nor Werther acknowledges it to the other or to himself. They are both involved in a conspiracy, a conspiracy which involves self-deception as well as deception of the other.

In this way the microworld of actual relationships is disguised behind cour-tesy, which often amounts to deception and self-deception. People ordinarily avoid "making a scene" by commenting on relationships. That is, they avoid risking embarrassment. The status quo in the microworld seems to be based on the avoidance of the risk of embarrassment, a shame dynamic.

Domination as a Joint Accomplishment

Structures of domination, such as those based on class, age, race, or gender may involve elements of coercion, but they may be joint accomplishments of both superordinates and subordinates. In his study of presidential press confer-ences, Wallace (n.d.) has shown that President Reagan ruthlessly dominated the press corps. He seldom answered a question, using various techniques of evasion. For example, when a reporter asked about certain questionable prac-tices the president was thought to have used, instead of denying or affirming them he simply asked the reporter a question in return: "A nice guy like me?" The president got a laugh, but the reporter got no information. When the next reporter was called on, he did not say * "Mr. President, that was a very funny line, but I noticed that you did not answer the question. I yield the floor to my colleague until he gets an answer from you." Instead, he introduced a new question, which in turn was evaded. The reporters, like most other partici-pants in conflict, stick to topics, never commenting on their relationship to the president.

Is the docility of the reporters in the face of such gross arrogance a product of bribery or coercion? I think not. The more successful members of the rul-ing class unconsciously learn to control members of the ruled class, and the ruled, also unconsciously learn to accept that control. We learn in our families of origin that one should be mesmerized by topics of discourse, that it is im-polite and offensive to discuss the microworld of relationships. The tech-niques of control that Reagan used with the press corps are invisible not only to him and to them but also to the watching public. We have all been down so long that it feels like up.

In her work on marital conflict, Retzinger (1988) has shown that in the transcripts of those couples where there is male domination, the discourse is completely devoted to topics; there is not a single reference to the relation-ship. By arguing about a never-ending series of topics—money, sex, chil-dren, and so on—rather than their relationship, both the man and the woman accomplish male domination. It is important to note that in these episodes there is no element of coercion or threat of coercion, not even a hint. The dominated wives, like the presidential press corps, are imprisoned by the invisible microworld of discourse tactics.

In the psychiatric interview discussed in chapter 6, several structures of domination are visible—domination based on profession, class, age, and gender. The therapist is a professional (a psychiatrist), middle class, older than the client, and a male. The patient enters the interview in the role of layperson (she is also subordinate to the therapist in her professional role, since she is a nurse); she appears to be of working-class background, she is younger than the therapist, and she is a woman.

The voice of the therapist is the voice of authority. It is assured, fluent, and grammatically correct. Word selection and pronunciation announce ruling-class, rather than working-class, membership. There is virtually no hint of regional dialect or patois. The patient's voice announces the ruled class. It is not just that her stammering and fragmentation suggest lack of self-confidence, although that is evident. Her pronunciation, word selection, and grammar suggest region and class, that is, Boston working class. The occasional struggles in these areas also suggest one source of the embarrassment which pervades her utterances: at several points she seems to be seeing her own discourse from T's point of view, since she corrects some of her errors of pronunciation and phrasing. As James (1910) long ago insisted, evaluating one's self negatively from another's point of view causes painful feeling, in this case embarrassment (shame).

More even than the subtle markers of class, the content of the conflict between the two suggests gender and age structures of domination. The patient wants to talk about, and even to express, emotions. Like a prototypical adult responding to a child, and a prototypical man responding to a woman, the therapist wants her to be less emotional and to talk less about emotions. Although the therapist no doubt has a professional justification for his tactics, they nevertheless also maintain the status quo of the adult, male middle class: domination of the microworld of relationships through the repression of emotion.

Perhaps this case can serve as a prototypic example of the core process which maintains the status quo—*repression of emotion*. The bare conflict between expressing and repressing emotions is quite near the surface in this particular dialogue but is more hidden in the others I have discussed. In every case, however, avoiding commenting on the relationship can be seen as driven by repression: by sticking to topics, the participants are denying the feelings aroused by inadequate deference, but they are not noticing, or avoid commenting on the relationship.

Avoiding comment on the relationship seems to be the basic means of maintaining the status quo. It does not matter whether the conflict is overt, as in an interminable quarrel, or covert, as in silent impasses. Interminable quarrels are quarrels about topics rather than about relationships. Impasses avoid forbidden topics altogether. But in neither case is the relationship itself commented upon. Both quarrels and impasses force the participants outside history. Domination can hardly be ended if its manifestations receive no notice or comment.

Concepts at the level of the macrostructure of domination, such as capitalism or patriarchy, are certainly necessary for grasping the idea of social structure, but they are insufficient by themselves. The discussion here suggests two further requirements. Concepts at the level of microstructure are equally necessary. Each level by itself is necessary but not sufficient for understanding. As I suggest below, there is also a third component necessary for understanding—performance or practice. Perhaps these three components together may be necessary *and* sufficient for understanding and change.

The second point is a more subtle one. To the extent that macroconcepts like capitalism and patriarchy are reified, that is, to the extent that they are not related, point for point, to the microworld, they serve to mystify rather than empower. Suppose that P understands that her inability to get help or even ordinary respect from T is a manifestation of macrostructures of domination based on expertise, age, class, and gender. Such knowledge might be of some help to her; depending on her turn of mind, it might comfort her to know that she is not alone.

However, it is extremely unlikely that abstract understanding of macrostructure, no matter how complete, would help her to get what she wants. On the contrary, it might impede her. How can a single individual, or, for that matter, a large group of her fellow sufferers, take on the vast structures of professional and age dominance, capitalism, and patriarchy? Reified analysis without organic connection to the *lifeworld* has had uncertain and only sporadic influence in the struggles of the ruled groups, the working class, students, women, and the consumers of professional service.

Knowledge of discourse tactics in the microworld, by contrast, may have immediate practical effects. For example, P could have said, * "Look, I'm not sure what you are after. Maybe it would help me cooperate if you would explain your goals, and I could explain mine." A crash course in discourse tactics for consumers might help ease the increasing impasse in the use of professional services. I am thinking here not just of psychiatry, but more broadly of physicians, lawyers, and so on. A similar argument could be made about relationships between students and teachers, men and women, workers and bosses.

Such a movement would surely encounter resistance from ruling groups, but it might also find support. For example, in psychiatry, Lazare (1979) has developed a system for teaching psychotherapists to empower patients, "consumer-oriented psychotherapy," a system which complements the analysis of discourse tactics presented here. He teaches that the first move for the therapist is to elicit the patient's request, to find out what kind of service the patient wants. The next step is to negotiate with the patient in order to reach a decision about the course of therapy.

The therapist may suggest alternative services that the patient has not mentioned. In a typical session, the therapist may elicit a patient request for medication, often a tranquilizer. After telling the patient the limitations and possible side effects of such medication, the therapist might mention other directions, such as psychotherapy. It is relevant to this discussion that frequently resistance to empowerment comes from the patient's side: "You want me to tell you what I want? You're the doctor, that's why I came here. I want you to tell me what's best" (Lazare 1985). In the kind of analysis done in family systems (Bowen 1978), the patient's response is called a "changeback" message. That is, attempts to change may be perceived as threatening, even change that would be beneficial.

This example raises an important question. Perhaps reform which comes only from one side might be very slow. The most effective mode of change would involve cooperation between ruled and rulers. If men changed overnight, seeking to empower women in the microworld of discourse so that negotiation about the sharing of power could occur, there might be resistance comparable to that described by Lazare. Capitalism and patriarchy are complex, overdetermined systems. For all their faults, they bring a measure of security and order. Perhaps effective change requires that every step be negotiated.

I am not saying, of course, that one side must wait for the other before changing. On the contrary, change must begin somewhere, even if only in a single relationship. But it will be speeded up if it is negotiated. Perhaps the most rapid rate of change occurs when tactics are used which bring immediate relief to both sides. This idea leads to my next topic: the importance of practice for both everyday and theoretical mastery.

The Part/Whole Ladder

So far I have argued that both micro- and macroanalysis is necessary for understanding human affairs. There is one more component that must be stressed to complete the picture: practice. Analysis and interpretation are part of human intelligence, but they are incomplete without the trial of performance, of practice in the complex world of everyday life.

To illustrate this idea, I need to return to one of the basic themes of the early chapters, the management of ambiguity through abduction. The distinction between topic and relationship is useful for understanding discourse tactics, but it is only a part of a larger system. As suggested in chapter 3, intelligence at its most effective involves part/whole relationships. In an open system, any part implies a larger whole, which is in turn part of a still larger whole, and so on, up the ladder. Applied to discourse, this idea suggests a movement back and forth between small concrete parts and ever-larger abstract wholes.

Concrete Level
   1. Single words and gestures
   2. Sentences
   3. Exchanges
   4. Conversations
   5. Relationship of the two parties (all their conversations)
   6. Life histories of the two parties

Societal Level
   7. All relationships of the same type: therapist-patient, man-woman, and so on
   8. The structure of the host society: all relationships
   9. The history and future of the host civilization (the world system)
   10. The history and destiny of the human species

Practical intelligence in the lifeworld appears to involve abduction, that is, the rapid, effortless shuttling up and down this ladder. The system can be visualized as Chinese boxes, each box containing a smaller one and nesting within a larger one. Indeed the concept of *nested contexts* is crucial for understanding discourse.

The distinction between topic and relationship hints at this larger system: the topic is at level 2, since it involves sentences; the relationship, at level 5. However, all levels are implied in the actual understanding and practice of discourse. The process is awkward to describe in explicit language, but it takes place constantly, effortlessly, and instantaneously in discourse.

Contemporary scholars and scientists seem to have difficulty visualizing part/whole relationships. In the current division of labor, the organic connection between part and whole is lost in the division of intellectual labor: theorists deal with wholes but not parts; researchers deal with parts but not wholes. The contributors to an interdisciplinary colloquium on parts and wholes (Lerner 1963) seemed to have difficulty in even approaching the topic. Only two of the papers convey some sense of the relationship: Roman Jakobson's (on natural language as an organic system), and I. A. Richards's (on poems as organic wholes).

Even Jakobson and Richards fail to give a minimal sketch, however. They locate the system in the verbal parts rather than in the social-cultural whole. Richards discusses only the integrity of the poem, rather than its relationship to social and psychological processes in author and audience. Like the subjects in the dialogues in this book, he sticks to topics rather than relationships. This same difficulty continues to haunt current discussion. The structuralists have discovered the ambiguity of expressions: they show that various expressions are "undecidable" and that translations may be "indeterminate." As already indicated here, when the social context is shorn away, as it is in most structuralist interpretation, all expressions become ambiguous. But in context, interpretive deciphering can result in consensual understanding.

As indicated earlier, a clear evocation of the contextuality of understanding can be found in Levine's examination of sociological theory (1985). By showing the contradictions which result from the attempt to eliminate ambiguity from expressions, he makes a case for the role of intuition in understanding the relationship between parts and wholes.

Goffman's technique of "frame analysis" (1974) also can be used to expand on part/whole process. His "frames" can be seen as contexts in the nested-context structure of thought. Goffman, however, limits himself to the analysis of the *social* aspects of framing, missing the opportunity to connect the social and the psychological. His analysis of "frame breaking" nevertheless suggests an important issue. The framing structure itself, the particular set of Chinese boxes that is tacitly assumed in a group, however limited, takes on a sacred character. Under these conditions, frame breaking, the use of a different part/whole structure, may be taken as an affront.

The theorist who came closest to the core of the part/whole approach is C. Wright Mills, with his idea of the *sociological imagination* (1959). At first glance at his book, one might think that Mills did not advocate the kind of analysis of systems and subsystems proposed here, one involving equity between the microworlds and macroworlds. Mills certainly has no such reputation. He is seen rather as an analyst of the macroworld, like most sociologists.

A closer look, however, suggests a strong affinity between his view of the sociological imagination and the perspective advocated here. Mills suggested that the link between personal troubles and public issues, the intersection between biography and history, should be the core of the sociological imagination (pp. 11–20). He defined that imagination as

> the capacity to shift from one perspective to another—from the political to the *psychological;* from examination of a single family to comparative assessment of the national budgets of the world; from the theological school to the military establishment; from considerations of an oil industry to studies of contemporary poetry. It is the capacity to range from the most impersonal and remote transformations to the *most intimate features of the human self*—and to see the relations between the two.
>
> (emphasis added, p. 7)

His reference to the psychological perspective in the first phrase seems not to have been merely pro forma. In the next to last phrase, he proposes the importance of "the most intimate features of the human self." Mills enthusiastically subscribed to the potential of psychoanalysis (pp. 159–60) for understanding these intimate features.

In his last chapter, on Intellectual Craftmanship, Mills advocates that all social scientists should keep a *file,* an intimate daily journal in which the researcher constantly searches back and forth between her own personal life and her professional work. Never stated explicitly, the implication is strong in this chapter that in order to understand the macroworld, one must struggle to understand one's own microworld. For example, to analyze the complex mixture of attunement, engulfment, and isolation in social bonds, the researcher would probably need some awareness of that mixture in her own bonds. Although Mills did not himself conduct the kinds of micro-macro studies suggested here, he seems to have visualized their potential.

To illustrate these abstract ideas, I call upon a part/whole analysis implied in a study of poetic form. Flexing part/whole muscles in her introductory comment, Smith (1968, vii) outlines a structure of nested contexts (level numbers added):

> This study is concerned with how poems end. It grew out of an earlier one that was concerned [1] with how Shakespeare's sonnets both go and end; and although the child has consumed the parent, it testifies to its lineage throughout these pages, where sonnets, Shakespearean and other, will be rather frequently encountered. In my earlier attempts to describe and to some extent account for the strengths and weaknesses of Shakespeare's sonnet endings, I found myself involved at almost every point with more general considerations of poetic structure and with what I finally recognized as a subject in its own right, [2] poetic closure. I also found that, although literary theorists from Aristotle on have been occupied with beginnings, middles, *and* ends, there had not been (aside from a brief and somewhat whimsical essay by I. A. Richards) any treatment of this subject as such. The questions and problems that pushed outward from sonnet endings to lyric closure in general continued to move out toward even broader considerations of closure in all [3] literature, in all [4] art, and finally in all [5] experience. Having bumped into a continent, however, and even having set a flag upon the shore, I realized that I was equipped to explore and chart only a bit of the coastal area. It seemed wise, then, to hold the line at poetic closure.

Smith locates her work within a larger structure. A *part/whole ladder* with five levels is implied: closure (1) in Shakespeare's sonnets, (2) in poetry, (3) in literature, (4) in art, and (5) in experience. She puts her particular study at level 2, poetry, in a structure of nested contexts: it is broader than just Shakespeares sonnets (level 1) but not as broad as literature (level 3). She does, however, make a number of significant comments about levels 4 and 5. I will use one of these comments to show the strength and limitation of her analysis.

The use of nested contexts, Chinese boxes, one within the other, involves *recursion,* as Hofstadter (1980) suggests. This kind of part/whole structure may be a way of giving concrete meaning to the abstract concept of reflexiveness, the kind of self-referencing which gives rise to self-awareness. A discussion like Smith's is reflexive to the extent that it locates its own argument within a part/whole structure, a total rather than a special frame of reference.

Smith seems to take an important step in this direction on the very last page. Her main argument has established that traditional poetry depends on a large variety of techniques for closure to establish that the poem is ending. These techniques are mostly conventions of rhyme and syntax. She notes that most modern poetry involves not only closural devices but also suggestion of rebellion against these devices. That is, many modern poets seem to want their poems to appear open-ended or continuing rather than closing with a snap. She locates this tendency in poetry and also in literature and art, particularly in painting and music (e.g., John Cage's serial or random music), as a rebellion not only against closure, but against all structure. In this way, she relates her description of the conflict between poetic closure and anticlosure to a larger context—the conflict between structure and antistructure within art as a whole.

Her analysis ends with a very brief reference to a still larger whole. In trying to make sense of the conflict over structure in art, she argues that the traditional structures of poetry, which press toward closure, have a hidden ally which gives them their staying power (271):

> . . . poetry is not without a sustaining vitality continuously fed and renewed by its relation to the rather formidable institution of language itself—and that as long as we continue to speak at all, no matter what new uses are made of language, there will remain revelations and delights to be found in the old uses. Poetry ends in many ways, but poetry, I think, has not yet ended.

Her comment implies conflict between social institutions. In seeking freedom for new forms within the social institution of art, poets pit themselves against another institution, "the rather formidable institution of language itself." The implication is that poetry will always press toward closure because it is based on language itself, and language, that is, the natural language that is used in everyday life, will always press toward closure. (It should be noted that discussion of linguistic closure could be grounded in the studies of turn taking discussed in chap. 6.) Her comment suggests the value of an additional part/whole level, higher than art (4) but before the leap to all experience (5), the level of social institutions.

Studies like those of Smith might be used to give concrete meaning to the abstract concept of *reflexivity*. Her study is reflexive in the sense that she carefully located her particular study within a broad and deep structure of nested contexts. She could have easily avoided that responsibility. Her study would have met the expectations in her genre had she made only passing reference to levels 3 and 4, and no reference at all to the level of institutions, and to level 5. Such a restricted study would probably give the alert reader a feeling of claustrophobia, as do most conventional scholarly and scientific studies. Overspecialization means the failure to establish responsible structures of nested contexts, of not exploring the relevant part/whole ladder.

Perhaps it was tactful of Smith not to get involved in what Goffman would call frame breaking. Had she said much more about the conflict between the institutions of art and language, most of the members of her audience, quite content with the conventions of the genre, might have been puzzled. She would have found herself in a "no-person's land" between two genres—literary interpretation and sociology. Perhaps the line between intellectual creativity and responsibility, on the one hand, and deviance, on the other, is vanishingly thin.

This discussion suggests an exact definition of reflexivity; the traversing of complete part/whole structures. To the extent that thought and creative effort travel the entire part/whole ladder, they are freed of their purely local dependence and become optimally useful and stimulating. However, as already indicated, they also run the risk of antagonizing the conventional structures of context and in this way becoming puzzling and opaque.

To understand the significance of an expression in context, the researcher, like the participants, needs to refer it to other levels. To understand the meaning of the words and manner of her lover's farewell, a woman might not only observe the exact words and gestures (level 1) but also compare them with how other lovers might have responded, a counterfactual (level 7). The interpretive decipherment of natural language, to use Steiner's phrase, requires part/whole thinking.

Does an understanding of the micro- and macroworlds of discourse contain the seeds of liberation? Only under the condition that performance is added to interpretation. Analysis is only theoretical; it does not ensure the kind of fluency needed to escape from structures of domination. Suzanne Retzinger has suggested a musical metaphor. One may be a great musical theorist, but to play Mozart, one must practice at the keyboard. Effective tactics for change in a classist, patriarchic society require understanding and practice at every level. Electing a president with vision or reforming the divorce law are small parts of a vast functioning system. These changes need to be augmented with changes at other levels, especially at the microlevel.

Because they have been neglected, understanding and practice involving the microworld of discourse tactics may be strategic in our era. If workers, women, students, and other members of dominated classes could learn new tactics, the conditions for wholesale change in the larger systems might be prepared for. One great incentive is that these tactics, if sufficiently understood and skillfully practiced, often give immediate practical returns: one's relationship with family members, boss, or subordinates improves. In interminable quarrels and impasses, improvement benefits both sides: teachers as well as students, bosses as well as workers, men as well as women. To be sure, change involves losses on both sides, but if these can be negotiated, they may not be as threatening as they seem when discussed in the abstract.

These ideas apply to researchers as well as to members of the society. In our research, we need to understand the part/whole abduction that our subjects use, practice it ourselves in conducting research, and acknowledge it openly in reporting our findings. Perhaps in this way we can escape from the prison of formal rationality, with its attendant overspecialization. If so, our work might have more immediate relevance to the struggle of our civilization to survive.

It is easy for us to recognize in nationalism a kind of runaway specialization. The citizens of each country are overspecialized; they are concerned mostly with their own country, less with the larger issues that threaten the globe. The war between Iran and Iraq did not arouse our interest the way war between California and Arizona would. Anarchy between states is not tolerated, but anarchy between nations is. The ruling majority of every nation is under an emotional spell, nationalism, which precludes understanding.

In the academy, disciplines and subdisciplines have become strongholds of a similar kind of overspecialization. Knowledge has been divided up among nations, tribes, and clans, that is, disciplines, subdisciplines, and "schools," each ignoring or at war with the other. By basing its work on premises and methods acceptable only to its own tribe or clan, each group is contributing to the onset of stasis. (Fallows (1989) terms this system "Confucianism.") As the history of science has shown repeatedly, it is the very premises that are being taken for granted in each group that need to be overthrown before advances in knowledge can occur. What can be done about this kind of nationalism?

The approach to research advocated in this book suggests a move away from overspecialization. By using and acknowledging abduction, and by making it a focus of research, the researcher is acting as a generalist, as well as a specialist, as suggested in Chapter 8. That is, human beings are capable of integrating all points of view, as well as specializing in just one, and they are at their best when they are doing so. Otherwise, one gives up too large a part of one's self, the part that is most emotional and most brilliant.

Intensive-Extensive Research Designs

My final topic concerns research designs of the future. In order to *test* a theory, the more general (and therefore abstract) the data, the better. But in order to *construct* a theory, the more concrete (and therefore particular) the data, the better. Concrete episodes of behavior, since they involve sequences, necessarily contain clues to causal sequences, and empirical markers for abstract concepts, both of which must be absent from aggregate data. Most of the sequential events and empirical markers have been sheared away by the act of aggregation. Analysis of concrete episodes can help to build theoretical models by specifying causal sequences and by specifying empirical markers for concepts.

The Micro-Macro Study of Suicide

How could study of concrete episodes contribute to the construction of a general theory of suicide? We know from the Durkheimian studies of suicide that the rate of suicide among Catholics is consistently lower than among Protestants. We also know, however, that the difference is not great. Suicides occur among Catholics; each of these events may point to a causal process omitted from Durkheim's theory. Perhaps the study of deviant cases, like Catholic suicides, could lead to theoretical models of the causal process broader and more precise than Durkheim's.

Attempts have been made to locate patterns of causation through the analysis of individual case histories, as in Kobler and Stotland (1964). In this study, the authors provided a detailed review of four cases of suicide and one near suicide, about forty pages for each case. On the basis of this review, they formulate a "hopelessness-helplessness" model: (1) An individual comes to feel that his future is devoid of hope, (2) he or someone else brings the alternative of suicide into his field, (3) he attempts to gain reassurance from other(s), and (4) for suicide to occur, the response of other(s) must be characterized by hopelessness and helplessness, usually communicated through an implicit or explicit expectation that the troubled person will kill himself. (I have restated their narrative formulation [252] as four propositions, but left the gendered language.)

This model involves two *internal states,* (1) hopelessness and (2) perception of suicide as a possible recourse, and two *behavioral events,* (3) the attempt to gain reassurance and (4) the hopeless/helpless response of the other. Note that this model does not draw on any general theory, and its terms are closely tied to suicide itself. One of the components (2) is so closely related to suicide that it is tautological.

Even limited as this theory is, one immediately notes several problems if one wished to test it. The most important is the absence of empirical markers. How can it be determined, for example, whether an individual feels that "his future is devoid of hope" or, in proposition 4, whether the expectation of suicide was communicated *implicitly* or *explicitly?* Another problem with the authors' formulation is that the full causal sequence is not specified. What is offered instead is four events in a sequence, without indicating how these events are linked.

The absence of a full causal sequence and of empirical markers may both result from the manner in which the authors treat their cases. Although they provide considerable information about each case, it is spread over a very large amount of time, that is, the subject's entire life. Perhaps more intensive study of verbatim discourse would have provided more information about causal sequences and empirical markers. Both Shneidman (1980) and Atkinson (1978) have taken steps in this direction. Both studies, however, lack ties to general theory. Like the Kobler and Stotland study, they are concrete and micro, in contrast to Durkheim's study, which was abstract and macro. How could one investigate suicide in a way that would retain the micro-macro link?

In chapter 7, I used an episode of fictional discourse to model the causal links between humiliation and suicide. If a person is (1) deeply humiliated,

(2) does not acknowledge the humiliation, and (3) has no one to whom to turn in her adversity (no secure social bond), then suicide (or some other desperate act) is likely to result. This formulation is a zeroth approximation of a theory of suicide, a beginning. In his edited volume on suicide, Gaylin (1968) reported a study of his on gender and suicide which seems to support the conjecture that humiliation may play a key role in suicide. Sacks's (1966) study of phone calls to a suicide prevention center also hints at the role of shame and the absence of social bonds.

Two further steps would be necessary for a complete micro-macro study. Step 2 would be an additional microstudy, but this time of actual, rather than fictional, cases. Although only a few cases would be needed, they should be from the population that is to be studied in Step 3, a large-scale test of the theory. One would need verbatim records, as in the Shneidman (1980) study, or better yet, verbatim accounts of discourse. Such accounts might be gathered from family members in the case of successful suicide and from the suicidal person in the case of failed attempts. Step 2 presumably would generate a precise causal model to be tested and the empirical markers that would make it possible to test the theory in a population. Step 3 would be an extensive study, using a large number of cases to assess the extent to which the theory is true or false.

The theory implied in the analysis of *Werther* claims to be quite general since it assumes unacknowledged shame-rage sequences to be a basic part of human attachment systems. That is, these sequences are expected to be an inevitable pancultural aspect of social solidarity and alienation. The theory is not redundant since it is based on processes which underlie the surface of everyday experience, processes of which the participants themselves are usually unaware. Finally, the theory is not limited to the phenomenon of suicide, but suggests that feeling traps of shame and rage can lead to other outcomes as well, such as homicide, vendetta, or psychosis. Perhaps a more efficient design would be to investigate all these outcomes in the same study. Even if limited to a single outcome, a three-step study of the type outlined here would mark a new departure in theoretically driven, micro-macro research.

The approach urged here involves more than just new directions in research, however. I propose a novel conception of human nature, one that brings into high relief its social character and its all but overwhelming complexity. The principal ideas concern the social bond, the premier role of low-visibility pride and shame as determinants of behavior, and the use of part/whole thinking and social organization to solve complex and pressing problems. Our era demands that we gather resources to solve the problems that threaten our survival. I propose the ideas in this book in that spirit.

Glossary

Abduction: Rapid (millisecond) alternation between imagination and observation, inner and outer worlds, deduction and induction. Role taking is abduction applied to the specific problem of understanding another person. Abduction subsumes all problem-solving activity, including coping with the physical world.

Association: Mental processing of information; association can be either *classificatory* (logical), which is based on similarity, or *total*, which is based on "mere" contiguity as well as on similarity. Imagination seems to be largely intuitive, produced by total association.

Attunement: Mutual understanding; joint attention to thoughts, feelings, intentions, and motives between individuals but also between groups. The degree and structure of attunement and lack of attunement (misunderstanding or nonunderstanding) is the degree to which society exists, as against being in a state of anarchy.

Context: The immediate context of social interaction is the dialogue itself and its physical environment. The *extended* context, however, is everything that has happened before, could have happened instead, and might happen after. Attunement involves the inner world of imagination as much as it does the outer world of physical reality.

Counterfactuals: Any imagining of what might have happened but did not. Counterfactuals are useful in research to the extent that they help us understand the archaeological layers of gestures, implicature, feelings, intentions, and motives underlying what did happen.

Differentiation: A concept developed by Bowen (1978). He proposed that level of differentiation is the crucial characteristic of a family. An optimal level involves balance between the individual and the group. In an underdifferentiated family, the individual's needs are sacrificed to the demands of the group; the individual is *engulfed*. In an overdifferentiated family, the needs of the group are sacrificed to those of the individual; the individual is *isolated*.

Domain: An array of items. A *closed* domain is composed of a relatively few items, each of which is unambiguous. The games of tick tack toe and checkers are closed domains. An *open* domain is composed of a very large number of items, most or all of which are ambiguous. Any natural language is an example of an open domain. (On the concepts of open and closed domains, see Dreyfus and Dreyfus [1986].)

Feeling trap: An emotion that is bound by unacknowledged shame. Normal anger, grief, fear, and shame may be intense but are also quite brief, perhaps lasting for as little as a few seconds. But if one is ashamed of an emotion, and this shame goes unacknowledged and undischarged, then a repeating loop of self-perpetuating emotions may occur. Such a repeating sequence may take the form of an inner loop, a feeling trap; of an outer loop between persons, which is called contagion; or of loops both within and between persons, a *triple spiral:* one loop within each of the participants, and one between them.

Ideology: In Mannheim's (1936) sense, an ideology is a total commitment to the existing status quo. Ideologically oriented persons are completely emeshed in existing conventions in the host society in terms of thoughts, feelings, and emotions. Utopians, by contrast, are totally alienated from the status quo, completely committed to an image of a different social order.

Implicature: A verbal statement of what was implied by words and gestures but was not expressed in words. Ordinary conversation, like poetry, runs mostly on implicature. (For a disciplined analysis of the implicature in actual discourse, see Labov and Fanschel [1977].)

Intuition: The facility for virtually instantaneous solution of a complex problem. Probably based on total association in an open domain, which allows parallel, as well as serial, processes. System involves analytical reasoning, which is concept based, that is, uses classificatory association based on similarity. (I take this concept of system from Pascal's *Pensées* (1656), in which he contrasts "the spirit of finesse," intuition, with the "spirit of system" [my translation of *l'esprit de géométrie*].)

Manner: The nonverbal component of discourse, its paralanguage and accompanying bodily gestures. In discourse, *topics* usually are conveyed by words; the state of the relationship, the *bond*-relevant information, by manner. Parties to protracted conflict are usually entrapped in topics, unaware that the conflict is driven by lack of deference, since it is usually conveyed by manner.

Markers: Outer indicators of inner emotions, verbal and nonverbal (paralanguage and bodily gestures). For the emotion of shame, for example, verbal markers would be overt terms like embarrassment or humiliation, or coded terms such as "awkward" and "insecure" (see *shame construct*). Most of the nonverbal markers of shame involve some type of *hiding behavior:* gestural cues such as covering the eyes or mouth, touching the face or hair, or averting the gaze, and paralinguistic cues such as speech disruption or static, silence, or oversoft speech.

Message stack: The package of information made up of words, manner, implicature, and emotion. Abductive technique, the shuttling between imagined and observed events, allows participants (and researchers) to infer implicature and emotions from observed words and manner.

Lifeworld: Term for the representation of experience in ordinary language. Such a representation can be effected only in an open domain.

Part/whole thinking: Glissando from the smallest detail up to the most abstract concept and down again; seeing the relationship between the parts and the whole. Consensual understanding of ordinary language inevitably involves part/whole thinking. The signifier is a small moving part in an enormous whole, the context. Finding the correct reference of an ambiguous term involves understanding its relation to the whole, the extended context. To put it another way, the part implies the whole, and vice-versa, in open domains. This relationship is suggested in Wittgenstein's analysis of what is implied in correctly following a rule, which, he says, involves the "mastery of practice," that is, being a functioning member in a complex society. An extraordinary glimpse of the functioning of such open systems is implied by Goethe's theory of metamorphosis, how the microcosm and the macrocosm imply each other. Living things—plants, animals, and humans—are involved in continuing exchanges between part and whole. Part/whole thinking requires an analysis of the parts and subsystems which make up a social system. For a brilliant part/whole analysis of crime in various countries, see Braithwaite, 1989.

Prospective-retrospective method of understanding: Schutz's phrase for one of the movements of the imagination. Understanding an expression by scanning forward, to what might (or does) occur after the expression, and scanning backward to what occurred before the expression.

Search: *Inner* search involves memory or imagination, or both, seeking the reference of an ambiguous expression. *Outer* search involves visual or verbal activity, seeking the reference of an expression in the environment or by questioning another.

Shame construct: In the work of Helen B. Lewis, shame involves not just the rare and intense emotion that comes with public disgrace, but a whole *family* or class of related affects. For example, embarrassment is different in some ways from humiliation, but there is also an underlying similarity: both are discharged by spontaneous good-humored laughter. The members of the shame family all have the same underlying physical basis, the shame response cycle. The shame construct involves both acknowledged shame, an emotion that is experienced, and unacknowledged shame, an emotion that is outside awareness. Lewis divided *unacknowledged* shame into two types: *overt*, undifferentiated shame, and *bypassed* shame. The former involves emotional pain which is misnamed ("I felt uncomfortable"); the latter, successful distraction from the pain through hyperactive thought, speech, or behavior. Shame plays a prominent role in this book because it signals social disconnection, that is, disruption of or threat to the social bond. Normal shame is an unavoidable affect for any social system. Unacknowledged shame is pathological since it leads to spirals of intra- and interpersonal shame which have no natural limit of intensity or duration.

Social bond: A bond is intact to the extent that it involves mental and emotional attunement between persons. Attunement consists of not only joint knowledge of meanings evoked during contact, but long-range considerations involving intentions and character. The same kind of attunement between groups is referred to as social solidarity. Bonding is maintained by an elaborate system of deference and demeanor. Bond-relevant signals occur mostly in manner. Bonds are continually tested in interaction: they either are being built/maintained/repaired or damaged. Society exists to the extent that bonds are intact between persons and groups. When most bonds are severed or threatened, anarchy occurs.

Status quo: The total system of social conventions of a particular society at a particular time in history. The majority of the members of society have an ideological attitude toward this system; they are emeshed in it if they think its components are absolute and inevitable. Despite this conviction, however, any existing status quo is not equivalent to *social order*. Any of an infinity of alternative systems would also be possible.

System: See entry under *intuition* (system vs. intuition).

Translation: The term *translation* is usually used to refer to the transformation of expressions from one language to another. However, since all human expressions are general and ambiguous, a process of internal translation is necessary in all communication in any given language.

Bibliography

Abeles, G. 1976. "Researching the Unresearchable: Experimentation on the Double Bind." In C. E. Sluzki and D. C. Ransom, eds., *Double Bind: The Foundation of the Communication Approach to the Family.* New York: Grune and Stratton.

Adler, A. 1956. *The Individual Psychology of Alfred Adler.* New York: Basic.

Alexander, J., B. Giesen, R. Muench, and N. Smelser. 1987. *The Micro-Macro Link.* Berkeley: University of California Press.

Amrine, F., F. Zucker and H. Wheeler. 1987. *Goethe and the Sciences: A Reappraisal.* Boston: D. Reidel.

Anderson, John R. 1983. *The Architecture of Cognition.* Cambridge, Mass.: Harvard University Press.

Asch, S. 1956. "Studies of Independence and Conformity: 1. A Minority of One against a Unanimous Majority." *Psychological Monographs* 70: 1–70.

Atkinson, J. M. 1978. *Discovering Suicide.* Pittsburg: University of Pittsburg Press.

Atkinson, M., and J. Heritage. 1984. *Structures of Social Action.* Cambridge: Cambridge University Press.

Bateson, G., et al. 1956. "Toward a Theory of Schizophrenia." *Behavioral Science* 1: 251–64.

Bateson, G., D. Jackson, J. Haley, and J. Weakland. 1951. "Information and Codification: A Philosophical Approach." In J. Ruesch and G. Bateson, eds., *Communication: The Social Matrix of Psychiatry.*

Blumer, H. 1969. *Symbolic Interactionism: Perspective and Method.* Englewood Cliffs, N.J.: Prentice-Hall.

Bohm, D. 1980. *Wholeness and the Implicate Order.* London: Ark.

Boltzmann, Ludwig. 1899. "The Recent Development of Method in Theoretical Physics." *Monist* 11: 229–30.

Boudon, R. 1986. *L'idéologie.* Paris: Fayard.

Bowen, M. 1978. *Family Therapy in Clinical Practice.* New York: J. Arenson.

Bowen, M., and M. Kerr. 1988. *Family Evaluation.* New York: Norton.

Bowlby, J. 1969. *Attachment and Loss.* Vol. 1: *Attachment.* New York: Basic.

———. 1973. *Attachment and Loss.* Vol. 2: *Separation: Anxiety and Anger.* New York: Basic.

———. 1980. *Attachment and Loss.* Vol. 3: *Loss.* New York: Basic.

Bradley, R. B. 1987. *Charisma and Social Structure.* New York: Paragon.

Braithwaite, J. 1989. *Crime, Shame and Reintegration.* Cambridge: Cambridge University Press.

Bruner, J. 1983. *Child's Talk.* New York: Norton.

Burlingham, D., and A. Freud. 1942. *Young Children in Wartime London.* London: Allen and Unwin.

Chomsky, Noam. 1957. *Syntactic Structures.* The Hague: Mouton.

———. 1965. *Aspects of a Theory of Syntax.* Cambridge, Mass.: MIT Press.

———. 1969. *The Acquisition of Syntax in Children from 5 to 10.* Cambridge, Mass.: MIT Press.

Cicourel, Aaron. 1974. *Cognitive Sociology: Language and Meaning in Social Interaction.* New York: Free Press.

Collins, R. 1981. "On the Microfoundations of Macrosociology." *American Journal of Sociology* 86: 984–1014.

Cooley, C. H. 1909. *Social Organization.* New York: Schocken.

———. 1922. *Human Nature and the Social Order.* New York: Scribner's.

Cox, Catherine M. 1926. *The Early Mental Traits of 300 Geniuses.* Stanford, Calif.: Stanford University Press.

Darwin, C. 1872. *The Expression of Emotion in Men and Animals.* London: John Murray.

Dewey, J. 1958. *Experience and Nature.* New York: Dover.

Dodds, E. R. 1951. *The Greeks and the Irrational.* Berkeley: University of California Press.

Dreyfuss, H., and S. Dreyfuss. 1986. *Mind over Machine.* New York: Free Press.

Durkheim, E. 1897. *Suicide.* London: Routledge (1952).

———. 1902. *The Division of Labor in Society.* New York: Free Press (1933).

———. 1906. *Sociology and Philosophy.* In G. Simpson, *Emile Durkheim.* New York: Thomas Crowell (1963).

———. 1915. *The Elementary Forms of the Religious Life.* New York: Free Press (1965).

Eissler, Kurt. 1963. *Goethe: A Psychoanalytic Study.* Detroit: Wayne State University Press.

Ekman, P., and W. Friesen. 1982. "Felt, False and Miserable Smiles." *Journal of Non-Verbal Behavior* 6: 238–52.

Ekman, P., W. Friesen, and P. Ellsworth. 1972. *Emotion in the Human Face.* New York: Pergamon.

Elias, Norbert. 1978. *The History of Manners.* New York: Pantheon.

Eliot, George. 1872. *Middlemarch.* New York: Washington Square Press (1963).

———. 1876. *Daniel Deronda.* New York: John W. Lovell.

Emerson, R. W. 1837. *Essays and Lectures.* New York: Library of America (1983).

Etzioni, A. 1989. "Toward an I-We Paradigm." *Contemporary Sociology* 18: 171–76.

Fahlman, S. 1981. "Computers and Implicit Knowledge." In G. Hinton and J. Anderson, ed., *Parallel Models of Associative Memory.* Hillsdale, N.J.: LEA.

Fallows, J. 1989. *More like Us.* New York: Houghton Mifflin.

Feuer, Lewis S. 1982. *Einstein and the Generations of Science.* New Brunswick, N.J.: Transaction.

Feynman, R. 1985. *Surely You're Joking, Mr. Feynman.* Toronto: Bantam.

Freud, S. 1927. *The Future of an Illusion.* In *Standard Edition*, vol. 21. London: Hogarth.

Freud, S., and J. Breuer. 1895. *Studies of Hysteria.* New York: Avon (1966).

Galton, Francis. 1869. *Hereditary Genius.* Cleveland: Meridian.

Garfinkel, Harold. 1967. *Studies in Ethnomethodology.* Englewood Cliffs, N.J.: Prentice-Hall.

Gaylin, W. 1968. *The Meaning of Despair.* New York: Science House.

———. 1979. *Feelings.* New York: Harper and Row.

――――. 1989. *The Rage Within: Anger in Society*. New York: Penguin.

Geertz, C. 1983. *Local Knowledge*. New York: Basic.

Giddens, A. 1984. *The Constitution of Society*. Berkeley: University of California Press.

――――. 1987. *Social Theory and Modern Sociology*. Stanford, Calif.: Stanford University Press.

Gill, M., R. Newman, and F. Redlich. 1954. *The Initial Interview in Psychiatric Practice*. New York: Norton.

Goethe, J. W. 1774. *Die Leidendes Jungen Werthers*. In *Gedankausgabe der Werke: Briefe und Gespraeche*. Zurich: Emil Beutel (1949).

――――. 1785. *Philosophical Studies*. Quoted in B. Fairley, *A Study of Goethe*. Oxford: Clarendon, 1963.

――――. 1786. *The Sorrows of Young Werther*. New York: Norton (2d ed., 1963).

――――. 1796. *Wilhelm Meister's Apprenticeship*. London: Robertson (1901).

Goffman, E. 1959. *The Presentation of Self in Everyday Life*. New York: Anchor.

――――. 1963. *Behavior in Public Places*. New York: Free Press.

――――. 1967. *Interaction Ritual*. Garden City, N.Y.: Anchor Doubleday.

――――. 1974. *Frame Analysis*. New York: Harper.

――――. 1981. *Forms of Talk*. Philadelphia: University of Pennsylvania Press.

Goleman, D. 1985. *Vital Lies, Simple Truths: The Psychology of Self-Deception*. New York: Simon and Schuster.

Goodman, Paul. 1969. *New Reformation*. New York: Vintage.

Goodspeed, D. J. 1977. *The German Wars: 1914–1945*. Boston: Houghton-Mifflin.

Gottschalk, L., C. Winget, and G. Gleser. 1969. *Manual for Using the Gottschalk-Gleser Content Analysis Scales*. Berkeley: University of California Press.

Grice, H. P. 1981. "Presupposition and Conversational Implicature." In H. P. Cole, ed., *Radical Pragmatics*. New York: Academic.

Guntrip, H. 1971. *Psychoanalytic Theory, Therapy, and the Self*. New York: Basic.

Heisenberg, W. 1974. *Across the Frontiers*. New York: Harper Torchbooks.

Heritage, H. 1984. *Garfinkel and Ethnomethodology*. Cambridge: Polity.

Hinton, G., and J. Anderson, eds. 1981. *Parallel Models of Associative Memory*. Hillsdale, N.J.: LEA.

Hofstadter, D. 1980. *Goedel, Escher, Bach*. New York: Vintage.

Horney, Karen. 1950. *Neurosis and Human Growth*. New York: Norton.

James, W. 1910. *Psychology*. New York: Henry Holt.

Johnson, Pamela H. 1971. "Triumph over Time." In Peter Quennell, ed., *Marcel Proust: 1871–1922*. New York: Simon and Schuster.

Kelley H., et al. 1983. *Close Relationships*. New York: W. H. Freeman.

Kemper, T. 1978. *A Social Interactional Theory of Emotions*. New York: Wiley.

Kobler, A. L:, and E. Stotland. 1964. *The End of Hope*. New York: Free Press.

Koestler, Arthur. 1951. *Darkness at Noon*. New York: Random House.

Kohut, H. 1979. *The Search for Self*, vol. 2. New York: International Universities Press.

Labov W., and D. Fanshel. 1977. *Therapeutic Discourse*. New York: Academic.

Lazare, A. 1979. *Outpatient Psychiatry*. Baltimore: Williams and Wilkins.

――――. 1985. Personal communication.

Lerner, D., ed. 1963. *Parts and Wholes*. Cambridge, Mass.: Harvard University Press.

Lessing, G. E. 1772. *Emilia Galotti*. London: Blackwell (1965).

Lévi-Strauss, C. 1966. *The Savage Mind*. Chicago: University of Chicago Press.

Levine, D. 1985. *The Flight from Ambiguity.* Chicago: University of Chicago Press.

Lewis, H. B. 1971. *Shame and Guilt in Neurosis.* New York: International Universities Press.

———. 1976. *Psychic War in Men and Women.* New York: New York University Press.

———. 1983. *Freud and Modern Psychology.* 2 vols. New York: Plenum.

Lukács, G. 1953. *Goethe and His Epoch.* Berlin: Aufbau Verlag.

Lynd, H. M. 1958. *Shame and the Search for Identity.* New York: Harcourt Brace.

Magnus, R. 1949. *Goethe as a Scientist.* New York: Harry Schuman.

Mahlendorf, U., and T. Scheff. "Public Issues and Private Life: Critical Responses to *Werther.*" Typescript.

Maine, H. 1887. *International Law.* London: S. Murray.

Mannheim, Karl. 1936. *Ideology and Utopia.* London: Routledge and Kegan Paul.

———. 1952. *Essays on the Sociology of Knowledge.* New York: Oxford University Press.

McDougall, W. 1908. *An Introduction to Social Psychology.* London: Methuen.

Mead, George Herbert. 1934. *Mind, Self, and Society.* Chicago: University of Chicago Press.

Mills, C. W. 1959. *The Sociological Imagination.* New York: Oxford University Press.

———. 1963. *Power, Politics, and People.* New York: Oxford University Press.

Neisser, U. 1981. *Memory Observed.* San Francisco: W. H. Freeman.

Nietzsche, Friedrich. 1886. *Ecce Homo.* London: Foulis.

———. 1887. *On the Genealogy of Morals.* New York: Russell and Russell (1963).

Olson, D. H. 1972. "Empirically Unbinding the Double Bind: A Review of Research and Conceptual Reformulations." *Family Process* 11: 69–94.

Pascal, B. 1656. *Pensées.* New York: Penguin (1966).

Peirce, C. S. 1896–1908. "Abduction and Induction." In J. Buchler, ed., *Philosophical Writings of Peirce.* New York: Dover (1955).

Piers, G., and M. B. Singer. 1953. *Shame and Guilt: A Psychoanalytic and Cultural Study.* New York: Norton.

Pittenger, R., C. Hockett, and J. Danehy. 1960. *The First Five Minutes.* Ithaca, N.Y.: Paul Martineau.

Quine, W. O. 1960. *Word and Object.* Cambridge, Mass.: MIT Press.

Raphael, B. 1976. *The Thinking Computer.* San Francisco: W. H. Freeman.

Retzinger, Suzanne. 1985. "The Resentment Process: Videotape Studies." *Psychoanalytic Psychology* 2: 129–51.

———. 1987. "Marital Conflict: Case Study of an Escalating Quarrel." Typescript.

———. 1987a. "Resentment and Laughter: Video Studies of the Shame-Rage Spiral." In Helen B. Lewis, ed., *The Role of Shame in Symptom Formation.* Hillsdale, N.J.: Erlbaum.

———. 1988. "Marital Conflict: The Role of Emotion." Ph.D. diss., University of California, Santa Barbara.

Ricks, C. 1984. *Keats and Embarrassment.* Oxford: Oxford University Press.

Rommetveit, R., and R. Blakar. 1979. *Studies of Language, Thought, and Verbal Communication.* London: Academic.

Sacks, H. 1966. "The Search for Help: No One to Turn To." Ph.D. diss., University of California, Berkeley; Ann Arbor: University Microfilms.

Sacks, H., E. Schegloff, and G. Jefferson. 1974. "A Simplist Systematics for the Organization of Turn-taking Conversation." *Language* 50: 696–735.

Satir, V. 1972. *Peoplemaking*. Palo Alto, Calif.: Science and Behavior.

Scheff, T. J. 1966. *Being Mentally Ill*. Chicago: Aldine (2d ed., 1984).

———. 1967. "Toward a Sociological Model of Consensus." *American Sociological Review* 32: 32–46.

———. 1967a. "A Theory of Social Coordination Applicable to Mixed-Motive Games." *Sociometry* 30: 215–34.

———. 1976. "Audience Awareness and Catharsis in Drama." *Psychoanalytic Review* 63: 529–54.

———. 1979. *Catharsis in Healing, Ritual, and Drama*. Berkeley: University of California Press.

———. 1984. "The Taboo on Coarse Emotions." *Review of Personality and Social Psychology* 5: 156–69.

———. 1986. "Toward Resolving the Controversy over 'Thick Description.'" *Current Anthropology* 27 :408–9.

———. 1986a. "Microlinguistics: A Theory of Social Action." *Sociological Theory* 4: 1.

———. 1987. "The Shame-Rage Spiral: Case Study of an Interminable Quarrel." In H. Lewis, ed., *The Role of Shame in Symptom Formation*. Hillsdale, N.J.: Erlbaum.

———. 1989. "Emotions and Understanding: Toward a Theory and Method." In S. Wapner, ed., *Emotions in Ideal Human Development*. Hillsdale, N.J.: Erlbaum.

———. 1989a. "Cognitive and Emotional Conflict in Anorexia: Analysis of a Classic Case." *Psychiatry* 52: 147–61.

———. 1989b. "War and Emotions: Franco-German Relations, 1871–1945." Typescript.

———. 1989c. "Hitler's Appeal: Alienation, Shame/Rage, and Revenge." In *Revenge: Studies of Humiliated Fury*. Typescript.

Scheff, T. J., and D. D. Bushnell. 1984. "A Theory of Catharsis." *Journal of Research in Personality* 18: 238–64.

Scheff, T. J., and U. Mahlendorf. 1988. "Emotion and False Consciousness. Analysis of an Incident from *Werther*." *Theory, Culture, and Society* 5: 57–80.

Scheff, T. J., and S. M. Retzinger. 1991. *Emotions and Violence: Shame and Rage in Destructive Conflicts*. Lexington, Mass.: Lexington Books.

Schegloff, E. 1984. "On Some Questions and Ambiguities in Conversation." In J. Atkinson and J. Heritage, eds., *Structures of Social Action*. Cambridge: Cambridge University Press.

Schutz, A. 1962. *The Problem of Social Reality*. The Hague: M. Nijhoff.

Shibutani, T. 1955. "Reference Groups as Perspectives." *American Journal of Sociology* 60: 562–69.

———. 1961. *Society and Personality*. Englewood Cliffs, N.J.: Prentice-Hall.

Shneidman, E. 1980. *Voices of Death*. New York: Harper and Row.

Simon, H. 1977. "What Computers Mean for Man and Society." *Science* 195: 1186–91.

Smith, B. H. 1968. *Poetic Closure*. Chicago: University of Chicago Press.

Steiner, George. 1975. *After Babel*. New York: Oxford University Press.

Steiner, R. 1926. *Goethe's Science*. Berlin: Goetheanum.

Stern, D., L. Hofer, W. Haft, and J. Dore. 1984. "Affect Attunement: The Sharing of Feeling States Between Mother and Infant." In J. Field and N. Fox, eds., *Social Perception in Early Infancy*. New York: Elsevier.

Terasaki, A. 1976. "Pre-announcement Sequences in Conversation." Social Sciences
  Working Paper 99. University of California, Irvine.
Thoits, P. 1985. "Self-Labeling Processes in Mental Illness: The Role of Emotional
  Deviance." *American Journal of Sociology* 91: 221–48.
Thomas, L. 1974. *Lives of a Cell*. New York: Bantam.
Toennies, F. 1887. *Community and Society*. London: Routledge.
Tomkins, S. S. 1963. *Affect/Imagery/Consciousness*. Vol. 2: *The Negative Affects*.
  New York: Springer.
Tronick, E. Z., M. Ricks, and J. Cohn. 1982. "Maternal and Infant Affect Exchange:
  Patterns of Adaptation." In T. Field and A. Fogel, eds., *Emotion and Early Interac-
  tion*. Hillsdale, N.J.: Erlbaum.
Updike, John. 1984. "Emersonianism." *New Yorker*. 60 (June 4): 112–32.
Vaihinger, H. 1924. *The Philosophy of "As If."* London: Kegan Paul.
Vietor, K. 1950. *Goethe the Thinker*. Cambridge: Cambridge University Press.
Wagner, Cosima. 1976. *Diaries*. Vols. 1–2. M. Gregor-Dellin and Dietrich Mack,
  eds. New York: Harcourt Brace Jovanovich.
Wallace, G. n.d. "Presidential Press Conferences." Typescript.
Watzlawick, P., J. Beavin, and D. Jackson. 1967. *Pragmatics of Human Communica-
  tion*. New York: Norton.
Weber, E. 1968. *The Nationalist Revival in France, 1905–1914*. Berkeley: University
  of California Press.
Weber, Max. 1946. *From Max Weber: Essays in Sociology*. H. Gerth and C. Mills,
  eds. New York: Oxford University Press.
———. 1947. *Theory of Social and Economic Organization*. Oxford: Oxford Univer-
  sity Press.
Wells, G. 1967. "Goethe and the Intermaxillary Bone." *British Journal for the His-
  tory of Science* 3: 348–61.
Wiley, N. n.d. "The History of the Self." Typescript.
———. n.d. "Notes on Goedel's Proof." Typescript.
Winkler, R., and A. Murphy. 1973. "Experiments in the Laboratory and in the Real
  World." *Organizational Behavior and Human Performance* 10: 252–70.
Winograd, T. 1984. "Computer Software for Working with Language." *Scientific
  American* 251: 130–45.
Wittgenstein, L. 1953. *Philosophical Investigations*. New York: Macmillan.
Wurmser, L. 1981. *The Masks of Shame*. Baltimore: Johns Hopkins University Press.
Wye, R., and T. Krull. 1986. "Human Cognition and Its Social Context." *Psychologi-
  cal Review* 93: 322–59.
Ziman, J. 1969. "Information, Communication, Knowledge." *Nature* 224: 318–24.

Index of References

Subject Index